Voicing desire

ALSO IN THE VOLTAIRE FOUNDATION'S VIF PAPERBACK SERIES

Vif

Etudes sur 'Le Fils naturel' et les 'Entretiens sur le Fils naturel' de Diderot
Sous la direction de Nicholas Cronk

ISBN 0 7294 0751 9

Jeanne Marie Le Prince de Beaumont, Contes et autres écrits
Edition présentée par
Barbara Kaltz

ISBN 0 7294 0705 5

The Darnton debate
Books and revolution in the eighteenth century
Ed. Haydn Mason

ISBN 0 7294 0653 9

Beaumarchais et la chanson
Musique et dramaturgie des comédies de Figaro
Philip Robinson

ISBN 0 7294 0652 0

Rhétorique et roman au XVIIIe siècle
L'exemple de Prévost et de Marivaux (1728-1742)
Jean-Paul Sermain

ISBN 0 7294 0654 7

For Ana

Diderot, anonymous eighteenth-century engraving
(Bibliothèque nationale de France)

Voicing desire

Family and sexuality in Diderot's narrative

J. E. Fowler

Vif VOLTAIRE FOUNDATION
OXFORD · 2000

ISBN 0 7294 0738 1

Voltaire Foundation Ltd
University of Oxford
99 Banbury Road
Oxford OX2 6JX U.K.

http ://www.voltaire.ox.ac.uk

Distributed in France by PUF

Printed in England

Contents

Preface

FIRST of all my thanks are due to Martin Hall, whose scholarly guidance and steadfast friendship have been equally important during the formation of this project. I should also like to thank Peter France for his general encouragement as well as valuable advice on key chapters, and the late John Lough for his generous support. Others who have offered constructive comments on various chapters or related articles are Naomi Segal, Robin Howells, David Adams, Haydn Mason, Anthony Strugnell, and Tony Williams. My thanks are also due to Nicole Masson for facilitating research undertaken at the Ecole normale supérieure, Paris in 1989-1991.

Earlier versions of chapters or parts of chapters have appeared in published form, as follows: 'Diderot's family romance: *Les Bijoux indiscrets* reappraised', *Romanic review* 88 (1997), p.89-102; 'Reading *Le Fils naturel* as a narrative', *SVEC* 323 (1994), p.167-92; 'Competing causalities: family and convent in Diderot's *La Religieuse*', *The Eighteenth century: theory and interpretation* 37 (Spring 1996), p.75-93; 'Suzanne at Ste-Eutrope: negation and narration in *La Religieuse*', *Diderot studies* 27 (1998), p.83-96; and '"Je m'entretiens avec moi-même": self versus other in *Le Neveu de Rameau*', *Dalhousie French studies* 42 (Spring 1998), p.77-88. Certain ideas contained in Chapter 5 were first presented in '"Ce cher oncle": L'Œdipe dans *Le Neveu de Rameau*', *Sexualité, mariage et famille au XVIIIe siècle*, ed. Olga B. Cragg and Rosena Davison (Quebec, Presses de l'Université Laval 1998), p.243-50.

Introduction

Diderot: a weathervane?

In a well-known passage of the correspondence, Diderot asserts that the people of his home town have the intellectual constancy of weathervanes: 'La tête d'un Langrois est sur ses épaules comme un coq d'église au haut d'un clocher. Elle n'est jamais fixe dans un point; et si elle revient à celui qu'elle a quitté, ce n'est pas pour s'y arrêter.'[1] He then presents himself as a case in point: 'Pour moi, je suis de mon pays' (p.207). Much has been made of this by commentators who emphasise the digressive or disorderly aspects of the *philosophe*'s thinking. However, closer attention to the passage indicates that Diderot does not characterise himself as simply changeable. Though this is not where the emphasis is placed, the weathervane's spinning is set against its recurrent return to certain points by the words: 'si elle revient à celui qu'elle a quitté'. Moreover, in his continuation of the passage in question, Diderot only admits to *having been* a typical *Langrois*, stressing that since he has lived in Paris, he has become rather different: 'Pour moi, je suis de mon pays; seulement le séjour de la capitale, et l'application assidue m'ont un peu corrigé. Je suis constant dans mes goûts'. In the end, then, Diderot is telling us that the vane that spins also has its sticking points.

I begin with this passage because the image of the weathervane summarises a common wisdom on Diderot which has been fruitful but which it is important to relativise in order for other perspectives to emerge. On the occasion of the bicentenary of Diderot's death, a volume of essays appeared whose title was: *Diderot: digression and dispersion*.[2] Two hundred years on, it seemed, some of the most recognised Diderot scholars associated the famous *philosophe* with a productive lack of focus. Such a view has informed studies of Diderot's work as a whole, as well as analysis of various Diderotian corpora (the philosophical, the aesthetic, the political, and so on). We will focus exclusively on narrative fiction; but here too the weathervane casts its shadow.

1. Denis Diderot, *Correspondance*, ed. Georges Roth and Jean Varloot, 16 vols (Paris, Editions de Minuit 1955-1970), ii.207-208 (10 or 11 August 1759). For comments on this famous passage see Jacques Chouillet, *Denis Diderot – Sophie Volland. Un dialogue à une voix* (Paris, Librairie Honoré Champion 1986), p.75.

2. *Diderot: digression and dispersion: a bicentennial tribute*, ed. Jack Undank and Herbert Josephs (Lexington, Kentucky, French Forum 1984).

It has become customary to represent Diderot's novels as belonging to a series of discontinuous phases. According to this view, Diderot first tried his hand at the pseudo-oriental fairy tale, then the Richardsonian novel, and finally the comic self-reflexive novel. As one influential critic puts it:

> Son 'à la manière de' Crébillon fils, Diderot l'écrivit en 1748 et ce furent les *Bijoux indiscrets* [...] Son 'à la manière' de Richardson, il l'écrivit douze ans plus tard, et ce fut *la Religieuse* [...] Son 'à la manière' de Sterne, il l'écrivit au temps de son voyage de Saint-Pétersbourg, entre 1773 et 1775 et ce fut *Jacques le fataliste et son maître* [...] Son 'à la manière' de Denis Diderot, il le commença en 1761-1762, et ce fut *le Neveu de Rameau* qui ne fut terminé qu'une douzaine d'années plus tard.[3]

Critics who stray from this orthodoxy by attempting a more synthetic approach to Diderot's narratives risk provoking strong reactions. For instance, a study by Roger Kempf, who emphasises the recurrence of certain themes across Diderot's novels, has drawn the following condemnation from a more traditional scholar: 'En rangeant dans des catégories arbitraires, au mépris de toute chronologie, selon une problématique toute subjective et, par rapport à Diderot, anachronique, des œuvres hétérogènes, il brouille les perspectives et les idées, risquant d'accroître la confusion là où la précision serait nécessaire.'[4] The question-begging phrase 'des œuvres hétérogènes' indicates a point of dogma which will be fiercely defended. To 'despise' chronology; to ask what affinities exist between works written at different stages of Diderot's career; such actions are presented here as a reprehensible rocking of the scholarly boat.

The present study does not attempt to deny that Diderot is in many respects digressive, nor that it can be useful to map into phases Diderot's experimentation in narrative form. It does however seek to identify a significant set of resemblances between his major narratives, regardless of divisions of subgenre and chronology. In a word, the narratives can be shown consistently to explore the role of desire in human discourse and action. More precisely, they represent or dramatise the interplay between sexuality and various other forces which Diderot presents as determining private and social experience. At the same time, as we will see, the theme of family relationships recurs frequently and is interwoven with that of desire.

3. See Georges May, *Quatre visages de Denis Diderot* (Paris, Boivin 1951), p.160. As if in accordance with this perspective, critics have tended to treat the major novels separately, devoting full-length studies to *La Religieuse*, *Jacques le fataliste* and *Le Neveu de Rameau* in particular.

4. Jean Fabre, '*Jacques le fataliste*: problèmes et recherches', *SVEC* 56 (1967), p.485-99 (p.485-86).

The trace of desire in Diderot's fiction

The principal theme and structuring device of Diderot's first novel, *Les Bijoux indiscrets*, is quite clearly an investigation into desire. The sultan Mangogul receives a magic ring with which he can cause women's *bijoux* (genitals) to speak the truth concerning female sexuality. On one occasion, the women on whom he turns the ring ignore the genital voice, conversing as normal in the hope of drowning it out. This image of an unofficial, 'true' voice of sexuality subverting the voice of social propriety is a striking one indeed.

Though Diderot never again resorts to the device of genital prosopopeia, the irruption of desire into a discourse which would disavow it constitutes both structuring principle and major theme in subsequent narratives. According to the fiction of *Le Fils naturel*, Dorval writes an autobiographical play in which, as hero, he abjures a passion for his friend's intended wife Rosalie in favour of a marriage based on virtue. As it turns out, Rosalie is his half-sister, so incest is narrowly avoided. It is Dorval's father who requests him to write the play, in order that it can be performed annually by the family as a means of recalling the terrible danger which threatened them. Thus an official discourse of authority and taboo, associated with the father, is designed to guard against the catastrophe of incest. The trace of sexuality subsists, however, within the very discourse designed to neutralise it. For in various gaps and contradictions we discover the persistence of Dorval's incestuous attachment, along with a fierce if disguised hostility towards the father whose return has confirmed the impossibility of access to the sister.

La Religieuse contains similar tensions. Narrator and heroine of her own story, Suzanne Simonin writes a moving letter in which she argues that she should never have been forced into the monastic system. As an important part of her anti-conventual rhetoric, she shows herself narrowly escaping seduction by a sapphic Superior, as though such seduction were a perversion to be avoided at all cost. Since the risk of lesbianism is magnified within the convent, she manages to imply, she should be rescued at once, or her innocence may be compromised. Yet her writing bears the trace of the sexuality she would deny. Not only does she record the ways in which her body responds to the Superior's advances; her discourse throughout implies a compromise between disavowal and avowal. Moreover, on the level of plot her familial and social relationships manifest the share which sexuality has in her motivations. So this novel too involves an opposition between sexuality and the forces which would keep it in check.

As for *Le Neveu de Rameau*, Lui argues that appetites such as hunger and sexuality are imperative, and that the moral codes which tend towards their transcendance are specious. This is one of the main issues of the famous dialogue. Moi by contrast represents himself as belonging to a breed of philosophers who can rise above the snares of desire in order achieve the *belle page*, or better still the *belle action*; and when Lui exposes his own attitudes concerning morality, sexuality, money and their interconnections, Moi reacts with horror. Indeed, Moi's later incarnation, the narrator who supposedly records, introduces and comments on the dialogue, goes to some lengths to disavow all possibility of identification between himself and Rameau's nephew. Once again, an official, censuring voice enters into conflict with an unofficial discourse on sexuality and its ramifications.

This opposition is worked out in yet another way in *Jacques le fataliste et son maître*. Few characters in this narrative which contains so many suggest that celibacy or constancy is to be valued, or even hoped for. Instead, the official discourse is that of a certain disabused heterosexuality recounted from the man's point of view – as when Jacques and the Master discuss their experience of women. Within such a system, the inevitability of changing object constitutes an orthodoxy, distilled for instance in Jacques's fable of the *Gaîne* and the *Coutelet*.[5] However, if a liberal heterosexual code seems here to enjoy official status, a new unofficial discourse is also present to subvert it. For while Jacques relates the story of his exclusive love for Denise, as a narrator with a fatalistic point to prove he is effectively enacting a loving identification with the lost Captain; and the relations of the lost Captain with his comrade, double and duelling-partner are emphatically presented by the narrator as revealing the latent truth of relations between men, and by extension of relations between men and women. In this sense the trace of desire in *Jacques* is that of 'homosocial' desire.[6] At the same time, the dichotomy of the virtuous versus the promiscuous woman, so pervasive in *Les Bijoux indiscrets*, is present as a ramification of homosociality.

Enough has been said to suggest that the tension between on the one hand various forms of sexuality and on the other various anti-sexual forces or codes constitutes an important recurrent theme in Diderot's narrative, and indeed provides a basic structuring element in given works. However, we can scarcely pursue this family resemblance without noticing its intimate connection with another theme – the theme, precisely, of family.

Any representational novel will inevitably permit discussion of the family

5. Denis Diderot, *Œuvres complètes*, ed. by Herbert Dieckmann, Jean Varloot *et al.* (Paris, Hermann 1975-), xxiii.129-30. References will be to this edition, in the form *ŒC*, unless otherwise indicated.

6. I borrow this term from Eve Kosofsky Sedgwick, *Between men: English literature and male homosocial desire* (New York, Columbia University Press 1985), whose definition of homosociality will be discussed in greater detail in Chapter 4.

theme, since characters are in the main represented in their social milieu, determined by their familial origins; and even if they are orphans or foundlings, quasi-familial relationships are normally present.[7] In Diderot's case, however, the theme of family is not only present but strongly foregrounded. *Le Fils naturel* deals of course with a bastard son, as indicated by the title, and includes a long disquisition on the respectability of the bastard who makes his contribution to society. *La Religieuse* is a novel whose initial situation is similarly explained by the daughter's status as bastard. She then moves from her original family to the 'family' of the convent, where the nuns are sisters and mothers. The significance of family is equally prominent in *Le Neveu de Rameau*, as Lui frequently speaks of his relationship to his uncle, attempting to come to terms with the fact that in the eyes of society he may have fallen short of the illustrious forebear.[8] On the other hand, *Les Bijoux indiscrets* and *Jacques le fataliste et son maître* may seem to emphasise family relationships far less. However, as I intend to show, in those works non-familial relations are worked out as extensions of the familial. Mangogul's attitude towards women, at once misogynous and idealising, suggests an anxious nostalgia for the mother; and the homosocial relationship between Jacques and the Master is structured on an oedipal model.[9] Thus, on condition that we accept that many non-familial relationships in Diderot's narrative are represented as 'family-like' (i.e. metaphorical enactments of family relationships), the full sense in which family is intertwined with sexuality becomes clear.

Dates and manuscripts

Whilst the approach adopted here is synthetic in that it ignores the traditional division of fictions into sub-genres of the novel (the licentious novel, the Richardsonian, and so on), this does not mean that it is synthetic

7. Marthe Robert analyses *Robinson Crusoe* in order to argue that the origins of the modern bourgeois novel are to be explained in terms of familial relationships. See *Roman des origines et origines du roman* (Paris, Gallimard 1972).

8. A sideways glance at titles of various fictions tends to confirm the importance of this theme. We have already mentioned *Le Fils naturel*; in addition Diderot's writings include *Le Père de famille* and the *Entretien d'un père avec ses enfants*. It should be added that whilst Diderot probably did not name his famous dialogue *Le Neveu de Rameau* himself, the title seems particularly apt, a point to which we will return in Chapter 5.

9. Lynn Hunt has recently read the French Revolution itself as an extension of familial relationships, arguing that the execution of the king in particular resembles the patricide effected by the 'primal horde' as imagined by Freud in *Totem and taboo*. See Lynn Avery Hunt, *The Family romance of the French Revolution* (Berkeley, University of California Press 1992).

in other respects. In particular, Kempf's approach, to which we have already referred, is not reproduced here; instead of moving back and forth between the various fictions in pursuit of a given theme, I have devoted one chapter to each fiction studied.

Given this structure, it is scarcely possible to show how the role of desire varies throughout the corpus without implying some kind of progression in terms of Diderot's practice as an author. However, the question of progression is a difficult one, given that the dating of certain major works is notoriously complicated. In particular, *La Religieuse*, *Jacques le fataliste* and *Le Neveu de Rameau* are works of overlapping gestation. On the other hand, it may seem relatively easy to date *Les Bijoux indiscrets* and *Le Fils naturel* in themselves and so in relation to each other and the other works of our corpus. However, the fact that Diderot added important chapters to *Les Bijoux indiscrets* some years after its original composition complicates even this point, so that placing the latter work before *Le Fils naturel* is no longer an entirely straightforward matter.

It is tempting simply to recognise the difficulty, and to invite the reader to see the choice of disposition of the chapters which follow as in some respects arbitrary. Nevertheless, I do propose to outline a progression on Diderot's part. Considerations of two kinds can be adduced in support of this. First, what we do know about the gestation and publication of the works considered implies the reasonableness of treating them in the order chosen. In other words, though the provisional chronology used here is not the only possible one, it is a sound one. Second, whilst the question of chronology must ultimately remain open, to treat the texts for the present purpose *as though* they were written in a particular order permits greater clarity of exposition.

In order to demonstrate these points, we will first indicate how the order of texts was arrived at, then show its usefulness for a clearer exposition of Diderot's practice. The method chosen here was in fact extremely simple: where the gestation of a given work was uncertain, the earliest date at which a substantial version is known or can be reasonably supposed to have existed was used in order to place the works in relation to each other. The situating of *Le Neveu de Rameau* in relation to *Jacques le fataliste* remains an intractable problem, but at least the situating of these two works in relation to the rest of the corpus is feasible. If the gestation of each work is taken to be a more or less protracted working-out of an original theme or idea, this method affords a reasonable approximation of what Diderot's progression as an author of narrative fiction might well have been.

Let us then review what is known of the composition of each work of our corpus, beginning with the case of *Les Bijoux indiscrets*. It is generally accepted that 1748 is the original date of publication. For the Hermann edition, Jean Macary restores the organisation of the chapters in two volumes, which Naigeon suppressed and which later editors failed to restore.[10] The vital point here is the question of three chapters written by Diderot after 1748. The Hermann edition presents these chapters (of which copies are to be found in the 'fonds Vandeul') separately from the rest. They are: 'Le rêve de Mangogul', 'De la figure des insulaires et de la toilette des femmes', and 'Des voyageurs'. The Hermann edition does not commit itself to a date for their composition. It is nevertheless appropriate to analyse the chapters in question as an integral part of the work of 1748, for the concept of progression, whilst excluding the possibility of anticipation (as soon as a textual possibility is 'anticipated', it is already realised) allows for the possibility of regression. In other words, if long after 1748 Diderot was inclined to compose certain passages for inclusion in a work of that year, it is quite possibly the case (and our analysis seems to confirm this) that the structures and properties of the original work were intrinsically suited to expansion by such a supplement.[11]

Le Fils naturel poses no serious problems of dating. There is no known existing manuscript, but the 1757 published edition seems to follow closely upon the work's composition. During the winter of 1756, the work was examined by Grimm, and it first appeared in published form in February 1757.[12] There is no reason to posit that the work was begun before 1756. The dating of *La Religieuse*, however, is considerably more complicated. Experts vary in their reconstruction of this work's genesis, possibly more radically than is justified. As far as we can infer from the correspondence, a version of the novel existed in 1760. In a letter of that year, which might well have been written at the beginning of November, Diderot tells Mme d'Epinay:

> Je me suis mis à faire *La Religieuse*, et j'y étais encore à trois heures du matin. Je vais à tire-d'aile. Ce n'est plus une lettre, c'est un livre. Il y aura là-dedans des choses vraies, de pathétiques, et il ne tiendrait qu'à moi qu'il y en eût de fortes.

10. See *Œ C*, vol.iii. It should be mentioned that David Adams subjects the Hermann edition's choice of manuscript to critical scrutiny, stressing 'the difficulty of assigning an order of precedence to various editions of the work which appeared in 1748'. See D. J. Adams, 'An English printing of *Les Bijoux indiscrets*', *Diderot studies* 22 (1986), p.13-15 (p.13).

11. Such a position is harmonious with Aram Vartanian's comment in the Hermann edition (p.17): '[La structure de l'œuvre] opère en même temps une convergence entre la curiosité érotique et la recherche scientifique; on n'a donc pas à s'étonner de ce que Diderot ait inséré dans ce roman voué à l'experimentalisme sexuel le célèbre "Rêve de Mangogul" (t.i, ch.29), où fut proclamé justement le rôle décisif de la méthode expérimentale dans le progrès des sciences.' In other words, the properties of the 1748 version made it the most natural home, so to speak, for the later chapters.

12. See *Œ C*, x.3-10.

> Mais je ne m'en donne pas le temps. Je laisse aller ma tête; aussi bien ne pourrais-je guère la maîtriser.[13]

As May argues (p.3), this passage suggests that if the first letters from the fictitious Suzanne to the Marquis de Croismare were composed during the spring of 1760, by the end of that year a first version of the novel was already in existence.

These indications are to be matched to the extant manuscripts. We quote May once again at some length, since he states the situation clearly and succinctly (p.9-10):

> Ce processus évolutif, interrompu sans doute pendant une vingtaine d'années en raison des autres occupations de l'écrivain, devait reprendre en 1780. De cela, les manuscrits qui nous sont parvenus apportent le témoignage, et principalement les deux suivants (lesquels font l'un et l'autre partie du fonds Vandeul). D'abord l'autographe, qui correspond à la version du roman la plus ancienne de celles qui nous sont connues. Ensuite la mise au net par un copiste professionnel de cet autographe, lui-même abondamment corrigé et raturé par Diderot. Cette mise au net, confiée à Roland Girbal, devait être à son tour corrigée de la main de Diderot avant d'être remise à Meister pour être 'publiée' dans la *Correspondance littéraire*. Cette revue diffusait alors toute une série d'ouvrages inédits de Diderot. *La Religieuse* y parut en neuf livraisons [...]. Le 27 septembre 1780 Diderot écrivait à Meister pour l'aviser que le début du manuscrit était à sa disposition et notait: 'C'est un ouvrage que j'ai fait au courant de la plume et sur lequel j'ai été rappelé par mon travail actuel'.

May goes on to argue that the process of revision occurring in 1780 went far beyond a tidying-up of the version of the novel which was already in existence. He argues instead that the 1760 version of the novel was far more rudimentary than the manuscript which Diderot made available for transcription by Girbal some twenty years later. This idea is largely based on the fact that Diderot's phrase 'fait au courant de la plume' is not suited to describe a manuscript as finished as that which, transcribed and corrected, became the basis of the text of the *Correspondance littéraire* in 1780-1782: 'il y a lieu de penser que le billet à Meister fait peut-être allusion à une première version hypothétique du roman antérieure à celle présente dans le manuscrit autographe, et non à l'état actuel de l'ouvrage au moment où le billet fut écrit' (p.10).

In brief, May is effectively setting out a case for seeing *La Religieuse* as a novel written in large part around 1780 rather than 1760. This would imply that we should have placed it after *Jacques le fataliste* and *Le Neveu de Rameau*. However, it is difficult to see the necessity of inferring the existence of an earlier, lost manuscript version of the novel (substantially different from the version transcribed by Girbal). It is true, as May points out, that in the

13. See *ŒC*, xi.9-10.

Préface-Annexe of 1770 Grimm writes: 'ce roman n'a jamais existé que par lambeaux et en est resté là'; but it is also true, as Herbert Dieckmann points out, that Diderot himself made two additions to the same part of the manuscript: first, 'ce roman, je l'ai achevé', and then, more mischievously, 'Et j'ajouterai, moi, qui connais un peu Mr. Diderot, que ce roman, il l'a achevé ...' (*Œ.C*, xi.17). Surely if we add any weight to Grimm's statement, we must add even more to Diderot's. Moreover, May has a great deal hang on the possibility that Diderot's phrase 'au courant de la plume' implies a version unsuited to publication in the *Correspondance littéraire*. Yet this is not a conclusive argument. For instance, the phrase suggests above all that the writing of the novel was rapid; but rapid composition does not necessarily lead to a fragmentary result. Moreover, even assuming that Diderot does mean to suggest this, he might have done so for a variety of reasons. He may have been motivated by false modesty, or by anxiety concerning his novel's reception resulting in an apologetic reflex. Finally, it is widely known how fond Diderot was of *mystifications*, including those in which he represented his own activity as a creator of literature inaccurately in order to create effect.[14] Perhaps here he wished to project the image of an author in the grip of inspiration, or swept along by his finer feelings. In consequence of such considerations, whilst May makes out a valid case, it is not an overwhelming one, and it seems at least defensible to maintain that what Diderot had written in 1760 was substantially if not entirely what he submitted for transcription in 1780.[15]

The question of dating *La Religieuse* is further complicated by the existence of the piece generally known as *Préface-Annexe*, at least if we accept that the latter is to be seen as part of the novel itself. This point of view was first suggested by Dieckmann, who argues that 'the documents, which we publish here for the first time, prove that Diderot not only carefully revised the *Préface-Annexe* in later years, but even transformed it into an integral part of the novel'.[16] The problem thus introduced is that the Preface

14. See Jean Catrysse, *Diderot et la mystification* (Paris, A. G. Nizet 1970).

15. In any case, even if we followed May in assuming that subsequently extensive revisions were made, we have no reason to suspect that such revisions altered that aspect of the text which concerns us here: the tension within Suzanne's discourse between the presence of an unofficial 'voice' of desire and the disavowal of that voice. The internal evidence of the text is reassuring in this connection; the contradictions in Suzanne's account appear frequently within the space of a page, and such pages are to be found from beginning to end, though with increasing frequency towards the end (as our analysis will show). It would seem perverse to postulate that such contradictions were largely or entirely introduced by additions and corrections effected after 1760.

16. See Herbert Dieckmann, 'The *Préface-Annexe* of *La Religieuse*', *Diderot studies* 2 (1953), p.21-147 (p.22).

was published in 1770, and this might make of *La Religieuse*, including the Preface, a work contemporaneous with *Jacques le fataliste*. However, two considerations might incline us against such a view. First, as Dieckmann himself makes quite clear, the piece includes 'the authentic letters of the Marquis de Croismare and Grimm's account of the plot' (p.31). It is not desirable to view a collaborative effort, be it carefully reworked by Diderot himself, as an integral part of a fiction written by him alone, even if the two pieces do have a single heroine. Second, even had we been able to view the *Préface-Annexe* as Diderot's exclusive work, it is difficult to see how the piece might radically alter anything we might have to say about the main body of the novel. We refer once again to Dieckmann himself to confirm this point: 'while in *Jacques le fataliste* [subjective elements] are introduced into the novel itself and often become a considerable nuisance, in *La Religieuse* they remain outside of the story proper and are all incorporated into the *Préface-Annexe*' (p.31). For both these reasons, inclusion of the Preface has been avoided, together with the complications which such inclusion would have brought to our proposed order of chapters.[17]

Now let us consider the case of *Jacques le fataliste*. In his introduction to the Hermann edition of this work Jacques Proust writes:

> L'histoire de la genèse de *Jacques le fataliste* reste en grande partie inconnue. La seule information sûre que nous ayons sur elle, avant la publication du roman dans la *Correspondance littéraire*, est une lettre de Meister le père à Bodmer, datée du 12 septembre 1771 et publiée en 1903 dans les *Lettres inédites de Mme de Staël à Meister*: 'Diderot a fait un conte charmant, *Jacques le fataliste*. L'auteur en a lu l'autre jour à notre homme pendant deux heures'.[18]

This is all we need to set out for the present purpose. There is no evidence that a version of *Jacques* existed much before 1771, and so we place it after the first version of *La Religieuse*.[19] As we are attempting to date the first versions of the works of our corpus in relation to each other, we need not speculate what form *Jacques* took in 1771, nor what revisions took place

17. It should be added that Jean Parrish is one of the editors of the Hermann edition of *La Religieuse*, and has elsewhere reproduced the earliest manuscript version of the novel. See Denis Diderot, *La Religieuse*, ed. Jean Parrish, *SVEC* 22 (1963). Careful attention to the variants highlighted by this scrupulous research prove especially important for any reading of the novel.

18. See *ŒC*, xxiii.3.

19. Adams argues that whilst *Jacques* continued to evolve between 1770 and 1782, the first version was probably written in 1770-1771. See D. J. Adams, 'Style and social ideas in *Jacques le fataliste*', *SVEC* 124 (1974), p.231-48 (p.237). See also J. Undank, 'A new date for *Jacques le fataliste*', *Modern language notes* 74 (1959), p.433-37, and Jean Varloot, '*Jacques le fataliste* et la *Correspondance littéraire*', *Revue d'histoire littéraire de la France* 65 (1965), p.629-36.

before its publication in 1778-1780. (Jacques Proust does not fail to give an account of the various possibilities in this respect.)

So far the simple method of choosing the earliest date for a first version of each work has allowed us to treat *Les Bijoux indiscrets* as anterior to *Le Fils naturel*, the latter as anterior to *La Religieuse*, and *La Religieuse* as anterior to *Jacques le fataliste*. However, the problem of situating *Le Neveu de Rameau* in relation to the other works of the corpus remains. It is reasonable to infer on available evidence that in its earliest version it postdates, be it quite narrowly or by a space of many years, the 1760 version of *La Religieuse*. However, as stated above, the question of its positioning in relation to *Jacques le fataliste* remains intractable. Scholars tend to disagree on a date for a first version of *Le Neveu de Rameau*. Henri Coulet decisively opts for 1773, and his argument is as follows (*ŒC*, xii.33-36). In a letter of 22 July to Sophie Volland, Diderot refers to the composition of 'deux ou trois petits ouvrages assez gais' (which one editor of the correspondence has taken to include *Le Neveu de Rameau*). In a letter of 18 August of the same year, written from La Haye to Mme d'Epinay, Diderot mentions 'une petite satire'. Coulet mentions the views of various scholars who have tended to resist the conclusion that the text mentioned here is *Le Neveu de Rameau*, also known as the 'Satire seconde'.[20] He, however, turns to yet another letter, dated, like the letter to Sophie Volland, 22 July 1773, but addressed to Mme d'Epinay, in which Diderot mentions 'deux ou trois [...] guenilles'. Coulet concludes: 'Etant donné le caractère de brièveté prêté aux "petits ouvrages" ainsi évoqués et l'imprécision de leur nombre, nous rangerons volontiers *Le Neveu de Rameau* parmi ces guenilles' (p.33).

Whatever the intrinsic merits of the views of various scholars on this point, it is unwise to choose between them; Diderot's allusions are here simply too vague to permit any degree of certainty. All we know is that the composition of *Le Neveu de Rameau* cannot predate the spring of 1761; this is not to say, however, that we know a version existed as early as that date.[21] Nor can the internal evidence of the text help us decide; as Coulet points out there are references to clusters of events spanning the period 1760-1773 or

20. According to Coulet, Fabre rejects the idea that the satire in question is *Le Neveu de Rameau*, arguing instead for the possibility that it is either the *Satire contre le luxe à la manière de Perse* or the *Satire première*. L. G. Crocker opts for an apocryphal work, the *Satire sur Colbert*, and G. Roth joins Fabre in arguing for the *Satire première*. See *ŒC*, xii.33.

21. One of the Vandeul copies does contain the closing line: 'en juillet 1762', which may be taken to indicate that a version of the manuscript may have been completed then. However, as Coulet argues, the date may be given as an indication of when the encounter between Diderot and Rameau's nephew is supposed to have taken place. See *ŒC*, xii.34.

beyond. This can only tell us that Diderot could not have completed the version which we know before 1773, without telling us whether he wrote the work in stages, or all at once around the latter date. Coulet concludes: 'nous préférons croire qu'en 1773 ou 1774, assez rapidement, Diderot a écrit d'affilée ce qui fera les cent trente-quatre pages de sa copie autographe, en voulant ressusciter l'atmosphère des années 1759-1762'; but this is indeed a preference rather than a firm conclusion.

The preceding discussion suggests that according to our method *Jacques le fataliste* and *Le Neveu de Rameau* should be treated as posterior to *La Religieuse* and the other texts, but should not be placed in any chronological relation to each other at all. If I have placed one before the other, this is merely in order to preserve the pattern of devoting a single chapter to a single text. So the method of seeking the earliest possible substantial version of each text works well enough, if we remember that the last two texts dealt with should be seen as being treated 'in parallel'.

I argued above that the disposition which follows has the added advantage of permitting thematic tendencies within and across the fictions to emerge with greater clarity. To present *Les Bijoux indiscrets* as the first text is to begin with an allegorical exploration of the role of desire which points up starkly oppositions which will subsequently be treated in more subtle and complex fashion. The placing side-by-side of *Le Fils naturel* and *La Religieuse*, on the one hand, and of *Jacques le fataliste* and *Le Neveu de Rameau*, on the other, is equally useful. The former two fictions are thematically related, given that they both explore the question of what it means to be born outside the sanction of marriage; and, as we will show, this question is not without its oedipal aspects.[22] Both fictions also deal with what might be viewed as 'experimental conditions', as the principal action takes place in each case within a closed environment: there is Clairville's home with its limited domestic cast, on the one hand, and there are the stifling prisons of family and convent, on the other. Subsequently, we would argue, Diderot moves on to investigate in what respects oedipal relations may obtain in the world at large between persons unrelated by family ties: that is, in what respects the social world is built on familial structures which correspond to those experienced by Dorval and Suzanne.[23]

22. Of course, Diderot seems concerned to work out the same question with important variations: first, Suzanne is passed off by the Simonin family as M. Simonin's daughter, whilst Dorval is born out of wedlock; and second, there is the difference which the sex of the central figure introduces.

23. Suzanne's tale more than Dorval's already opens out onto the world, by presenting the relation to the various Mother Superiors, for instance, as a re-enactment of the relation to the original mother; however, the fact that this re-enactment takes place within an institution which deliberately reconstructs the

The question of approach

It is implicit in what has been said so far that I have adopted an approach which owes certain concepts and terms to psychoanalysis. It scarcely seems possible in our age to discuss desire in literature without some reference to Freud, who argues that the role of sexuality far exceeds functions such as bodily pleasure or reproduction. Freud connects desire with language on the one hand and the unconscious on the other, and it is this double connection which is of interest here. In addition, Freud provocatively expands loving desire into an ambivalence forged of desire and aggression. Desire thus understood has many implications for the analysis of discourse. It drives discourse yet manifests itself only indirectly within it. Condensation and displacement, negation, gaps and contradiction: such are the paths to expression available to unconscious desire. Discourse, at its most consciously controlled, its most rational, or its most rhetorical, is but a compromise-formation in which the mechanism of repression must continually permit a return of the repressed. This is the unsettling Freud who, by providing a radical view of language and desire, is of continuing importance for literary studies.

It hardly needs stating that any use of the Freudian heritage within literary studies is regarded by many with suspicion. In an argument based on the worst excesses of the tradition, it is often claimed that such an approach leads to reductionism. It is especially important, then, that critics who use psychoanalysis explain their methodology. The present study is not intended as a restatement of Freudian or post-Freudian dogma, but as an attempt to understand how psychoanalysis and narratology might illuminate each other. The most impressive practitioner of such an approach is probably Peter Brooks. On the other hand, several of his general statements on methodology are slightly at odds with his own practice, as a result perhaps of a prevailing orthodoxy which dictates that certain types of literary psychoanalysis are outmoded. I have addressed such questions, if somewhat briefly, in the Conclusion. Meanwhile, it will suffice to say that the study which follows is informed by a variety of theorists of psychoanalytic and narratological orientation. Freud and Lacan are a rich source of reflection on the relationship between desire and language. Brooks's insistence on using Freudian models to read narrative as being shaped (as if) by desire provides proof of the fact that psychoanalysis and narratology can vivify each other. Echoing, however mutedly, Freud

family by its use of the maternal, paternal, and fraternal metaphors, places the text 'between' *Le Fils naturel* and those texts whose characters move outside the limits of both family and family-like institution.

and Lacan, René Girard argues that the relationship between the desire of the subject and the desire of the Other is vital for an understanding of the novel in general. Finally, Eve Kosofsky Sedgwick shows how Girardian triangulation can and often does assume what she calls a homosocial aspect. The importance of these various thinkers and critics will emerge more clearly in due course.

The need to include some discussion of theory should not obscure the fact that this remains above all a study of Diderot. This having been said, whilst it must be recognised that any student or critic will read the available biographies with profit, any attempt to define Diderot the man remains outside our concerns. It is not an historical figure but a recurrent mode or tendency of writing which is examined here; and in this sense there are many 'Diderots'. Alongside the materialist, the moralist, the political thinker, the art critic, the dramaturge, the lover and the various other Diderots which can be constructed, we need to find space for Diderot, poet of desire.

1. *Les Bijoux indiscrets*

As stated in the Introduction, Diderot's first novel derives a certain structural and thematic underpinning from the fact that its central character, the sultan Mangogul, receives a magic ring with which he is able to pursue a protracted investigation into female desire. If we read the text naively, we might simply ask ourselves what it tells us of women. Women's *bijoux* speak; they speak of female sexuality; therefore we can glean a number of messages with a minimum of interpretive effort. If we do read in this manner, however, we are likely to be disappointed when we come across a small number of truisms, repetitively demonstrated in the course of some thirty trials of the ring: women are deceitful, and they are naturally promiscuous; women can be homosexual, or hypocritically prudish, or coquettish. However, a more fruitful approach is possible. We can ask, not what the text tells us of female sexuality, but what it betrays of male desire. What is at stake in the textual construction of a desiring woman? What does the need to know 'what woman wants' tell us of male sexuality, the sexuality of the sultan who pursues his quest and that of the narratorial figure who organises the text?

Two papers by Freud provide a suitable frame for such questions. In the first, entitled 'On the universal tendency to debasement in the sphere of love', Freud analyses certain ways in which men desire women. He suggests that many men experience a certain inhibition when they become attached to any woman who recalls the mother or sister, since the resemblance arouses the guilt attached to the incestuous choice of object. The mother can be recalled in any way whatsoever; however, it is particularly common for this to happen when the woman in question commands respect and affection. Freud infers the existence of a split in male desire; the 'whorish' woman is desirable but despicable, whilst the respectable woman is idealised but sexually less interesting: 'there are only a very few educated people in whom the two currents of affection and sensuality have become properly fused; the man almost always feels his respect for the woman acting as a restriction on his sexual activity, and only develops full potency when he is with a debased sexual object'. This dichotomy is neatly expressed in French by the shorthand phrase *maman/putain*. The second paper which is of interest here is entitled 'A special type of choice of object made by men'. Here, Freud seems concerned with establishing the incestuous basis of the respect which he claims so inhibits male desire.

He also intensifies the kind of emotion which is likely to recall attachment to the mother. With disarming simplicity he asks how it is possible that when men love women, they are capable of idealising the loved one beyond all reason, assigning her qualities which she does not possess. Freud's answer is that such a response is derived from the relation to the mother: 'the trait of overvaluing the loved one, and regarding her as unique and irreplaceable, can be seen to fall [...] naturally into the context of the child's experience, for no one possesses more than one mother, and the relation to her is based on an event that is not open to any doubt and cannot be repeated'.[1] Consequently, if any subsequent object is regarded as irreplaceable, that quality will have been conferred by an unconscious identification of that object with the mother. The desiring male does not emerge well from such an analysis; threatened with 'psychic impotence' unless he couples with women he despises, he is unable to encounter women except as projections of an inner split instituted by guilt.

One response to Freud's reasoning is to suggest that, whilst his observations may tell us a great deal concerning his own affective life they have no force when generalised (to cover all but 'a very few educated people'). However, his concepts do prove useful as a frame for reading *Les Bijoux indiscrets.* Especially if we read both authors with due suspicion, the convergence of the theorist and the novelist illuminates the writing of each. Like Freud's desiring male, Diderot's sultan ultimately divides women into two categories: the whorish on the one hand and the ideal, unique and irreplaceable on the other. By definition, the second category can only admit one woman, and that woman is Mirzoza. If we persist in asking why this should be so, we discover that Diderot's first novel expresses an infantile plaint, a nostalgia for the mother, which constantly subverts the surface rhetoric of a misogynous discourse.

Reading desire in 'Les Bijoux indiscrets'

The desire of difference

The plot of *Les Bijoux indiscrets* suggests that Mirzoza is virtuous, and also that all other women resemble each other in not being so. They are not by any means identical; but they are equally marked by an inexorable sexual impulse which prevents them from being satisfied either with celibacy or

1. See respectively: 'On the universal tendency to debasement in the sphere of love', in Sigmund Freud, *The Standard edition of the complete psychological works*, ed. and translated by James Strachey *et al.*, 24 vols (London, Hogarth Press 1957-1974), xi.177-90; and 'A special type of choice of object made by men', in *The Standard edition*, xi.163-75 (p.169).

with fidelity. This similarity, confirmed by experimentation with the ring, allows Mangogul to construct a taxonomy of women (labelled 'la morale de Mangogul') which is based entirely upon the differing vicissitudes of the all-present sexual instinct:

> Si j'accordais une âme aux femmes, je supposerais volontiers [...] que les bijoux ont parlé de tout temps, bas à la vérité, et que l'effet de l'anneau du génie Cucufa se réduit à leur hausser le ton. Cela posé, rien ne serait plus facile que de vous définir toutes tant que vous êtes;
>
> La femme sage, par exemple, serait celle dont le bijou est muet, ou n'en est pas écouté.
>
> La prude, celle qui fait semblant de ne pas écouter son bijou.
>
> La galante, celle à qui le bijou demande beaucoup, et qui lui accorde trop.
>
> La voluptueuse, celle qui écoute son bijou avec complaisance.
>
> La courtisane, celle à qui son bijou demande à tout moment, et qui ne lui refuse rien.
>
> La coquette, celle dont le bijou est muet, ou n'en est point écouté; mais qui fait espérer à tous les hommes qui l'approchent, que son bijou parlera quelque jour, et qu'elle pourra ne pas faire la sourde oreille.[2]

There are two categories here which require further elucidation. For both the 'femme sage' and the 'coquette' are said either not to listen to their *bijoux*, or to possess *bijoux* which do not speak. This may be understood in one of two ways. First, such women may not experience desire, if their *bijou* is silent – but this would follow most awkwardly on Mangogul's universal premise that 'les bijoux ont parlé de tout temps'. Second, they may for whatever reason suppress their desire – they do not 'listen to' the *bijou*. Now, Mirzoza does not belong anywhere in Mangogul's system, not even in the category of 'femme sage'. For when her *bijou* does speak, it is to reveal that there is no distinction possible in her case between spoken and unspoken desire. She experiences desire, but exclusively for the sultan (p.258), whilst as we have just seen the 'femme sage' either experiences no desire or suppresses it. Mirzoza in fact is to be qualified as a 'femme tendre', to use her own term: 'La femme tendre est celle [...] qui a aimé sans que son bijou parlât, ou [...] dont le bijou n'a jamais parlé qu'en faveur du seul homme qu'elle aimait' (p.100).[3]

Mirzoza, then, is what she is because she is not the others, whilst the others resemble each other too closely to be as distinct from each other as she is from them. In these circumstances, the desire whose object is Mirzoza

2. Diderot, *ŒC*, iii.99.

3. Here, Mirzoza's definition of the 'femme tendre' initially overlaps with one side of Mangogul's definition of the 'femme sage': a woman who, lacking sexual instincts, nevertheless experiences love. However, she then discards this definition in favour of one according to which sexual instincts and love are co-present, and the closing chapter shows that this is the case which she herself illustrates.

will be prevented from slipping metaphorically from like to like. Such slippage of course characterises relations between women and men other than the central couple, as is repeatedly demonstrated by the trials of the ring, for these reveal a world where sexual objects are constantly exchanged. In brief, a single, truly dyadic relation exists in a world of shifting desires.

This is less a contribution to an ongoing debate on women than the expression of a wish and the defence against an anxiety. This can be confirmed by a review of basic elements of the plot. First, out of dissatisfaction with his life, Mangogul acquires the magic ring and promises not to test Mirzoza; second, he tests other women; third, he tests Mirzoza, on the pretext of saving her life; fourth, he relinquishes the ring, and is dissatisfied no longer. Now, such events might well prompt a number of questions. How precisely is the dissatisfaction of the opening replaced by satisfaction at the close? Is Mangogul happy because he has had the opportunity to prove that Mirzoza desires him alone, and did the trials of the other women represent a mere delay of the only trial that mattered? Or is the testing of the other women equally important in the movement towards the happy ending, and would Mangogul never have relinquished the ring had he not tested both Mirzoza and the others?

Answers to such questions can be inferred from the nineteenth and twentieth chapters of the second volume (p.246-55).[4] In Chapter 19, the sultan discovers that a certain Zaïde seems to be completely devoted to her lover, to the exclusion of all other men. His reaction betrays a wish and an anxiety, interconnected: 'Le sultan fut dans un étonnement incroyable; il n'avait jamais vu de femmes tendres que la favorite et Zaïde. Il se croyait aimé de Mirzoza; mais Zaïde n'aimait-elle pas davantage Zuleïman? Et ces deux amants n'étaient-ils point les seuls vrais amants du Congo?' (p.246-47). This passage implies that there is and can only be one woman whose love is at once absolute and exclusive, for, according to Mangogul's reasoning, if Zaïde's love is these things then Mirzoza's cannot be. Correlatively, of course, there can only be one individual who is loved, absolutely and exclusively, by the woman in question. Now, this conviction that there is one such woman only is far from empirical; it is not based on all or indeed any of the trials of the ring, since up to this point these trials have only pointed towards the conclusion that the existence of such a woman is doubtful.[5] Yet not only is this conviction anti-empirical; it is also wishful,

4. As stated in our Introduction, the Hermann edition re-establishes the work's division into two volumes, which Naigeon and subsequent editors suppressed (see *ŒC*, iii.19-20).

5. For a perceptive discussion of the theme of experimentation in the work, see D. J. Adams, 'Experiment and experience in *Les Bijoux indiscrets*', *SVEC* 182 (1979), p.303-17.

which is shown here *a contrario*. For it is clearly indicated that not to belong to the one truly dyadic couple is experienced by Mangogul as intensely disturbing. Until the closing chapter, then, Mangogul does not discover but posits the existence of one true couple, and he does so *in order to belong to it.*

Once again, such emphasis on uniqueness points in the direction of the mother. We have seen that Freud connects the uniqueness of the mother with the tendency of men to idealise the woman they love. However, the same conclusion can be reached from a slightly different starting point. Quite simply, not to be able to bear the metaphorical substitution of one (female) object for another is a tendency which can be read in terms of a clinging to the first object of all, a fixation in the attachment to the mother. Moreover, if Mangogul cannot conceive of two women equalling each other in their capacity for exclusive love, it is perhaps because he cannot bear to conceive of two men being equally loved. This in turn points in the direction of rivalry towards father and siblings on the part of the infant who experiences the division of his mother's love as traumatic, so fiercely does he require to be loved exclusively. Zaïde alone is metaphorically connected to Mirzoza in that both women represent the 'femme tendre' (that category which escapes Mangogul's taxonomy); as we have just seen, the narrator informs us that 'Mangogul [...] n'avait jamais vu de femmes tendres que la favorite et Zaïde'. As a result, they can be read as representing a single woman – that unique woman whose love is valuable – 'split' by the division of her love between two objects.[6]

Mangogul's final satisfaction is ensured in two ways. First, Zuleïman is shown to be impotent, with the result that Zaïde's attachment to him is doomed to survive only as Platonic love (p.248). Second, Mangogul and Sélim join forces to prove to Mirzoza through an elaborate allegory that Platonic love is in fact an impossibility (p.249-55; we will return to this allegory below). Zuleïman's impotence, then, assures the anxious sultan of a future alteration in Zaïde's devotion to her lover. This points the way from the 'false' ending in which Zuleïman is to be envied to the 'true' one, in which Mangogul proves to be the only one who is loved as he requires to be.[7] The novel's three closing chapters, then, show that what is at stake is

6. This split permits a disavowal; it is not she (Mirzoza) who loves another (Zuleïman); it is another (Zaïde) who does so. This allows for a second split and a second disavowal: it is not I (Mangogul) who am impotent (or desire the forbidden object, my mother); it is another (Zuleïman) who is so. Reversed, these disavowals become: I desire my mother, who desires another. Thus the oedipal situation is disavowed yet manifested in the pattern of (false) doubles contained in the work's penultimate chapter.

7. There is an intriguing play of letters and sounds between the names of the four characters concerned. Not only does each couple share names beginning with the

not ultimately scientific knowledge (a statement on women), but a compensation of the anxiety connected with the threat to the dyadic relation which is posed by the mobility of desire; and by the same token, the text manifests a fixation on the mother with whom subsequent objects are either identified (Mirzoza) or contrasted (women in general). Implicit in this is an antagonism directed towards the rival for the mother or her surrogate: the father or his surrogate. The fundamentally oedipal structures of the text will be explored in greater detail below.

Two types of object

As we have just seen, Mirzoza is opposed to Zaïde and defined to some extent by her difference from her; and this takes place just before the close of the work, modifying the sense of the ending. Curiously enough, this sequence is a repetition of the manner in which the first volume is brought to a close; for there too a potential double for Mirzoza is presented, only to be contested: Eglé, who at first seems faithful and loving, but is later proved to be as changeable as the rest. These two false doubles, to be differentiated at all cost from Mirzoza, may be seen as punctually resuming all the other women in the novel at a climactic moment of the narrative. We suggested above that what is at stake in the opposition between Zaïde and Mirzoza is the notion that there is only one dyadic couple, immune from the contagion of a world of change. However, something else is also at stake: the divisibility of the female gender ultimately into two and only two truly important categories. For whilst Mangogul may invent a taxonomy of women with six categories, these can all be subsumed in the category defined by 'difference from Mirzoza', thanks to their being either sexually unresponsive or fickle, whilst Mirzoza is neither. Eglé and Zaïde confirm, not only that Mirzoza is unique, but also that there is no middle ground between the ideal and the debased woman. The anxiety generated by Zaïde's case in particular suggests that no woman can resemble Mirzoza without 'becoming' her (so that Mirzoza ceases to be herself, the one ideal woman); and both cases suggest that no woman can differ from her in the slightest without being relegated to the category of 'all the rest'.

same initial letter, but the last and first letters of their names overlap: ZuleïMAN, MANgogul, MirzoZA, ZAïde. It is tempting, if tendentious, to suggest that this shows that Zaïde is indeed 'split off' from Mirzoza, and that Mangogul risks being a second version of Zuleïman. However, the pattern of these names does at least suggest by its play of sounds the risk of reduplication of (partial) identity which is apparently so disturbing to Mangogul, given that he needs to establish that the two couples are absolutely non-identical, and that only the couple to which he belongs is unique.

Whatever objections may be raised against the conception of a *maman/putain* dichotomy in other circumstances, it seems appropriate to adduce it here. For we have seen how strong the tendency is to distinguish between the two categories, and to eliminate any middle ground at the concluding moment of each volume of the narrative. Moreover, there can be no doubt that Mangogul debases the women who differ from Mirzoza. His investigation into the nature of women involves the evaluation of the genders in terms of a 'better' and a 'worse'. For women to be capable of desiring different men is not presented as a morally neutral characteristic which they share with men, but as whorishness. Thus Mangogul's quest, which is sporadically presented as a disabused scientific inquiry, shades off repeatedly into moralistic evaluation.

The clearest example of this slippage between apparent empiricism and moralistic censure is afforded in Chapter 21 of volume i. Mangogul here discovers that a battle was lost as Zermounzaïd, a colonel, made love to Thélis, wife of Sambuco, a general. This incites Mangogul's rage; the sexual instinct is presented here as profoundly unpatriotic: 'Que d'horreur! s'écria tout bas Mangogul: un époux déshonoré, l'Etat trahi, des citoyens sacrifiés, ces forfaits ignorés, récompensés même comme des vertus, et tout cela à propos d'un bijou!' (p.94). It is the woman who, Eve-like, proffers the forbidden fruit and tempts the man from his proper course: 'tout cela à propos d'un bijou!' And throughout the work, when women's secrets are out, they generally respond with shame, occasionally defiance; but either way they are laughed at, by the men first, but also by other women with as much to fear.

In contrast, when men are ridiculed, it is because they claim conquests which they have not made, or because they foolishly believe in attempting to live out a partnership of mutual fidelity (which is especially foolish in the case of older men). The latter point is illustrated by the case of Sambuco, as made clear by the following gloss: 'Thélis fut ou parut vertueuse pendant six semaines entières après son mariage. Mais un bijou né voluptueux se dompte rarement de lui-même, et un mari quinquagénaire, quelque héros qu'il soit d'ailleurs, est un insensé, s'il se promet de vaincre cet ennemi' (p.92). Sélim too illustrates this truism, as we shall see below. As for (young) men claiming false conquests, this is the subject of the chapter on the *petits-maîtres* (p.149-54; book II, Chapter 3).

Furthermore, it seems clear that a *maman/putain* dichotomy is precisely what sets the narrative underway in the first place. The attachment between Mangogul and Mirzoza is presented as precarious, and in need of a supplement in order to subsist; particular emphasis is placed on the insufficiency of the erotic attachment, for Mirzoza has 'peu de tempérament': 'La favorite, qui possédait au souverain degré le talent si nécessaire et si rare de bien narrer, avait épuisé l'histoire scandaleuse de Banza. Comme elle avait peu de tempérament, elle n'était pas toujours disposée à recevoir les caresses du sultan, ni le sultan toujours d'humeur à lui en proposer' (p.40).

Up to this point, Mirzoza has compensated for the deficiency of this 'peu de tempérament' by telling scabrous tales of other women; others' sexuality supplements her own. Now, however, her tales of the 'aventures galantes de la ville' have run dry, and by the same token the erotic attachment is threatened with being weakened once again. The further supplement which she proposes is to obtain erotic stories, not of the women of the town but of the women of the court, and it will be up to someone other than Mirzoza to narrate these tales: 'Qui que ce soit qui vous les raconte, je suis sûre que Votre Hautesse gagnera plus par le fond, qu'elle ne perdra par la forme' (p.41). Yet as Derrida has argued, the supplement may replace rather than complete its object.[8] Mirzoza is now doubly detached from the content of the erotic tales; not only do they speak of others, they are spoken by others. It is clear that Mangogul's erotic interest is henceforth to be directed exclusively towards those 'whorish' women who confess to their own exploits under the influence of the ring. Though the interest takes the form of listening rather than participating, it is clear that it is rooted in sexual curiosity as well as in the (connected) need to despise women for their sexual appetite.[9]

Thus a split is instituted at the outset; others (the possessors of the *bijoux indiscrets*, as it turns out) will provide erotic satisfaction for the sultan, whilst Mirzoza, lacking 'tempérament', is relieved of this obligation. This split sets the narrative into motion, as the sultan shuttles to and fro between Mirzoza and the others, first listening pruriently then reporting back scornfully. In this way the *maman/putain* dichotomy is afforded expression in and as a narrative structure. Almost of necessity, the narrative closes as the split is healed, and all other women abandoned afresh in favour of Mirzoza. The latter henceforth offers all satisfactions comprehended by the term 'amour': 'Génie tout-puissant, lui dit Mangogul, reprenez votre anneau, et continuez-moi votre protection. – Prince, lui répondit le génie, partagez vos

8. For Derrida's discussion of *suppléer* and his application of it to Rousseau's *Confessions*, see Jacques Derrida, *De la grammatologie* (Paris, Editions de Minuit 1967), p.203-34.

9. Whilst Mangogul usually merely listens to the *bijoux* speaking, occasionally the listening is combined with looking, as in the case of Thélis (p.93). Touching, however, is avoided, as we shall see below. Nevertheless, the sexual nature of the looking and listening can scarcely be mistaken, and in this sense the 'whorish' women who are not Mirzoza do indeed provide the sultan with sexual excitation and a kind of gratification.

jours entre l'amour et la gloire. Mirzoza vous assurera le premier de ces avantages, et je vous promets le second' (p.258).

This happy ending represents a wishful transcendence of the *maman/putain* split. Now that her *bijou* has finally spoken and echoes her mouth, Mirzoza is to be the source and satisfaction of all erotic and 'higher' impulses equally.

Sexual difference and the castration motif

As critics have pointed out, there are precedents for the conceit of the *bijou* in the work of Caylus, Crébillon *fils* and others.[10] However, this does nothing to diminish the striking quality of the concern with the female genitals manifested in the extended use of the conceit. Literary tradition notwithstanding, this implies an obsessive attention to sexual difference and its anatomical basis.

Indeed, in a psychoanalytic perspective certain questions are inevitable. Why this curious emphasis? Does it screen some disavowed anxiety? Is it connected with a defence of some kind? In its most rationalised form it is presented as a scientific quest, and the culmination of this tendency is the 'morale de Mangogul' to which we referred above. But we can also read this *morale* as follows: 'there must indeed be an anatomical distinction setting women apart from men; for it is possible to perceive it in every aspect of women's behaviour, however varied. In fact, the whole of women's behaviour is nothing but an expression of the genital difference.' More generally, we can read the repetition of the trials of the ring as the expression of a similar affirmation: 'There must indeed be an anatomical distinction; for however many times I test it, I will surely find it to exist.' And in such propositions we can detect the negated presence of the idea against which they are directed: 'The distinction between the sexes is not founded.' In other words, it can be argued that Mangogul's attention to the genital difference as expressed (he asserts) in all kinds of behavioural extensions is underpinned by the subsistence of a difficulty in respect of accepting the anatomical distinction. Such a difficulty may be anxious or regretful: the distinction may be emphasised either because it is felt to be threatened, or because its reversal is desired.

If this is a negated expression of a difficulty in respect of accepting sexual difference, a positive expression is also present in the form of the motif of castration, both male and female. For passages dealing with castration of course imply a neutralisation of the genital difference which is so obsessively asserted elsewhere. The passages in question vary in presenting

10. See, for instance, R. J. Ellrich, 'The structure of Diderot's *Les Bijoux indiscrets*', *Romanic review* 52 (1961), p.279-89.

castration either as a wounding, or as a painless, magical suppression of difference. Chapter 25 of volume i opens as follows: 'Le viol était sévèrement puni dans le Congo [...] Le coupable était condamné à perdre la partie de lui-même par laquelle il avait péché, opération cruelle dont il périssait ordinairement' (p.112). There follows the story of Fatmé, whose lover Kersael is in the process of leaving her for another woman. She accuses him of rape; he is convicted, and his punishment is to be castration. At the eleventh hour, however, Mangogul uses his ring to discover the truth, and Kersael is set free. Fatmé's punishment is to wear a chastity belt, which is attached 'publiquement et sur l'échafaud même dressé pour l'exécution de Kersael' (p.118). This seems to be intended as a kind of poetic justice, and by the same token is a symbolic castration; Fatmé had intended Kersael to be castrated; instead, symmetry is instituted for she is 'castrated' (prevented from having sex). The link between Kersael's projected and Fatmé's actual punishment is reinforced by a kind of condensation; the 'échafaud' used for one was to be used for the other.[11]

The doubling of male by female castration recurs in Chapter 20 of volume ii, in the allegory on Platonic love. A young man, Hilas, fails to genuflect the customary seventeen times before the 'grande Pagode'. The latter punishes him as follows: 'le pauvre Hilas se trouva tout à coup enflammé de désirs les plus violents, et privé, comme sur la main, du moyen de les satisfaire'. He is to remain castrated until he finds a woman who will love him nevertheless. After a period of fruitless search he meets Iphis, who tells him: 'il y a deux ans que j'eus le malheur d'offenser une pagode, qui m'ôta tout'. Hilas and Iphis fall in love; their castration is therefore magically reversed and they become lovers. However, the threat of male castration returns, if on an ironic and ribald note: 'Pendant plusieurs mois qu'ils séjournèrent ensemble dans le désert, ils eurent tout le temps de s'assurer de leur changement: lorsqu'ils en sortirent, Iphis était parfaitement guérie; pour Hilas, l'auteur dit qu'il était menacé d'une rechute' (p.255). In this allegory, castration is painless and institutes a genital and situational symmetry between Hilas and Iphis which was incomplete in the case of Fatmé and Kersael.

Finally, the chapter entitled 'Le Rêve de Mangogul' (p.261-66) presents an account of a vision of Mangogul's. This vision incorporates a dream in which the threat of an emasculation which may well involve castration looms. For the dreamer sees a woman fleeing before a *menuisier*, who 'se

11. Rank mentions this episode in a discussion of incest and castration which involves extended use of his concept of literary doubles. See Otto Rank, *The Incest theme in literature and legend*, trans. Gregory C. Richter (Baltimore and London, Johns Hopkins University Press 1992), p.237-38.

dispose à lui percer un trou où il devait y en avoir deux et où il n'y en avait point'. The woman is more or less willing to submit to the painful operation, but the dreamer attacks the *menuisier*, who turns instead on him, crying: 'Demande grâce ou je t'en fais deux'. In his waking life, the dreamer is left with the delusion that he has 'deux trous au cul', which is effectively, to judge by the preceding dialogue between the *menuisier* and the woman, to be female.[12]

It should further be noted that the threat of castration normally arises as punishment, and indeed as the punishment of illicit desire. It is Kersael's desire for another woman, of course, which incites Fatmé's wrath. In the Platonic allegory, Hilas fails to genuflect seventeen times before the *grande pagode* because he is inflamed by desire as he sees 'la beauté dont il était épris' passing by (p.251). As for Mangogul's 'vision', it seems there that the threatened feminisation is a punishment for gazing at a thinly disguised sexual (primal?) scene, and so perhaps also for the desire which such a scene arouses in the dreamer.

Such considerations raise a more general question. If there is a threat (of castration, mutilation or more generally punishment of any kind), are there co-present indications that the threat comes from a specifically paternal figure, suggesting that the father is a hostile presence and a rival for the mother? The stories of castration neither confirm nor invalidate such a link. Fatmé is the one who requests Kersael's castration, but it is the sultan, father of the people, who must approve or lift the punishment. As for the tale of Hilas and Iphis, the 'grande pagode' is a figure of indeterminate sex. Finally, in Mangogul's dream, both the *menuisier* and his master are male, but not necessarily paternal. Elsewhere, however, the father and his substitutes are represented in their own right, and it will be revealing to examine those figures in order to establish whether they are hostile, passive, or both. If ambivalence towards the father emerges, this provides an interesting point of reference from which to review the desire for the mother on the one hand and the fear of or wish for castration on the other. Without it being possible to connect these various aspects of the text in too positive a fashion, their co-existence obviously suggests a patterning of desire and anxiety along the lines of family relationships.

12. Within this dream, incidentally, all male-male relationships are conceived on the model of subjugation of the weak by the strong. The *menuisier* claims to be the forerunner of one greater than himself, and one who will inflict greater pain. There is an especial emphasis laid on the punishing figure, since from the dreamer's point of view he is double.

The father and his substitutes

An oedipal relation to the father, in both its affectionate and hostile manifestations, is expressed in a fairly clear fashion throughout the novel. Whilst Mangogul's actual mother is not mentioned in the novel, his father is. Erguebzed seems to display nothing but affection towards his heir, supervising his education with the best intentions and stepping down from the throne to allow his accomplished and attractive young son to reign in his place. The father-son relationship would seem to be perfectly harmonious thanks to Erguebzed's recognition of Mangogul's superior vigour (p.38), and the emphasis on this at the opening of the novel can be read as a disavowal of all possibility of oedipal hostility or rivalry. There is no need for the father to die in order for the son to reign; instead he lives on somewhere in the kingdom, quiet and voluntarily powerless, and not in the least a threat (p.39). He is scarcely mentioned after the opening chapter, and at one point there is a casual allusion to his death (p.222), though this death is nowhere narrated.[13] However, if Mangogul lives in perfect harmony with Erguebzed, his birth is the occasion of the death of many of his sultan father's peers, as though his birth had a mysterious connection with their deaths: 'Le trépas de plusieurs souverains fut, comme on voit, l'époque funeste de sa naissance' (p.36). This curious detail suggests that the oedipal hostility which is so ostentatiously diverted from Erguebzed is visited magically upon his peers or substitutes.

In the father's absence a man of his generation, Sélim, is introduced, and becomes, with Mangogul and Mirzoza, the third main character of the text. Sélim is closely associated with the father, for he states: 'Le prince Erguebzed était monté sur le trône: j'avais sa bienveillance longtemps avant son règne: il me l'a continuée jusqu'à sa mort, et j'ai tâché de justifier cette marque de distinction par mon zèle et ma fidélité' (p.222). By virtue of this lifelong friendship, Sélim seems to elect himself the representative of the dead father, a mirror of his values and a perpetuation of his presence; and like the sultans who die at Mangogul's birth, as mere proxy he can safely become the butt of filial hostility. Sélim is not only presented as a version of the father, but also – if subtly – as a potential rival for Mirzoza. Rivalry is

13. The failure to narrate the father's death as an event in the son's life may be interpreted in a variety of ways. It may be seen as a 'bévue', if Diderot is assumed first to have intended the father to remain alive somewhere in the kingdom but then to have forgotten that intention. Otherwise it must be seen as an elision in the narrative. No rule exists, of course, to determine what may normally be elided in a given narrative. However, it is interesting to note that here the elision expresses a compromise or hesitation between a story in which the father would be killed, and another in which he would not. This implies a narratorial ambivalence towards the father.

naturally at stake in this text which involves a reflection on the conditions of possibility of fidelity. Mirzoza is shown to be worthy of Mangogul's fidelity by a lengthy denigration of all other women. Yet Mangogul is shown to be the worthy lover of Mirzoza over and above no crowd of men but one old man closely associated with the father, male rivalry being clearly conceived on the oedipal model. Possibly the humiliation of this 'father' is as necessary to the happy ending as the debasement of all women but Mirzoza. At least, it helps to prove the exclusive love of the 'mother' at the expense of what is in an infantile perspective the most important and forbidding rival of all.

If Sélim is present as a surrogate father, what kind of father does he represent? The ageing courtier is characterised initially by his vast sexual experience. Mirzoza enjoins him to relate the story of his past loves (p.198-99) and she displays great interest in his tales of his own potency, which include an episode where he impregnates a whole convent (p.214-15). Mangogul, on the other hand, displays a certain hostility towards the older man by raising doubts concerning his mistress Fulvia's fidelity: 'je n'ai point du tout de foi en elle' (p.229). When Sélim suggests that she should be put to the test, Mangogul forcefully concurs, in spite of Mirzoza's protests (p.229-30). In doing so, he places the older man in danger of being humiliated. Clearly what is at stake here is not only Fulvia's reputation and the ongoing debate on women, but also Sélim's belief that he remains potent and attractive enough to satisfy a young woman. Coming as it does at the end of a conversation in which Sélim has impressed Mirzoza with his boasts, Mangogul's challenge seems to be intended as a means of resolving their rivalry over the favourite.

Fulvia is duly exposed. Mortified, Sélim exiles himself from the company of Mangogul and Mirzoza. However, they reassure him that they need and enjoy his presence, and so he returns (p.234-35). Now he represents, not a potent figure who can threaten to seduce Mirzoza, but an impotent, humbled and controllable presence. All of this can of course be read as representing a wishful reversal of the oedipal situation; it is now not the father but the son who is of the same age as the mother, and her body is forbidden not to the son but to the father.

The ageing courtier thus affords the possibility of dramatising the oedipal hostility which is so carefully diverted from the true father at the opening of the novel. Initially a threatening father-rival, Sélim is constrained to follow the course voluntarily adopted by Erguebzed, the affectionate father-ally: renunciation of all claims to power or potency followed by exile or self-effacement. However, the situation is reversed in the 'Vision de Mangogul' which was, interestingly enough, one of the last two chapters to be added to the work. If in the case of the dream which we examined above the *menuisier* (and for that matter his master) are associated with the father, then there at least he refuses to efface himself or die but threatens rather to leap up and mutilate mother and son alike.

Ideal egos and mirror images

Mangogul does not take as his model men such as Sélim who can boast of the broadest sexual experience. Instead, he displays a certain inhibition in respect of sexual activity. For however many women Mangogul spies on and listens to, with the sole exception of Zaïde, who seems momentarily to displace Mirzoza as the true 'femme tendre', he is never tempted to make love to any of them. This inhibition is dramatised in volume ii, Chapter 12, in which he attends a masked ball. When he is approached by a young woman, although she is 'jeune et jolie', the sultan flees. He then changes costume with a guard who makes love to the woman in his place (p.209). Once the guard removes his mask, he reveals 'une physionomie armée de deux grands crocs, qui n'appartenaient point du tout à Mangogul' (p.209). This guard then mocks the young woman; her discomfiture is presented as comical and gratifying. This episode bespeaks a difficulty in respect of accepting women's desire, and indeed men's desire for women, since this grotesque double is substituted for the sultan in the sexual act, the impulse towards which is presented as squalid or punishable. Whilst the sultan throughout insists that women are driven primarily by their sexual appetite, which implies an intellectual acceptance of their sensuality, when it comes to touching rather than merely looking and listening a strong inhibition comes into play, and female sensuality is presented as sordid and risible. At the same time, by fleeing he chooses for himself chastity rather than contamination, there being no other options if men, no less than women, are debased by sex for sex's sake.

Other passages point in the same direction. For instance, Mangogul is conventionally endowed with a harem, as befits sultans in French-Oriental tales, but unconventionally throws it open to the world: 'Il brisa les portes du palais habité par ses femmes; il en chassa ces gardes injurieux de leur vertu; il s'en fia prudemment à elles-mêmes de leur fidélité: on entrait aussi librement dans leurs appartements que dans aucun couvent de chanoinesses de Flandres, et on y était sans doute aussi sage' (p.39). The passage is clearly ironic. Opening the harem is scarcely a gesture of trust in the world, but one of indifference to possessing women other than Mirzoza, in her absolute difference. The harem, which conventionally represents a situation in which one man is promiscuous whilst many women are faithful, now represents the converse.

Such consistent fidelity as this is a resounding contradiction in the character who does not cease to trumpet the impossibility of fidelity in others. By the same token, Mangogul clearly mirrors Mirzoza, for it seems that he like her is destined to love exclusively. At some point during the repetitive trials of the ring the reader may well reach a surprising conclusion: that Mangogul's apparently empirical investigation into the nature of women has been teleologically directed towards the discovery, not only of the one true woman, but also and especially of himself in another.[14]

It would be reasonable to connect these indications of symmetry between male and female with the castration motif we have already examined. What seems to be expressed is a wish, on the one hand, to belong to a dyadic couple, and on the other a fear that the price of such a belonging may be, however obscurely, castration. Perfect (genital) symmetry between partners serves to express the wish and the anxiety at once; for symmetry may result from painful castration or it may recall what seems in retrospect a lost paradise preceding (the original perception of) sexual differentiation, when mother and infant were yet to be separated by maturation and accession to culture, or indeed by the father.

We have suggested that Mirzoza stands in the text for a type of object-choice based on the mother, and we have traced the associated incest-guilt through the *maman/putain* split. Furthermore, we have explored the obsession with genital difference, the motif of castration and the ambivalent treatment of the father-figure. All of these elements are embraced in the notion of the Oedipus complex. They may in addition be lent a Lacanian bias. The 'mirror stage' involves an assumption of the rigid 'armour' of the ego by a process of specular identification preceding the business of anatomical distinction between the sexes, and prepares the way for the Oedipus complex with its attendant castration anxiety. Furthermore, Mangogul's wish to belong to a dyadic couple resistant to all possibility of change and substitution in terms of desire may well be read as a clinging to the Imaginary rather than a (salutary) surrender to the play of symbolisation.[15] But Freud and Lacan aside, the obsessions and tensions of *Les Bijoux indiscrets* are clearly suggestive of a dyadic object-choice defensively maintained, or comfortingly recalled, against a world where desire seems infinitely displaceable.

14. This mirroring is reinforced by other characteristics suggestive of symmetry; Mirzoza, like Mangogul, attempts to explain natural phenomena by philosophising on the location of the soul, dressing in men's clothes to do so (p.118-25); both the sultan and she narrate an allegorical dream (p.130-34; 172-77); and finally they are of similar age and exceptional beauty and charm.

15. The clearest exposition of Lacan's theory is probably the following: Malcolm Bowie, *Lacan* (Cambridge, Harvard University Press 1991). The mirror stage on the one hand and the Imaginary, Symbolic and the Real on the other are dealt with in Chapters 2 and 4 respectively.

The subversion of rhetoric

Les Bijoux indiscrets has traditionally been read as implying a statement on women. In the analysis of the work to which we have already referred, Ellrich situates it in a tradition of debate on women, 'the familiar opposition dating at least from the *Roman de la Rose*' (p.279). There is on the one hand the 'Platonic defence of women', and on the other 'an anti-feminist, naturalistic current' (p.282). The main speakers in this debate are of course Mangogul and Mirzoza, and Ellrich concludes in favour of Mangogul, asserting that ultimately it is 'difficult not to agree with' the sultan's anti-feminist point of view.

According to this type of reading, *Les Bijoux indiscrets* consists in an elaborate rhetorical structure designed to convey a message concerning women. The basis of such a reading is clear, since in several ways the central conceit of the *bijou indiscret* resembles a persuasive device with the most unambiguous of functions. First, there is the fact that the voice of the *bijou* enjoys authority within the text whilst the more 'official' voice of the mouth, or of social propriety, does not. This can be explained in part by the text's explicit appeal to the convention of prosopopeia. The reader is enjoined to accept the authority of the voice issuing from the woman's genitals on the grounds that, providing it speaks about female sexuality, it speaks of what it knows. This principle is made explicit; to Mangogul's question: 'lorsque la bouche et le bijou d'une femme se contredisent, lequel croire?' a courtier answers: 'jusqu'à présent ils ne se sont expliqués que sur un chapitre qui leur est très familier. Tant qu'ils auront la prudence de ne parler que de ce qu'ils entendent, je les croirai comme des oracles' (p.54).[16]

Second, from a structural point of view the *bijou indiscret* is bound to have amongst its effects the unmasking of woman as sexual hypocrite. For, unless it is to become perfectly redundant, it can scarcely speak except when it is contradicting the discourse of the mouth (where the latter concerns sexual behaviour); and the structure of the novel, which is an episodic one, depends on this contradiction being maintained for the duration of the narrative. According to the same principle, it would seem that the narrative must close (as it does) as the discourse of mouth and *bijou* come to match. It seems more or less inevitable, then, that thanks in part to its function as a structuring device, the *bijou* must expose the lying woman who pretends to purity, celibacy or constancy which are not in her nature.

A third way of viewing the *bijou* is to call it an allegorical device. The novel

16. D. J. Adams states: 'The undoubted reliability of their evidence is due to its being wholly coterminous with their experience; they tell only of what they know, and offer no remarks on matters foreign to their experience' (*Diderot: dialogue and debate*, Vinaver Studies in French 2, Liverpool, Francis Cairns 1986, p.105).

as a whole may be seen as an extended allegory, in which the voice of the *bijou* 'stands for' the disavowed drive of female sexuality and in doing so conveys the message that such a drive has universal existence, however often it is disavowed. As we have seen, Mangogul's *morale* takes such a position as its starting point, for he suggests 'que les bijoux ont parlé de tout temps, bas à la vérité, et que l'effet de l'anneau du génie Cucufa se réduit à leur hausser le ton. Cela posé, rien ne serait plus facile que de vous définir toutes tant que vous êtes' (p.99). In speculating that the voice of the *bijou* speaks always and everywhere, Mangogul shows the reader that the *bijou indiscret* is to be interpreted as an allegory for female sexuality in general, and so serves to found a discourse on 'vous toutes'.

If the the novel as a whole is an extended allegory, it serves to frame other allegories, and these too may seem to function as part of the rhetoric concerning femininity. For example, there is the story which we have already analysed, in which Hilas is magically castrated and must remain so unless he can find a woman who will love him platonically. His difficulties in doing so are intended by Mangogul to suggest the universal impossibility of the Platonic love of which women affect to be capable. There is also the chapter 'Des voyageurs', in which Mangogul reads extracts of an account of a journey written by his explorers. They relate that they have visited an island whose inhabitants' *bijoux* (those of both sexes) are of various geometric shapes. Accordingly, before two of these inhabitants marry, they are inspected by the local priests to establish whether they are physically compatible. This may be read as an allegorical re-statement of the message of the talking *bijoux*: that love cannot be abstracted from its sexual basis. In case we miss the point, it is reinforced. On the island special thermometers are used, and these too have a clear allegorical import. The priests apply these thermometers to the *bijoux* of the inhabitants who wish to marry 'pour déterminer le rapport nécessaire de chaleur entre deux époux', and marriage is only permitted between partners whose compatibility is established by this method. The geometrical genitals and the sexual thermometers seem designed to overdetermine the 'message' that what Mirzoza and others call love is only ever glorified sex.

All of these devices, then, may seem to be exploited in order to confirm the portrayal of women as hypocritical whores and the related message that love cannot be abstracted from its physiological basis. It seems then reasonable to argue that this is a text whose elaborate rhetoric tends towards the communication of a single, misogynous view of femininity and an associated vision of men.[17]

17. The *bijou* is also used to communicate satirical messages which have no connection with the sexual; for instance Catholic priests and members of the

Yet it must also be recognised that the work's overarching rhetorical scheme is powerfully subverted. There is, for instance, the conspicuous problem of the ending. However much evidence Mangogul has gathered during the novel to confirm his case, when he finally submits Mirzoza to a trial of the magic ring, the voice of her *bijou* speaks only words of fidelity. This complicates the question of what the text tells us of women; for as Mirzoza herself says 'or s'il y a une femme sage, il peut y en avoir mille' (p.143). The ending may then be read as following the logic of the proverb 'rira bien qui rira le dernier', with which Diderot will later close *Le Neveu de Rameau*. After all, from roughly halfway through the narrative Mirzoza has been Mangogul's debating partner, asserting that love can be at once complete and exclusive, or indeed Platonic. So she would seem to have the last laugh when her own fidelity is demonstrated.

Yet if Mirzoza wins the debate, will we discount the elaborate rhetoric manifest in all that precedes? Or do the ending and the rest simply cancel each other out, telling us nothing of women except that there is more than one view of them? Or are we to understand that virtuous and lascivious women exist in roughly the proportion of one to thirty? If this is all we can derive from the work, we may suspect we have been drawn into a book-length debate as futile as that which occurs between Jacques and his Master: 'Et les voilà embarqués dans une querelle interminable sur les femmes, l'un prétendant qu'elles étaient bonnes, l'autre méchantes, et ils avaient tous deux raison; l'un fausses, l'autre vraies, et ils avaient tous deux raison.'[18]

Critics have attempted several solutions to the problem of the ending. As already stated, Ellrich argues that Mangogul clearly wins the argument, notwithstanding the case of Mirzoza. Another critic has read the novel in terms of Diderot's views on probability, expressed in the *Encyclopédie*; the more women are tested with the same result, the more probable it is that they are all of a kind.[19] Whatever their merits, such readings have an air of wishing to dispose of the problem of the ending in order to salvage a message concerning women (and with it, no doubt, the general notion that clear messages are to be had from rhetorical narratives); but the ending of *Les Bijoux* undeniably subverts the rhetorical scheme of the whole.

The same applies to the two important framed allegories we mentioned

Académie des sciences are satirised. However, this use of the *bijou* is not relevant to the present discussion. It can conveniently be thought of as a supplementary exploitation of the device which is less 'natural', or more arbitrary, than when it is employed to convey a vision of sexuality.

18. *ŒC*, xxiii.42. No fewer than eleven pairs of oppositions are strung together in the passage in question.

19. See Roger Kempf, 'Des bijoux et de l'opinion', *Colloque international Diderot*, ed. Anne-Marie Chouillet (Paris, Aux amateurs de livres 1985), p.239-44 (p.240).

above, contained in the chapters 'Les voyageurs' and 'L'amour platonique'. For on close examination each of these tends to slip out of reach of the rhetorical scheme they seem designed to serve. Once again, the tale of the island of geometrical genitals and sexual thermometers may seem to be intended to convey the message that physiology is at the basis of all love relationships. Here is a utopian society whose laws and customs, like those of the Tahiti of the *Supplément au Voyage de Bougainville*, reflect a purely phyiosological conception of love: 'nos insulaires sont conformés de manière à rendre tous les mariages heureux, si l'on y suivait à la lettre les lois écrites' (p.268) states Cyclophile, an islander. However, the statement is paradoxical. It would be easy to understand why sexual legislation would be required if this were a society which wished to have its citizens act against (their) nature (i.e. nature's purpose as revealed in the geometrical genitals). But why are 'lois écrites' required in order to oblige the *insulaires* to act naturally when they select a partner? Why 'force nature' rather than surrender lawlessly to its promptings? The paradox suggests that what the islanders enshrine in Law is not Nature but only a conception of Nature, and by extension that there will be losses as well as gains wherever there is legislation of desire.[20]

Cyclophile signals quite explicitly that all is not well on his island, or in this allegory: 'Nous avons donc [...] des cocus autant et plus qu'ailleurs, quoique nous ayons pris des précautions infinies pour que les mariages soient bien assortis' (p.267). A little further on, we learn how it comes about that the concept of cuckoldry applies on the island. The testing of the *insulaires* in terms of the configuration of their *bijoux* on the one hand and their *degré de chaleur* on the other is not undertaken merely to advise lovers whether to marry. Instead, the physiological incompatability of two islanders, whenever it is established, becomes for the authorities the basis of a prohibition against marriage between them. It is when lovers unite in spite of this that cuckoldry arises.[21] This aspect of the travellers' tale subverts Mangogul's argument concerning the impossibility of Platonic love. For on an island whose legal system is built on the truism that all love is

20. Similarly, the Tahitians of *Le Supplément au Voyage de Bougainville*, as they are represented by Orou, feel they need to reinforce their 'natural' tendency towards heterosexual promiscuity by deploying a range of customs and prohibitions. See for instance Janet Whatley, '*Un retour secret vers la forêt*: the problem of privacy and order in Diderot's Tahiti', *Kentucky Romance quarterly* 224 (1977), p.199-208.

21. A similar type of transgression defines incest on the island. When two *insulaires* whose genitals are compatible are discovered to vary in respect of their *degré de chaleur*, the 'grand pontife' declares a 'défense à elles de s'unir, sous les peines portées par les lois ecclésiastiques et civiles contre les incestueux. L'inceste dans cette île n'était donc pas une chose tout à fait vide de sens' (p.269).

reducible to the physiological, a love which transcends physiology opposes love-as-physiology.

By its positioning just after Mangogul's anxieties concerning Zaïde and just before the testing of Mirzoza, the fable contained in the chapter 'L'amour platonique' would seem to hold a key position: surely, we might suppose, this is a set-piece allegory designed to resume the misogynous position at the closing stages of the narrative. Yet this allegory is subverted or problematised just as we saw 'Les voyageurs' to be. As long as Hilas cannot find a woman to love him in his castrated state, the tale confirms Mangogul's argument, for it suggests that women cannot enter into the Platonic love they praise so highly. However, Hilas does find love before his genitals are restored, and we are told quite clearly that Hilas and Iphis 's'aimèrent platoniquement' (p.255). At this point, far from suggesting the impossibility of Platonic love, the tale evokes such love and depends upon it for its narrative structure. Finally, their genitals restored, Hilas and Iphis make love. Barthes has argued with others that where narrative is concerned, succession implies causality, or that in reading we employ the principle 'post hoc ergo propter hoc'.[22] If this is the case, the organisation of Hilas's tale represents Platonic love as the *sine qua non* of non-Platonic love. For the narrative sequence implies that it is only on condition that we first experience Platonic love that we can reach the stage of physical love, as though the latter were only conceivable as a development of the former. It is physiological compatibility, not Platonic love, whose existence is represented as less probable, more difficult to attain, and more precarious once attained.

Enough has been said to show that if the novel and its intercalated tales are allegories, their allegorical function is subverted.[23] Now this point

22. 'Tout laisse à penser, en effet, que le ressort de l'activité narrative est la confusion même de la consécution et la conséquence, ce qui vient *après* étant lu dans le récit comme *causé par*; le récit serait, dans ce cas, une application systématique de l'erreur logique dénoncée par la scolastique sous la formule *post hoc, ergo propter hoc*' (Roland Barthes, 'Introduction à l'analyse structurale des récits', in Roland Barthes *et al.*, *L'Analyse structurale du récit*, Paris, Seuil 1981, p.7-33 (p.16). This collection was first published in *Communications* 8, 1966).

23. This might be explained as flawed rhetoric, by imagining the figure of Diderot the novelist-rhetorician, who fails for technical reasons to fulfil his (conscious) intentions. Alternatively it might be explained as clever writing by constructing the figure of Diderot the ludic author, who already in his first novel wishes to problematise the task of the reader in search of an easy read. However, intentionalist constructions are not relevant here. We do not need to decide either that the text shows us the subversion of rhetoric or that we must arrive at such subversion by adopting the posture of a suspicious reader. Both possibilities are subsumed in the statement that rhetoric is subverted in *Les Bijoux indiscrets*.

brings us back to our main concerns. If rhetoric is subverted here, it is *as though* it is subverted by desire. More precisely, it is as though rhetoric is simultaneously fed and subverted by desire. For rhetoric here is apparently employed to convey what is admissible in respect of desire (its avowed objects and limits), whilst the rhetoric thus employed is apparently subverted by the return of the inadmissible in respect of desire (its disavowed objects and aims). The very possibilities which rhetoric seems to contradict (Platonic love, the ideal woman, and connected to both the desire of the mother) subsist at the margins and threaten to subvert the rhetorical structures of the text as a whole (and the vision of woman towards which they gesture). For instead of a single vision of women as whorish, we have discovered a tension between two visions of women which seems to correspond to an oedipal subject-position. Beneath the bragging, misogynous categorisation of women as available whores subsists an inexorable longing for the infantile relation to the mother, an unchallenged belonging within a dyadic couple existing before or somehow beyond sexual differentiation; and this kind of longing invades even those passages in which we can (otherwise) identify the clearest use of rhetoric in the service of the misogynous message.

Finally, the problem of the ending is cast in a new light by the notion that rhetoric is subverted by desire. It has been implicit throughout our reading that rhetorical flaws, inconsistencies, gaps and peculiar emphases, whilst disconcerting in various contexts of interpretation, are from a psychoanalytic point of view a privileged means of access to the workings of desire within discourse. From this point of view the question of a contradiction between the ending and the rest does not arise; both the ending and the rest, taken together, inform us of Mangogul's desire, precisely because their juxtaposition makes no sense in the novel's rhetorical scheme. In order to attain satisfaction, Mangogul must not only test Mirzoza but also test all other women and find them lacking.[24] In other words, the happy ending may be supposed to depend in equal measure on the idealisation of Mirzoza and on the debasement of all others. As we have already seen, she is desired, not for herself, but because she is different from the rest. Once Mirzoza has been tested by the ring, we realise that the others' *bijoux* have been saying, not: 'All women are worthless', but: 'We are worthless, but there is one who is not'. This can be read as a wishful construction dependent on a dialectical movement beyond the opposing terms which are the ideal and the debased

24. By 'Mangogul', I have throughout referred, not to a 'character' as the term is understood in the realist tradition of the novel, but to a (subject-)position in the text which permits the expression – or betrayal – of a narratorial cluster of desires, anxieties and obsessions; and the same applies to other characters' names.

woman. Or we might say that it is not a case of A being contradicted by B, but of A plus B equalling C, where A is the debased woman, B the unique, ideal woman and C a union affording the fullest satisfaction with no trace of incest guilt.

Conclusion

We have seen that it is possible to read *Les Bijoux indiscrets* as if it manifests a strong attachment to the mother with whom subsequent objects are either identified (Mirzoza) or contrasted (women in general). Implicit in this is an antagonism directed towards the rival for the mother or her surrogate: the father or his surrogate. In other words, desire here assumes an oedipal form.[25]

In this connection, it is useful to recall that the *maman/putain* opposition which we have used to analyse *Les Bijoux indiscrets* is a ramification of the oedipus complex. The opposition points towards the operation of incest guilt in respect of choice of object, in that the choice of object depends on avoiding resemblance to the mother. At the same time, the opposition is, for the unconscious, (also) an identity. Thus (consciously) to differentiate the mother from a whore can unconsciously serve the fantasy that she is after all whorish. In the case of *Les Bijoux indiscrets*, the whorish women would then represent Mirzoza as well as her antithesis. The text would then seem to express a wish to circumvent the incest taboo. The inhibition with respect to the mother/Mirzoza is dealt with by splitting off the idea of possessing her sexually along with the moral shame attached to that idea. These are then indulged (by looking and listening) in contact with the whorish women. Finally, the split is represented as superfluous; for in an alternative fantasy, Mirzoza becomes a woman sensually as well as platonically in love with Mangogul, as she speaks words of love from the *bijou* as well as the mouth.

Long decried, if constantly reprinted, *Les Bijoux indiscrets* began to be rehabilitated by scholars, not in its entirety, but for several of its chapters which were deemed worthy of separate study as indications of Diderot's early interest in various subjects (the theatre, dreams, experimental science, the development of human cognition). Subsequently, it was noticed that it

25. Freud's account of the Oedipus complex is problematic, as has been pointed out frequently. For instance, he takes as his starting point a supposed male point of view, that of the 'little man', and attempts – inadequately, by his own admission – to construct a female Oedipus complex which would be a variation on the male norm. Once again, we need not follow Freud in all details. Instead, it is a matter of adopting only those psychoanalytic concepts which seem to be invited by characteristics of Diderot's own text.

was not without self-referential or experimental aspects, and was presented as a 'laboratory for Diderot's later novels'.[26] In addition, it should now be recognised that Diderot's first novel in fact constitutes an elaborate exploration of a family complex which can be detected as a fundamental structuring factor in later narratives. Without having the status of an origin it is the first of a series of tellings of a tale of incestuous desire and its ramifications, the ignoring of which impoverishes any account of Diderot's narratives as a whole. The sultan's ring is far more than a picturesque device borrowed from the stock of the pseudo-oriental fairy tale; it is a way of narrativising desire, and to narrativise desire is a tendency which Diderot retains. Henceforth this tendency will be manifested in more subtle and intricate ways; but as stated in the Introduction, the notion of an unofficial 'voice' of sexuality subverting an official discourse, indeed an official rhetoric which would disavow it, is one which proves immensely suggestive for a reading of subsequent texts.

26. See L. J. Greenberg, 'Narrative technique and literary intent in Diderot's *Les Bijoux indiscrets* and *Jacques le fataliste*', *SVEC* 79 (1971), p.93-101; Vivienne Mylne and Janet Osborne, 'Diderot's early fiction: *Les Bijoux indiscrets* and *L'Oiseau blanc*', *Diderot studies* 14 (1971), p.143-66; and Ruth P. Thomas, '*Les Bijoux indiscrets* as a laboratory for Diderot's later novels', *SVEC* 135 (1975), p.199-211.

2. *Le Fils naturel*

It is well known that classifying many of Diderot's works according to genre is a difficult task, given his tendency to experiment with hybrid forms. Even so, it may at first seem tendentious to propose to read *Le Fils naturel* together with its framework as part of a corpus of his major narratives, as here. Yet Diderot himself invites us to do just this, in *De la poésie dramatique*. In the latter piece, which was attached to *Le Père de famille*, Diderot uses the term 'une espèce de roman' to characterise his earlier play together with the prologue and the *Entretiens*:

> Quoiqu'il en soit, de cette portion d'une farce en trois actes, j'en fis la comédie du *Fils naturel* en cinq; et mon dessein n'étant pas de donner cet ouvrage au théâtre, j'y joignis quelques idées que j'avais sur la poétique, la musique, la déclamation, et la pantomime; et je formai du tout une espèce de roman que j'intitulai *Le Fils naturel*, ou *les épreuves de la vertu*, avec l'histoire véritable de la pièce.[1]

Roger Kempf interprets the word 'roman' here as meaning 'matière brut, non raffinée'.[2] Other critics, however, have understood Diderot simply to mean 'novel' or 'narrative',[3] and several interesting if brief discussions of Diderot's 'espèce de roman' have been undertaken.[4]

1. Diderot, *ŒC*, x.364. This volume also contains *Le Fils naturel*, and subsequent references will be indicated by page numbers in parentheses in the main text of the chapter.

2. Roger Kempf, *Diderot et le roman, ou le démon de la présence* (Paris, Seuil 1964), p.58.

3. Jacques Chouillet argues that the text as a whole 'se rattache pour l'essentiel à la forme romanesque, comme l'ont souligné les critiques de l'époque [...], et comme Diderot l'explique lui-même dans *De la poésie dramatique*' (*Diderot*, Paris, Société d'édition d'enseignement supérieur 1977, p.142). Derek F. Connon argues a similar case, speaking of 'the "espèce de roman" [...] formed by *Le Fils naturel* and its attendant critical apparatus' (*Innovation and renewal: a study of the theatrical works of Diderot*, *SVEC* 258, 1989, p.127). Jay Caplan includes the work in his corpus of Diderot's narrative, *Framed narratives: Diderot's genealogy of the beholder* (Minneapolis, University of Minnesota Press 1985). Jeffrey Mehlmann refers to it as 'a play within a play', but analyses the narrative as a whole in his chapter 'Theater', in *Cataract: a study in Diderot* (Middletown Conn., Wesleyan University Press 1979), p.33-40 (p.33).

4. In addition to the publications already mentioned it is worth consulting Roger Lewinter, *Diderot, ou les mots de l'absence: essai sur la forme de l'œuvre* (Paris, Editions champ libre 1976), p.21-32, and Lucette Perol, 'Une autre lecture du *Fils naturel* et des *Entretiens*', *Revue d'histoire littéraire de la France* 76 (1976), p.47-58. These two discussions share a psychoanalytic orientation.

When read as a narrative, the text as a whole tells a very different story from the play in isolation from the rest. Few would disagree that in the play Dorval is represented as a champion of secular ethics, a faithful son to Lysimond and a loyal friend to Clairville. However, various aspects of the text as a whole tend to subvert such an account. The play is integrated into a structure which serves to emphasise its distance from, and its oblique relation to, the original events it supposedly portrays. The subversive aspects of the work are not foregrounded in any obvious way; they are to be detected in telling gaps, contradictions and incoherences. However, such disturbances of Dorval's rhetoric prove surprisingly consistent. They demonstrate that Dorval's ethical victory is hollow, and in particular it is undermined by an oedipal pattern of relationships. Dorval continues to love his sister Rosalie incestuously, though he claims to have surmounted such love; his much-vaunted friendship with Clairville, who marries Rosalie, veils a hostile envy; and his filial piety betrays a disavowed struggle for authority with the dead father. In order to demonstrate these points, we shall examine the various parts of Diderot's 'espèce de roman' in turn.

The prologue

The prologue of *Le Fils naturel* is in some respects similar to the preamble of *Le Neveu de Rameau*. The framing narrator, 'Diderot' or Moi, characterises an intriguing, ostensibly split character before allowing him to speak for himself. Moi's first impression of Dorval is that he is habitually melancholy, but subject to moments of brightness whenever he speaks of virtue (p.15). On their second meeting, Dorval relates to Moi the events on which his reputation for virtue is based: 'Il me raconta son histoire' (p.15). However, these events are not relayed to the reader for the moment. Moi suggests to Dorval that they might form the basis of a play; and Dorval reveals to him that his own father, now dead, had in fact commanded him to write such a play. These are the father's words, as conveyed by Dorval (p.15-16):

> Dorval, tous les jours je parle au Ciel de Rosalie et de toi. Je lui rends grâces de vous avoir conservés jusqu'à mon retour, mais surtout de vous avoir conservés innocents. Ah! mon fils, je ne jette point les yeux sur Rosalie, sans frémir du danger que tu as couru. Plus je la vois, plus je la trouve honnête et belle; plus ce danger me paraît grand. Mais le Ciel qui veille aujourd'hui sur nous, peut nous abandonner demain. Nul de nous ne connaît son sort. Tout ce que nous savons, c'est qu'à mesure que la vie s'avance, nous échappons à la méchanceté qui nous suit. Voilà les réflexions que je fais toutes les fois que je me rappelle ton histoire. Elles me consolent du peu de temps qui me reste à vivre; et si tu voulais, ce serait la morale d'une pièce dont une partie de notre vie serait le sujet, et que nous représenterions entre nous.

The ramifications of this speech are central to our reading, and need to be spelled out as clearly as possible. When the father says 'Je ne jette point les yeux sur Rosalie, sans frémir du danger que tu as couru', the word 'danger' refers beyond reasonable doubt to the danger of committing incest which subsisted (it is implied) as long as it was not known that Rosalie and Dorval were related. When he says 'Mais le Ciel qui veille aujourd'hui sur nous, peut nous abandonner demain', he implies first, that the danger of incest was only avoided thanks to the intervention of Heaven, and second, that Heaven might withdraw its help at any moment. This suggests that Lysimond entertains a Jansenistic conception of God. The words 'tout ce que nous savons, c'est qu'à mesure que la vie s'avance, nous échappons à la méchanceté qui nous suit', emphasise the near-total blindness of humanity and reinforce the warning against presuming that a *deus absconditus* will protect us from evil throughout our lives. Finally, when Lysimond says 'si tu voulais, ce serait la morale d'une pièce dont une partie de notre vie serait le sujet, et que nous représenterions entre nous', he clearly intends Dorval to write a dramatic version of the events preceding his father's return to France which would express the latter's vision of life as just set out: a blind, helpless humanity avoiding dangers such as incest only if Providence chooses to protect it. Of course, if any person is the instrument of Providence on this occasion, it is the father, whose return ensures the impossibility of Rosalie and Dorval marrying; and so his version of events accords him the most important role.

The father, then, makes it quite clear what moral is to emerge from the future play. He also expresses a stern opinion on artistic licence, enjoining Dorval to be accurate in his representation of events regardless of considerations of dramaturgy: 'Il ne s'agit point d'élever ici des tréteaux, mais de conserver la mémoire d'un événement qui nous touche, et de le rendre comme il s'est passé.' To the intended moral and the manner of the play he then adds an indication of its intended function. The annual performance in the family is to preserve the father's presence through the generations, in such a manner that he will never be eclipsed by any male descendant, but speak as if over their heads to their (male) children: 'Et je me survivrais à moi-même, et j'irais converser ainsi, d'âge en âge, avec tous mes neveux' (p.16). The performance of the play should ensure, then, that he is the earliest ancestor who matters, the head of the family through all generations; he aspires to the status of Alpha or origin. This might well seem appropriate from the point of view of his posterity if the play to be written by Dorval suggested that it is his timely return to France which determines the future shape of the family tree by ensuring that Dorval and Rosalie cannot marry.

In more general terms, the father wishes Dorval to write a play conveying a specific message unambiguously and persuasively. This is by no means an easy task. Drama is of course almost always composed of dialogue, and so no guiding narratorial presence obtrudes itself as privileged mediator of the events represented; in Nathalie Sarraute's phrase, dramatic dialogue 'se passe de *tuteurs*'.[5] In this respect the dramatic genre might be thought to have an intrinsic tendency towards open-endedness or 'openness'; the risk that a given authoritative message will become caught up in a dialogic play of voices seems great indeed.[6]

An analysis of the play will enable us to assess to what extent Dorval has conformed to the father's wishes. We will see that Dorval has indeed attempted to rise to the challenge of avoiding ambiguity in order to convey a message (and to the connected challenge of avoiding dramatic weakness). Were this the message intended by the father, more or less, then Dorval's efforts as playwright could serve as a measure of his filial obedience. When our analysis of the play is complete, however, we will consider its relation to the prologue in order to show that the message which Dorval is at pains to convey is not, in fact, the father's. On the contrary, the play represents a betrayal of Lysimond's intentions and a challenge both to his interpretation of Dorval's life and to the view of the world which underpins it.

The play

Certain critics have examined *Le Fils naturel* as drama and can be referred to for accounts of its failure as a stage play, for its importance for the history of dramatic theory and practice, and so on.[7] It is useful to stress that since we are examining the play as an integral part of the narrative whole, Diderot's dramaturgy falls outside our concerns, and the author of the play, for the present purpose, is the fictional Dorval. The immediate aim of our analysis is simply to show that Dorval has striven to disambiguate his drama in order to convey a clear message, and to identify that message.

We have no statistical or empirical basis for deciding this question, but it seems safe to assert that *Le Fils naturel* strikes most of its readers as having a fairly well-defined message concerning virtue. Daniel Mornet's reaction is typical:

> D'un bout à l'autre, nous avons des marionnettes chargées de nous débiter les sermons conçus par Diderot. Dans son résumé des caractères du théâtre

5. *L'Ere du soupçon* (Paris, Gallimard 1956), p.59; cited in Kempf, *Diderot et le roman*, p.61.

6. This is not necessarily to say that other genres and modes of discourse are intrinsically more 'closed' than drama; merely that the specific manner in which drama as a genre tends towards openness is connected with the fact of drama consisting largely of dialogue.

7. Connon's study has already been cited; see also Aimé Guedj, 'Les drames de Diderot', *Diderot studies* 14 (1971), p.15-95.

> nouveau, Diderot a oublié de nous dire que le genre bourgeois et sérieux devait être une tribune du haut de laquelle on ne cesserait de nous inviter à pratiquer les vertus de loyauté, de justice, de générosité et de sacrifice. Et sur cette tribune, c'est Diderot qui monte et qui pérore.[8]

Mornet is categorical; the play is so completely unequivocal, its author's message so perfectly clear, that he has the impression that he is listening to a series of sermons delivered by the author in person. On the other hand, Mornet's discussion contains no explanation of how this effect is achieved; he alludes to the content of various speeches without examining their context or their relation to other components of the work. Yet this question is worthy of attention. After all, a given speech or position contained or indicated in a literary work is generally interpreted either as authoritative or unsound according to its relation to other elements of the work.

We suggested above that the dramatic genre is particularly ill-suited to the conveying of a message, given the absence of a guiding narratorial presence. A solution which might suggest itself is to have the message expressed by a sympathetic character, by the hero if he is easily identifiable. Yet to attempt to guarantee that a given character will be treated sympathetically or a hero uncritically is clearly a precarious project. For the dramatist who wishes to be competent or better, this problem is compounded by the goal of artistic success.[9] For it is reasonable to suppose that a conflict must arise between the need to provide dramatic effect and the desire to convey a message univocally. A source of conventional satisfaction for the spectator of drama is the dialogue of confrontation; if it is true that 'Là, parler, c'est agir', as d'Aubignac suggests, verbal action is often a matter of contest, the struggle for power, the desire to persuade. If all the characters agree, there is no dramatic action of the verbal kind. In the light of this, the playwright wishing to convey a message may be confronted with a difficult choice. If he has other characters oppose his hero's position strongly and argue against it, he may create dramatic tension at the expense of ideological clarity. Conversely, the playwright may have all his characters agree, or secondary characters oppose the hero only weakly; but the drama may then lack tension.[10] We will now analyse the play in the light of these reflections, noting those elements of *Le Fils naturel* which work together with

8. *Diderot: l'homme et l'œuvre* (Paris, Boivin 1941), p.175.

9. That Dorval is concerned with good dramatic practice is of course amply illustrated by the *Entretiens* as a whole.

10. The illusion of reality may also be supposed to suffer; the use of certain characters as mere foils may be transparent to the audience, who may dismiss the play as an artificially constructed vehicle for the exposition of the author's ideas; and so it may turn out that the strategy is less persuasive for being more transparent.

the content of speeches in favour of virtue in order to constrain readers to identify this content as the message of the play.

In the play, Dorval is one of the characters who delivers what Mornet calls sermons; he also displays exemplary behaviour consonant with his moral precepts. Combining in the hero virtuous words and virtuous actions might well function as a strategy to help convey a moral message clearly and forcefully. Such a strategy can afford only a partial solution to the problem of disambiguating dramatic dialogue, however. For, as we have already noted, the need for dramatic effect might dictate that the voices of other characters oppose the hero's own, or indeed, as we have not yet noted, the hero's own voice might be split as he debates with himself in any soliloquies serving to expose his motivations. We must ask ourselves, then, what prevents the position expressed by the hero of *Le Fils naturel* from being caught up in a play of opposing voices and points of view.

When we attend to this question, we discover that, quite simply, no voice is raised in the dialogue in opposition to the voice of virtue. Explicit statement of the idea that love and sexuality might or must be pursued in preference to virtue, though it is surely at the forefront of many readers' minds as they observe Dorval's vacillations, is consistently avoided by the playwright.

The strategy may seem obvious, but from another point of view we might wonder that a playwright can manage to deploy it in a form which so clearly invites the use of dialogues of confrontation. The avoidance of confrontation is perhaps most remarkable in the two pivotal dialogues which occur between Dorval and Constance and Dorval and Rosalie. In the first of these (Act IV, scene iii), Constance argues against Dorval that Dorval should marry her. In the second (Act V, scene iii), Dorval argues against Rosalie that he should marry Constance and that she should marry Clairville. Yet during these two debates, neither Dorval nor Rosalie expresses the obvious counter-argument that love cannot necessarily be transcended in favour of virtue. Closer examination of these dialogues will help us to understand how the playwright manages this.

The first of these two dialogues has been prepared for by Constance's discovery of Dorval's unfinished letter to Rosalie, which she assumes is intended for herself. The *quiproquo* permits the playwright to motivate Constance's plea in favour of a marriage based not on love but on virtue. She argues that neither Dorval's illegitimacy nor his lack of a fortune ought to present an obstacle to their marriage; virtue alone can lead to fulfilment (p.66-67). In doing so, she fails to consider the opposition which is the essence of Dorval's dilemma, that is the opposition love/virtue. For she pleads for a marriage based on a harmony between love and virtue, assuming as she does that Dorval loves her; the opposition she considers is only that between society's norms and the individual's conscience. The *quiproquo* thus permits the displacement of the question of whom Dorval loves into the question of whether it is ethical for a penniless man to marry, and so avoids explicit indication of one horn of Dorval's true dilemma. In the absence of confrontation concerning the play's central issue, dramatic effect (of a weaker kind, perhaps) is provided by the fact that we know that Dorval does not dare to avow the truth; the scene relies on dramatic irony instead of confrontation.

As for the second pivotal dialogue, in which Dorval persuades Rosalie that they must not marry, Rosalie is there prevented from producing an antithesis to what has become Dorval's thesis by the simple means of having her saying nothing. Dorval silences her in advance by asking her 'La vertu a-t-elle pour vous quelque prix? L'aimez-vous encore?' To this Rosalie replies: 'elle m'est plus chère que la vie' (p.73-74). The dialogue continues as follows:

DORVAL

Je vais donc vous parler du seul moyen de vous réconcilier avec vous, d'être digne de la société dans laquelle vous vivez, d'être appelée l'élève et l'amie de Constance, et d'être l'objet du respect et de la tendresse de Clairville.

ROSALIE

Parlez. Je vous écoute.

Given the common touchstone that virtue is dearer than life, Rosalie is bound to be persuaded by what Dorval proceeds to say. He merely has to insist on ethical commonplaces, principally that the surest foundation for marriage is a union based on virtue, whilst passion fades. Rosalie proves to be consequent; she makes no objection to Dorval's apology of virtue, with the result that this pivotal scene of the play consists mainly of a monologue on Dorval's part.

This dialogue with Rosalie is prevented from being completely one-sided, for mime is called upon to compensate for the absence of verbal confrontation. As Dorval speaks, Rosalie first leans against an armchair in an attentive pose, then she sighs and is moved to tears, which she furtively wipes away. Next she appears downcast, and when she does finally speak it is in a trembling voice (p.74-76). We might say that verbal dialogue is replaced by an exchange between verbal expression on Dorval's part and physical expression on Rosalie's. This allows the playwright to imply a dramatic suspension between two courses of action without permitting one of these courses expression in a verbal and rational form.

Now let us turn from dialogues to soliloquies, and note that there too avoidance of an explicit antithesis to the play's 'sermons' is avoided.

Soliloquies, of course, are often constructed as a kind of dialogue with the self, producing dramatic effect by explicit examination of alternative courses. Dorval's soliloquies, however, reduplicate the pattern of his dialogues with Constance and Rosalie; the antithesis to the play's message is marginalised, covered by silence, or intimated at the most. Connon remarks: 'we will search in vain for any trace of confusion, or of that element of debate with oneself which is essential if a soliloquy is to be either involving or realistic, and which we will invariably find in the great soliloquies of a Corneille or a Shakespeare' (p.34). We can show this, for instance, by reference to the monologue of Act III, scene ix, in which Dorval is briefly tempted to marry Rosalie as a result of Clairville no longer being rich enough to do so (p.54):

DORVAL

> Un événement imprévu a ruiné Rosalie. Elle est indigente. Je suis riche. Je l'aime. J'en suis aimé. Clairville ne peut l'obtenir ... Sortez de mon esprit, éloignez-vous de mon cœur, illusions honteuses!

Here, each aspect of the situation which points towards the conclusion that Dorval should take Rosalie for himself is briefly alluded to. However, we are robbed of the momentous, scandalous conclusion, and must satisfy ourselves with suspension marks. Far from founding a display of Racinian oscillation, the thought is imperiously rejected before it is expressed: 'Sortez de mon esprit', etc. This is the pattern of each of Dorval's soliloquies. If he oscillates between two possibilities, only one of them is granted explicit verbal expression and an apology. If the reader of the play refers to the *Entretiens sur le Fils naturel*, he discovers that the use of fragmented speech is represented there as a means to achieve a realistic impression; broken sentences are the natural language of the passions: 'Qu'est-ce qui nous affecte dans le spectacle de l'homme animé de quelques grandes passions? Sont-ce ses discours? Quelquefois. Mais ce qui émeut toujours, ce sont des cris, des mots inarticulés, des voix rompues, quelques monosyllabes qui s'échappent par intervalles, je ne sais quel murmure dans la gorge, entre les dents' (p.102). Such fragmentation of speech may well produce a naturalistic effect; yet the playwright of *Le Fils naturel* obtains a secondary gain from the device, which is nowhere made explicit in the *Entretiens*. For when he constructs a monologue with gaps, the words and phrases obliterated are precisely those which might express the antithesis to the message concerning virtue, as we saw above.

Fragmented soliloquy, then, is exploited not only for its naturalistic effect but also for its potential to reinforce a message. The same can be said of the playwright's use of mime, as exemplified in the dialogue with Rosalie already discussed. In the *Entretiens* the use of mime (referred to as 'la pantomime') is justified from the point of view of dramatic effect; it is claimed to be more expressive than words at certain points of the action. However, in the play itself, as we have seen in the case of the dialogue of Act v, scene iii, the playwright uses it as a substitute for explicit statements against the apology of virtue. Innovations which the Dorval of the *Entretiens* presents as motivated purely artistically are used strategically to reinforce the play's closure. Conversion to virtue everywhere confers eloquence; hesitation between virtue and love gives rise to inarticulateness or silent mime. This is convenient indeed for the play's moral.[11]

The result of these various devices is that the antithesis to the play's message – the simple assertion that sexuality and love cannot be transcended for the sake of virtue – is not expressed in pivotal dialogues, whereas dramatic effect might well have caused it or required it to be discussed, sooner or later, in a less closed play. This seems to manifest an especial concern to protect the play's message from interference. And the message does indeed emerge with clarity, through a dialogue which, for being less dramatic in important respects, is all the more univocal. Throughout the play, whoever speaks for virtue holds authority. We have seen that when Constance argues for an absolute obedience to virtue as the only course towards fulfilment, Dorval opposes her without authority and that when he, in turn, pleads virtue's cause to Rosalie he enjoys authority and she defers. At the play's close, all the characters but the father admire and approve of Dorval's motives and actions. The cumulative effect is that the voice of virtue meets no resistance it cannot overcome; whoever borrows it enjoys an absolute power of persuasion.[12]

It is interesting to compare these observations on Diderot's use of dialogue in *Le Fils naturel* with Jean Starobinski's essay 'Diderot et la parole des autres'. Of *Le Rêve de d'Alembert*, Starobinski writes: 'Le transfert de la parole obéit à la loi qui veut que le discours de la science puisse être reçu et retransmis par tout esprit juste. L'hypothèse se fraie, littéralement, un chemin, d'un individu à l'autre; elle annonce ainsi son pouvoir d'appartenir à tous'; and of the *Lettre sur les aveugles* he writes: 'La vérité est un bien commun; elle est généralisable; l'énoncer, c'est aussitôt la

11. A detailed analysis of Diderot's theatrical dialogue can be found in one of the studies already mentioned: see Derek F. Connon, 'Stylistic aspects of Diderot's theatrical dialogue', *SVEC* 258 (1989), p.49-74. This includes a discussion of Diderot's use of gestures, *style rompu* and mime.

12. It could be remarked that if adherence to virtue is unequivocally conveyed as a positive value, what virtue amounts to remains ill-defined throughout. This contributes to the mystic quality of the characters' common belief in virtue; and it also protects the notion, for it escapes critical scrutiny thanks in part to being left vague.

communiquer, tenter de lui assurer la reconnaissance universelle.'[13] Such comments could aptly be applied to the discourse on virtue which passes from character to character in *Le Fils naturel.*

The various devices tending to render dialogue univocal do not in themselves guarantee the play's closure. The play's ending has a role of potentially pre-eminent importance in the reader's decisions concerning its message. For – obviously – the dénouement can help to confirm or overturn hypotheses concerning the play's message which the reader or spectator may have formed during its action.

It might seem safe to assert that the happy ending of *Le Fils naturel* confirms the message we have seen to emerge from the drama, where a tragic or neutral ending would have tended to overturn or complicate it. If we had been held in suspense at all with respect to whether Dorval has made the right choices in following virtue at each stage of the action, that suspense is likely to be resolved at the close, with its mood of triumph and finality. However, the question is not as simple as that.

Let us recall how this dénouement is prepared. In the pivotal dialogue with Rosalie to which we have already referred, Dorval has argued that total submission to virtue's dictates is, paradoxically enough, a kind of freedom; he implies that it permits him to transcend the sexual. He has learnt this by listening to Constance speak of virtue, and his hope that Rosalie will in turn learn this from him is fulfilled when she exclaims 'Je vous entends. Vous êtes mon ami [...] Oui, j'en aurai le courage [...] Je brûle de voir Constance [...] Je sais enfin où le bonheur m'attend' (p.77). Rosalie, then, is burning to announce the happy news to Constance, and Dorval pronounces a speech to close scene iii whose tone of joyful finality seems to qualify it to be the last of the whole play (p.77):

DORVAL

> Ah Rosalie, je vous reconnais. C'est vous, mais plus belle, plus touchante à mes yeux que jamais! Vous voilà digne de l'amitié de Constance, de la tendresse de Clairville, et de toute mon estime; car j'ose à présent me nommer.

This is the moral climax of a moral play. Dorval 'recognises' Rosalie, though this is not (yet) a *scène de reconnaissance*. In other words Rosalie has re-assumed the values she had temporarily lost from view as a result of falling in love. Moreover, the consequence of Rosalie's re-assuming her original values is that her marriage to Clairville will proceed. In that the transgression of social order with which the play opened is reversed in Rosalie's re-

13. 'Diderot et la parole des autres', in Denis Diderot, *Œuvres complètes*, ed. Roger Lewinter, 15 vols (Paris, Club français du livre 1969-1973), xiii.iii-xxi (first published in *Critique* 296, January 1972, p.3-22).

conversion to virtue, the moral climax corresponds to a resolution in terms of plot-structure. If the playwright is concerned with achieving structural and ideological closure, he could scarcely require of himself a dénouement more final than one which at one stroke confirms the message prepared throughout the play and resolves its central tension.

However, the play does not come to a close here; rather, Lysimond's entrance provides what might be called a second dénouement. Act v, scene v opens as Lysimond is led on to the following exchange (p.77-78):

ROSALIE

Mon père!

DORVAL

Ciel! que vois-je! C'est Lysimond! C'est mon père!

LYSIMOND

Oui, mon fils. Oui, c'est moi. (*A Dorval et à Rosalie.*) Approchez, mes enfants, que je vous embrasse... Ah, ma fille!.. Ah, mon fils!.. (*Il les regarde.*) Du moins, je les ai vus ... (*Dorval et Rosalie sont étonnés. Lysimond s'en aperçoit.*) Mon fils, voilà ta sœur... Ma fille, voilà ton frère...

ROSALIE

Mon frère!

DORVAL

Ma sœur!

ROSALIE

Dorval!

DORVAL

Rosalie!

The scene in which Dorval recognises Rosalie morally, then, is followed by a scene in which he recognises her as his sister. On reflection, each of these scenes has the function of a dénouement in relation to different aspects (or *nœuds*) of the plot; Dorval's moral recognition of Rosalie represents the culmination of the trials of virtue, whilst his recognition of her as his sister represents the resolution of the references to their respective fathers (and fortunes).

It is difficult to decide how to relate this closing scene to what precedes. We might argue that, although they are prepared for by different elements of the plot and so display different structural functions, the two dénouement scenes have a rhetorical function in common; they seem equally suited to confirm the position adopted by Dorval and with it the moral of the play. For as we consider this exchange, we cannot but imagine that the surprise of Dorval and Rosalie on learning that they are half-brother and -sister is accompanied by the realisation that if they had become lovers they would have committed incest. This seems to offer an additional point of reference to confirm the decision of Dorval and Rosalie that they should marry Constance and Clairville respectively. It is as though this twist in the play throws the spectator's probable aversion to incest into the scales on Dorval's (or virtue's) side.

The play has indeed been interpreted along such lines. Here a critic refers in the first instance to the play's closing scene:

> La scène est capitale; c'est la clé de voûte de la pièce, d'elle dépend sa réussite ou son échec. Il faut reconnaître tout d'abord que Diderot, avec une admirable probité artistique, a refusé la solution de facilité: il ne révélera le lien de parenté entre Dorval et Rosalie qu'après le succès de l'épreuve. En fait, la pièce a deux dénouements dont nous devons préciser les rapports et prouver la nécessité. Le second dénouement se présente en coup de théâtre. C'est parce que Dorval est un fils naturel qu'il ignore la nature profonde du sentiment qui le pousse vers Rosalie et que Rosalie ignore la signification naturelle de cette attirance instinctive [...] [Cette découverte] permettra, après, de constater avec un soupir – philosophique – de soulagement, que *l'ordre de la nature coïncide avec l'ordre moral.*[14]

However, the relation between the father's return and the rest of the play cannot be dealt with as simply as this. The universal law implied here – that siblings who first meet as adults 'naturally' feel an attraction which is not sexual yet which closely resembles the sexual – is questionable indeed.[15] Moreover, such a reading circumvents an awkward fact: the discovery that Rosalie and Dorval are siblings has no logical bearing on the question of whether their reasons for renouncing each other in ignorance of their

14. Guedj, 'Les drames de Diderot', p.70.

15. This reading is echoed in the Hermann edition by a curious footnote to Act II, scene ii: 'On prépare le dénouement de loin [...]. Rosalie porte en elle sans le savoir le *modèle idéal* de la perfection paternelle et cette *reconnaissance* n'est pas une chimère. La pensée de l'inceste est donc purifiée avant d'être formée' (*Œ C*, x.32). In contrast, Connon argues that the first dénouement is tinged with melancholy, and that the second is 'a false dénouement which does not represent a resolution of the emotional conflicts of the work, but which drowns the melancholy in a flood of tears of joy, providing an artificially happy ending' (*Innovation and renewal*, p.141). Approaching the interpretation offered here more closely still, Caplan speaks of the 'retroactive, unsettling way' in which Diderot puts incest to dramatic effect (*Framed narratives*, p.32).

connection are well founded in themselves. The incest-element is not only irrelevant, however; it is an element which has a force of its own. Such a powerful notion is more disturbing to many, no doubt, than the prospect of betraying a friend by falling in love with the woman he is to marry. If the element of incest outweighs the prospect of disloyalty, it risks diminishing the importance of Dorval's moral crisis by changing its terms after the fact. At the eleventh hour, Lysimond's entrance converts a play whose action had been concerned with the avoidance of a fairly routine betrayal, into a play whose action is suddenly, retrospectively and possibly *instead* concerned with the avoidance of incest. In supplementing Dorval's motives for renouncing Rosalie, the incest-element threatens to replace them.[16]

We might summarise our analysis of the play to this point as follows. A range of strategies is deployed in order to achieve a univocal effect (but not, incidentally, without the sacrifice of certain potential sources of dramatic effect). However, a problem in the play's rhetoric is to be detected in Lysimond's return, for whilst it might help to confirm Dorval's championship of virtue by drawing on our horror of incest, any such advantage is bought at the cost of obscuring what would otherwise have been the play's clear argument.

The relation of play to prologue

Once again, the analysis which precedes is concerned with the dramatic practice, not of Diderot, but of Dorval. This permits us to ask ourselves questions concerning this fictional author's motivations on the basis of our examination of his play, and to combine what we infer from this with what we infer from other parts of the text. With this in mind, we can now return to the question we raised during our discussion of the prologue: given the father's injunctions, to what extent does Dorval's play fulfil them; and if there is a respect in which he fails to fulfil them, what is at stake in that failure?

Dorval must write within certain constraints (not all of which are those of Diderot). In particular, he is beginning with certain 'facts', i.e. the original events, and in addition he is responding to his father's request in respect of the play's subject and moral. He can use a certain amount of licence in the manner of his representation of certain events; but he cannot avoid representing them. Amongst these events is the return of Lysimond.

16. This is reminiscent once again of Derrida's discussion of the *supplément* in *De la grammatologie*. Lysimond's reappearance may seem intended to complete a play which could not duly close without it, but by introducing the incest-element it displaces or decentres one area of concern in favour of another, so that 'incest' substitutes itself for 'loyalty'. In this respect, Lysimond's entrance 'supplements' Dorval's play, replacing what it supposedly completes.

However closed and complete the play may seem in both structure and ideas by the close of Act v, scene iv, it cannot be concluded until Lysimond has made his entrance and all the characters have realised that Rosalie and Dorval are half-brother and sister. However, if Dorval has no choice but to deal with the father's return, he does have a choice in respect of the emphasis, degree of relevance, amount of text and manner of representation accorded to it; and the same applies to the father's role in the play as a whole. Examination of these aspects of his writerly activity prove revealing.

Let us recall the father's project. He required Dorval to write a play which would show how Heaven alone had saved Dorval and Rosalie from the danger of incest, and convey the more general moral that none of us knows or controls his fate. When we compare this request with the result which is Dorval's play, we can only conclude that Dorval has signally failed to convey both the father's version of events and the father's moral. This failure can be highlighted by the question: to whom does the merit fall? In Dorval's play the merit falls to himself. In the play projected by the father, the merit falls to the clemency of Heaven. The difference in outlook is fundamental: the father's theodicy, possibly Jansenistic, enters into opposition with the secular ethics of the son.

Indeed, nothing less than an oedipal struggle for interpretive authority over the original events on which the play is based is inscribed in the gap between the father's intention and the son's text, since the latter consistently excludes Lysimond's vision. In particular, Dorval's representation of his father within the play can be seen as symptomatic of his anxious concern to contain the threat of paternal authority. A particular example is given by the manner in which Dorval chooses to represent Lysimond at the play's close. These are the play's final lines (p.80-81):

LYSIMOND

Mon fils, que te veulent-ils? Il faut que tu leur aies donné quelque grand sujet d'admiration et de joie, que je ne comprends pas, que ton père ne peut partager.

DORVAL

La joie de vous revoir nous a tous transportés.

LYSIMOND

Puisse le ciel qui bénit les enfants par les pères, et les pères par les enfants, vous en accorder qui vous ressemblent, et qui vous rendent la tendresse que vous avez pour moi.

At this point, all but the father are initiated in the truth that the son's heroism is the source of their wonder. Insight and the interpretive authority which depends on it are withheld from the father by the son as a character in the play (and of course by the son as the playwright who chooses to close the play before the father is enlightened). There is a hint of paternal reproach in the words: 'un grand sujet d'admiration et de joie [...] que ton père ne peut partager'. However, Dorval simply will not explain the true source of the others' transport, and indeed lies by ascribing it to the return of the father rather than his own heroism. This undercuts the father's final peroration, which is based on an acceptance of the lie, and might make us feel slightly embarrassed for the old man deluded into believing the homages offered to the son in fact signify joy at his own return. Indeed, there is a hint of irony in his wishing sons with a similar filial attitude on Dorval himself.

We have learnt from the prologue that the father had hoped Dorval would immortalise him as the instrument of Heaven, providentially returning in time to prevent incest. Instead, Dorval robs him of a basis for his interpretation of events as being determined by Heaven. The father's appeal to Heaven which closes the play is born of ignorance of the facts, and the father who has declared 'vous saurez tout' is most in need of enlightenment. (In fact, the text does not specify how much the father is subsequently told, and he could even be imagined to have retained the impression that his return had *preceded* and brought about Dorval's renunciation of Rosalie, which would certainly explain his version of events as expressed in the prologue.) It is in vain that Lysimond reveals himself to be the progenitor of Dorval and Rosalie at once, and later, as we learn from the prologue, tells Dorval that Heaven alone protected him from committing a terrible sin; by representing himself in the play as deciding independently of this to renounce Rosalie, Dorval has stolen the father's thunder.

In a word, the gesture of Dorval the playwright is to contain the father as an impotent, controllable, blind presence. This opens up a new perspective on the problem we discussed in the preceding section: the double dénouement and the relation between Lysimond's return, the incest-element and Dorval's heroism. Lysimond's return in Act v can be read as Dorval's unavoidable concession to the father's original project. However, the lateness of this incident, the tangential relation it bears to the rest of the play, and the irrelevance of Lysimond's paternity of Dorval and Rosalie to Dorval's crisis, can be seen as signs of Dorval's refusal to reflect his father's interpretation of the original events in the text of the play. So we can now see that what resembles a rhetorical flaw in the play in itself is enlarged and endowed with psychological significance in the relation between the prologue and the play, indicating there an oedipal tension.[17] This tension, as we will see below, is also manifested in the *Entretiens*.

17. William F. Edmiston argues that it is the 'unresolved conflict' between 'freedom and paternal authority' which finds expression in the *drames*, and that, 'viewed in terms of Diderot's personal conflict, this dichotomy [passion versus

The 'Entretiens'

The *Entretiens* signal by various means that Dorval's official account, contained in the manuscript play he has shown to Moi, is far from a transparent and objective account of the original events which it commemorates. First, we are told that it is only one of several possible and competing versions of the original events. We are told, for instance, that Clairville and Dorval have each penned an alternative version, the former in the comic, the latter in the tragic genre; moreover, Moi himself sketches out a new version which maintains the hero's dilemma for a greater part of the action; and André, a servant, criticises Dorval on the grounds of misrepresentation of the father's plight in England and proposes a revision in this respect. These various possible ways of representing the original events function as so many accounts of the circumstances of Dorval's sacrifice which modify each other; and they make of the text as a whole a narrative with several subsidiary narrators and as many points of view. Nor are we told which events Dorval has adapted for reasons of dramatic effect. Rather, we learn from the dialogue that here dramaturgical considerations have won out over fidelity to the truth and that there the converse is true; and since we are given only several examples of each case, we are not always authorised to decide whether a given speech is a reproduction of what was originally said or the result of a subsequent addition or edulcoration.

The result is not a transparent narrative; what might have constituted the 'original events' has become quite obscure beneath various narrative layers and mutually contradictory points of view. Over and above this, none of Dorval's statements concerning the original events, the play's accuracy, and indeed anything else is guaranteed by Moi as a faithful transcription. Instead, Moi emphasises the existence of flaws in his own account (p.84):

> Voici nos entretiens. Mais quelle différence entre ce que Dorval me disait, et ce que j'écris!... Ce sont peut-être les mêmes idées; mais le génie de l'homme n'y est plus... C'est en vain que je cherche en moi l'impression que le spectacle de la nature et la présence de Dorval y faisaient. Je ne la retrouve point. Je ne vois plus Dorval. Je ne l'entends plus. Je suis seul, parmi la poussière des livres et dans l'ombre d'un cabinet... Et j'écris des lignes faibles, tristes et froides.

The consequence of all of this is that a new, polyphonous account of the events represented in the play is suddenly instituted, retroactively. Various characters (or character-narrators) compete to contain the significance of the original events in the particular type of dramatic representation they

reason] reflects the opposition between the son's individual desire and the father's social virtue that opposes that desire' (*Diderot and the family: a conflict of nature and law*, Stanford French and Italian Studies 39, Saratoga Calif., ANMA Libri 1985, p.59).

champion or envisage. Other tensions and contradictions also emerge. In particular, if we recall the father's injunction in the prologue: 'il ne s'agit point ici d'élever des tréteaux, mais de conserver la mémoire d'un événement qui nous touche, et de le rendre comme il s'est passé' (p.16), we can represent any change in the original events for the sake of dramatic effect, *bienséance* or whatever as a departure from the father's project. What mattered to him was not whether the play might succeed as drama, nor the avoidance of embarrassment, but a repetition of the original events, 'warts and all'.

Attending to such tensions is revealing. Official, explicit statements of motivation on the part of Dorval or other characters can be shown to be shadowed by a range of purely implicit possibilities, many of a nature not easily avowed, and which we can only reconstruct thanks to the textual tensions in question. This will now be demonstrated by an examination of the contradictions between the various positions expressed in the *Entretiens*. Contradictions between the *Entretiens* on the one hand and the prologue and the play on the other will also be considered. We begin with the most important and persistent opposition of all – that of Dorval and his father, already inferred from the relation between play and prologue; we will also examine the opposition between play and performance, Clairville and Dorval, and tragedy and comedy.

Father versus son

Moi opens the first *Entretien* by asserting that Dorval's play diverges from his father's intentions; 'Je vous ai lu; mais je suis bien trompé, ou vous ne vous êtes pas attaché à répondre scrupuleusement aux intentions de monsieur votre père' (p.85). Later, the accusation of filial disloyalty is raised again, this time in Dorval's account of his servant André's criticism of his play. André suggests that his master has failed in commemorating the father and incorporating his outlook in the play. In particular, the servant tells Dorval that he might have extended the scene in which he, André, gives an account of Lysimond's captivity in England. André questions Dorval's motives for suppressing such details (p.108):

> Et l'endroit du correspondant? Vous l'avez si bien brouillé, que je n'y entends plus rien. Votre père me dit, comme vous l'avez rapporté, que cet homme avait agi, et que ma présence auprès de lui était sans doute le premier de ses bons offices. Mais il ajouta: 'Oh! mon enfant, quand Dieu ne m'aurait accordé que la consolation de t'avoir dans ces moments cruels, combien n'aurais-je pas de grâces à lui rendre?' Je ne trouve rien de cela dans votre papier. Monsieur, est-ce qu'il est défendu de prononcer sur la scène le nom de Dieu, ce nom saint que votre père avait si souvent à la bouche? – Je ne crois pas, André. – Est-ce que

vous avez appréhendé qu'on sût que votre père était chrétien? – Nullement, André.

André goes on to suggest that Dorval has systematically avoided reference to God because he is 'un peu [...] esprit fort' (p.108). Dorval dodges the question, replying merely: 'André, je serais obligé d'en être d'autant meilleur citoyen et plus honnête homme' (p.108). Yet it is clear that Dorval has a stake in not letting André quote his father's talk of God's influence. To introduce such an idea before the close of the play would have meant suggesting that Dorval did not enjoy sole responsibility for the moral victory which the father assigns, rather, to Heaven's intervention. In other words, Dorval prevents the idea that he saves himself and the idea that Heaven saves him from entering into competition within the play; and this amounts to suppressing the father's version of events.[18]

This point converges with our findings concerning the oedipal tension inherent in the gap between the father's intentions and the play in itself. We might even suggest that from a psychological perspective what is at stake in André's comment is not merely a question of subscribing or not to a belief in God. God is everywhere so closely associated with Dorval's father that for him to disbelieve in God is by extension to challenge his father's authority. Indeed, since God is of course by definition a father one might suspect that an oedipal hostility towards one's own father is easily displaced onto God.

This reading can be supported by further reference to the *Entretiens*. In the continuation of the passage just quoted, André asserts: 'Monsieur, vous êtes bon; mais n'allez pas vous imaginer que vous valiez monsieur votre père' (p.108).[19] This implies that André detects an element of rivalry in Dorval's failure to quote his father's talk of God. Much later in the *Entretiens*, Dorval betrays this rivalry more directly than when quoting André: 'Dorval mourra content, s'il peut mériter qu'on dise de lui, quand il ne sera plus: Son père, qui était si honnête homme, ne fut pourtant pas plus honnête homme que lui' (p.160). This rivalry may eventually culminate in identification; the whole of Dorval's reflection on theatre is not undertaken for its own sake, but in order that it might be crowned by his writing a play

18. In fact, Heaven in its providential guise is mentioned in the play by André: 'Cependant je me dépouille de mes lambeaux, et je les étends sous mon maître qui bénissait d'une voix expirante la bonté du Ciel'; but Dorval ripostes '(*bas, à part, et avec amertume*) – qui le faisait mourir dans le fond d'un cachot, sur les haillons de son valet!' (p.50).

19. A similar remark was apparently made to Diderot himself by an inhabitant of Langres, whom Diderot quotes as saying: 'Monsieur Diderot, vous êtes bon; mais si vous croyez que vous vaudrez jamais votre père, vous vous trompez' (*Œuvres complètes*, ed. Lewinter, viii.599).

entitled *Le Père de famille*. In describing this project, Dorval identifies himself with the father as subject of the play (p.161):

> Ce sujet me tourmente, et je sens qu'il faudra que tôt ou tard je me délivre de cette fantaisie; car c'en est une comme il en vient à tout homme qui vit dans la solitude... le beau sujet que le père de famille!... C'est la vocation générale de tous les hommes... Nos enfants sont la source de nos plus grands plaisirs et de nos plus grandes peines... Ce sujet tiendra mes yeux sans cesse attachés sur mon père... Mon père! J'achèverai de peindre le bon Lysimond... Je m'instruirai moi-même... Si j'ai des enfants, je ne serai pas fâché d'avoir pris avec eux des engagements.

This is, however, only a project. It is André once again who emphasises that in the play which has already been written, Dorval avoids representing the father too extensively or too favourably. He represents this as a wanton, disloyal usurpation of authority; 'Ailleurs, vous passez *de votre autorité* une des choses qui marquent le plus la bonté de feu monsieur votre père; cela est fort mal' (p.107; my emphasis).

We have seen how André's comments, and several other passages of the *Entretiens*, reinforce the case for arguing that an oedipal tension underpins Dorval's filial obedience. We should like to proceed by exploring the opposition between Dorval's play as a written text and the performance of it by the members of Clairville's household (a performance which Moi surreptitiously attends).

Play versus performance

If the play is read in isolation, or if it is watched in performance at the theatre, it will appear quite different from the play which is performed in Clairville's salon (according that is to the fiction of the 'espèce de roman' or the text as a whole). This difference is fundamental. It will be recalled that, according to the prologue, Dorval has written the play in order that it might be performed annually by the members of Clairville's household, in conformity to the dead father's wishes. On the occasion of its first performance it duly happens that the various members of the household play themselves a year after the original events. (The father, now dead, is of course the exception.) The play in itself creates no such effect; obviously, the characters are represented as living out the events of the play for the first time. A further distinction between play and performance consists in the fact that Clairville's household does not succeed in performing Dorval's text as it stands; the dénouement is not played out, for the actors are reduced to uncontrollable weeping as soon as Lysimond's stand-in enters.

Consequences for interpretation follow on these differences. First of all, the obvious should be stated; that since the time of the original events, all members of the household have learnt that Dorval and Rosalie are related, whilst at the time of the original events this only became known upon Lysimond's return. As a result, the play as performed in Clairville's salon can be imagined to impress itself upon all present – i.e. the actor-characters, other members of the household, and Moi concealed behind a screen – as the story of the providential avoidance of the terrible danger of incest, from the first to the last scene. (This cannot be the case for the first-time reader or spectator of the play in itself.) Under these circumstances, the audience may well have in mind the danger of incest to the point where the import of Dorval's representation of his heroic crisis, which 'originally' occurred independently of the question of incest, is destroyed. Moreover, if the incest-element is present in the minds of all from the beginning of the performance, so in fact are all the play's events known to its actor-characters from the beginning. This creates an effect of inevitability which is absent from the play in itself. It is the inevitability of the flashback; greater even than the inevitability of the often ambiguous oracle, it runs counter to Dorval's depiction of himself as freely choosing the course of virtue. In retrospect, it might well seem that he could not help renouncing Rosalie precisely because she was his sister, in the kind of teleological reading which we have already seen that certain critics have arrived at in order to square the element of incest with the rest.

In this respect, surprisingly enough, the performance conforms to the dead father's intentions concerning its meaning and reception where the play does not. The father requested a play showing the providential avoidance of the danger of incest. We saw in a previous section that the incest-element is added after the resolution of the play's crisis, creating a curious effect. However, we have just seen that the performance, in the precise circumstances of Clairville's salon, portrays the danger of incest from the first to the last. Moreover, as suggested, a sense of inevitability will weigh on the performance, and this accords well with the father's vision of Providence. In contrast, if the play is performed elsewhere, by other actors, incest is thrust in after the fact and Dorval's choices may well seem open rather than inevitable.[20]

However, if the father has his own way in the end, it is not without modification of his explicit wishes. We might now observe in this connexion

20. It is intriguing to reflect that since the performance mysteriously meets the dead father's intentions, his influence could be compared to his own conception of the equally mysterious working of Providence. For it is he who is at the origin of play and performance alike, and it is he who is ultimately responsible for the fashion in which the performance meets with his own intentions in spite of his son's attempts to write a play betraying them.

that the annual performance does not signify an absolute prohibition of the incestuous impulse; it is also something of a *concession* to that impulse. This paradox arises thanks to the fact that the children play their former selves (though nothing would have prevented Constance from playing Rosalie, for instance). This might be imagined to be intended by the household to produce a semblance of identity between the performance and the original events; but we can also imagine that it produces other effects. Extraordinarily enough, Rosalie and Dorval are permitted, indeed required, to make love once a year, as before Lysimond's return. Clairville and Constance will not only be present at these scenes, but will act as accessories; they facilitate the normally forbidden love-making by taking part in the collective ritual which alone creates the conditions in which such love-making is permitted. The performance may therefore be said to permit the subsistence of the incestuous impulse which the play in itself represents as having been definitively surmounted in Dorval's triumphant dénouement. We might indeed regard the ritual aspect of the performance as allowing distorted expression, and so a limited indulgence, of the very impulse which it is designed to prohibit.[21]

We have discussed several of the differences which mark the performance off from the play in itself. The most obvious difference of all, however, consists in the fact that the dénouement written by Dorval is not performed. Moi accounts for this as follows (p.83):

> J'ai promis de vous dire pourquoi je n'entendis pas la dernière scène, et le voici. Lysimond n'était plus. On avait engagé un de ses amis qui était à peu près de son âge, et qui avait sa taille, sa voix, et ses cheveux blancs, à le remplacer dans la pièce.
>
> Ce vieillard entra dans le salon, comme Lysimond y était entré la première fois, tenu sous le bras par Clairville et par André, et couvert des habits que son ami avait apportés des prisons. Mais à peine y parut-il, que, ce moment de l'action remettant sous les yeux de toute la famille, un homme qu'elle venait de perdre, et qui lui avait été si respectable et si cher, personne ne put retenir ses larmes. Dorval pleurait. Constance et Clairville pleuraient. Rosalie étouffait ses sanglots et détournait ses regards. Le vieillard qui représentait Lysimond, se troubla, et se mit à pleurer aussi. La douleur passant des maîtres aux domestiques, devint générale, et la pièce ne finit pas.

By dying, Lysimond has sabotaged Dorval's closing scenes. In our analysis of the play in itself, we saw that the double dénouement resembles a strategy to clarify the play's message (even if it tends to introduce a problem by throwing the incest-element into relief). The sense of freedom

21. Cf. Freud's imaginative discussion of the subject contained in *Totem and taboo* (*The Standard edition*, xiii.1-162). Mehlmann makes a brief reference to this; see *Cataract*, p.35.

and joy experienced by Rosalie and Dorval as they renounce each other is followed closely by the appearance of Lysimond, both incidents tending to confirm that Dorval has taken the only justifiable course. The performance which takes place in Clairville's salon undoes this effect; the sadness which arises as Lysimond's substitute enters succeeds the acting-out of joy which has just accompanied Dorval's renunciation of Rosalie. Mourning at the loss of the father displaces celebration of the virtue of the son. Concomitantly, the message that we can achieve happiness and moral freedom by embracing a code of secular ethics, or the possibility that we might perform actions which bring us into a happy ending which might prolong itself indefinitely, is displaced by a rather gloomier impression; and the general mourning into which the performance dissolves seems consonant with the father's Jansenistic statement: 'le Ciel qui veille sur nous aujourd'hui, peut nous abandonner demain'.

The fact that the performance is truncated does nothing to diminish the effects which distinguish the performance from the written text of the play in the manner already discussed. In order to reflect on the danger of incest from the beginning, those present have no need of the dénouement in which the returning Lysimond reveals that Rosalie and Dorval are related, since they know this in any case. As for the undoing of Dorval's heroic representation of himself as free creator of his own happiness, the annual performance can function as a warning against his kind of filial pride all the better if the performance dissolves into general grief at the close.

Clairville versus Dorval: comedy versus tragedy

Within the play, the relation between Clairville and Dorval is presented as one of mutual esteem and affection, indeed of ideal friendship. Dorval resolves to renounce the woman he loves purely out of duty to Clairville. He flies to Clairville's rescue when he becomes involved in a duel. He consoles him as he weeps on his shoulder. The impression we gain of the relations of Dorval and Clairville in the *Entretiens*, however, is rather different; there the two men seem to be locked into a relation of mutual incomprehension manifested in veiled attacks and tactless jokes.

This hostility is evident, for instance, in the two men's play-writing activities. In the course of a discussion of the new system of dramatic classification he proposes – principally, comedy, tragedy and the *genre sérieux* – Dorval tells Moi that 'la pièce dont nous nous sommes entretenus a presque été faite dans les trois genres' (p.135). He proceeds to explain that, some time after the events depicted in his own play, Clairville began to joke about them, and went as far as to write a parody of Act III. The manner in which Dorval speaks of this incident is revealing (p.135):

> Son ouvrage était excellent. Il avait exposé mes embarras sous un jour tout à fait comique. J'en ris; mais je fus secrètement offensé du ridicule que Clairville jetait sur une des actions les plus importantes de notre vie... Je me vengeai de Clairville, en mettant en tragédie les trois derniers actes de la pièce; et je puis vous assurer que je le fis pleurer plus longtemps qu'il ne m'avait fait rire.

The finished version of this tragedy has been burnt, but Moi requests and obtains the *canevas*. Moi summarises its opening lines for us as follows: 'Rosalie, instruite, au troisième acte, du mariage de Dorval et de Constance, et persuadée que ce Dorval est un ami perfide, un homme sans foi, prend un parti violent. C'est de tout révéler'. In the *canevas*, this situation precipitates Dorval's suicide, in spite of the united efforts of Clairville, Constance and the repentant Rosalie, all of whom are alerted by André to the danger to Dorval's life (p.136-39).

When we analysed the play in itself we analysed Dorval's incursion into the *genre sérieux*. Its central conflict is one between love and duty which is resolved by the decision on the part of Dorval and Rosalie to follow the virtuous course. This leads to general admiration of Dorval. Dorval's tragedy, on the other hand, represents a different resolution of the same conflict, as we have just seen; Rosalie does not successfully surmount her desire in favour of virtue, and Dorval dies. The two outcomes are, obviously, mutually exclusive in reality. However, the fiction of the framing text represents both these possibilities side by side, as projected outcomes neither of which was reached; it is simply that one was preferred as an official account. Their co-existence tells us something other than what we might have learnt from the independent existence of either one. For both versions together attest to the unresolved subsistence in Dorval of the very conflict between love and duty, or incest and taboo, which each version represents as having been resolved. Another way of putting this is to state that the official version of events, the play in the *genre sérieux* with its happy ending, is achieved on the basis of an attempted repression of the tragic possibility. Yet the very possibility disavowed in the writing of the official version returns, symptomatically enough, in the tragedy which Dorval also pens. Indeed, there is a double return of the repressed. Having written the tragedy which represents a first return, Dorval burns it. However, he has retained the *canevas,* which he shows to his new friend Moi, thus affording his resentment a second moment of expression. Nor does the reader have any indication that this type of repetition stops here.

Moreover, in all of this we are shown that Dorval deeply resents Clairville's making light of recent events through his comic version of them. Dorval's writing a tragedy more effective than his friend's comic version of his own play manifests a certain hostility; he is 'secrètement offensé' and his aim is revenge. The text indicates only one origin for this hostility: sexual jealousy directed towards the 'tranquille possesseur de Rosalie'. Dorval's jealousy of Clairville has therefore clearly outlived his heroic renunciation of Rosalie and indeed his discovery that she is his sister. We might usefully recall the words he had lent himself in the official version of events (p.76):

> Nous avons été malheureux, Mademoiselle! Mais mon malheur a cessé au moment où j'ai commencé d'être juste. J'ai remporté sur moi la victoire la plus difficile, mais la plus entière. Je suis rentré dans mon caractère. Rosalie ne m'est plus redoutable; et je pourrais sans crainte lui avouer tout le désordre qu'elle avait jeté dans mon âme, lorsque dans le plus grand trouble de sentiments et d'idées qu'aucun mortel ait jamais éprouvé, je répondais... Mais un événement imprévu, l'erreur de Constance, la vôtre, mes efforts m'ont affranchi... je suis libre.

In this speech Dorval aims to set an insuperable barrier between his former self, prey to the torment of his illicit love for Rosalie, and his present self, absolutely free and happy in his renunciation of her. Yet its words sound hollow indeed when we compare them with Dorval as presented in the frame; he has clearly not transcended his incestuous passion as long as he resents his sister's husband. The claim 'j'ai remporté sur moi la victoire la plus difficile mais la plus entière', read in the context of the text as a whole, can only be interpreted as a wishful construct, a disavowal of what is in fact an incomplete victory or indeed a defeat.[22]

This we learn, if from Dorval's own lips, yet only indirectly and, so to speak, in spite of himself. The same can be said of any inferences we draw which run counter to Dorval's assertion that his play is written to conform to his dead father's request; and of any elements which cause us to read suspiciously the text of the play performed by the household. So we might claim that Dorval is a clearly marked unreliable narrator.

Salon versus theatre

Dorval's position in the dialogue of the *Entretiens* is a shifting one. Moi opens it by putting to Dorval the fact that he has betrayed the intentions of his father by not representing 'les choses comme elles s'étaient passées', and

22. Connon remarks on the contrast between the triumphant Dorval of the play and the Dorval of the surrounding text: 'We find this same Dorval, still melancholic despite the apotheosis of the final scene, in the *Entretiens sur Le Fils naturel*, where he figures as the author of the play' (*Innovation and renewal*, p.143).

immediately Dorval defends his adjustment of events by reference to dramaturgy, in particular the three Unities: 'Les lois des trois unités sont difficiles à observer, mais elles sont sensées' (p.85). Here speaks the playwright defending his play as good theatre. At other times, however, he defends his play on the grounds that what he has written is simply what happened, as when Moi objects to Dorval's drinking tea at the opening of the play (p.90):

> 'Et le thé de la même scène, lui dis-je?'
>
> Je vous entends. Cela n'est pas de ce pays. J'en conviens; mais j'ai voyagé longtemps en Hollande. J'ai beaucoup vécu avec des étrangers. J'ai pris d'eux cet usage; et c'est moi que j'ai peint.
>
> 'Mais au théâtre!'
>
> Ce n'est pas là. C'est dans le salon qu'il faut juger mon ouvrage.

Dorval has apparently adhered in this connection to no constant principle of composition; dramatic imperatives on the one hand, and the imperatives of 'le fait comme il a été' on the other have alternately won out over each other. Nor does Moi in his questioning show more consistency than has Dorval in defence of his composition; now he requires justification of the play as theatre, now of Dorval's actual motivations at the time of the original events. Guedj comments: 'le va-et-vient est continuel entre la scène et le salon, et trop manifeste pour être involontaire'.[23]

This 'va-et-vient' can be interpreted in terms of an aesthetics of the theatre, as Guedj interprets it.[24] However, when read in the context of the work as a whole, and the work as narrative, it can be placed in relation to other elements tending to characterise Dorval. We have already seen how Lysimond had stipulated that Dorval must be accurate in his representation of events, regardless of considerations of dramaturgy: 'Il ne s'agit point d'élever ici des tréteaux', etc. We can recuperate any of the modifications Dorval claims to have made to the original events for the sake of artistic effect as indicating his failure to fulfil his father's wishes; as part, that is, of the oedipal tension we have already explored.

We have seen that Dorval is represented in the play, and to some extent in the prologue, as an ideal friend and dutiful son whose case seems to suggest that virtue is the only road to happiness. However, our reading shows that this account is consistently undermined in the text as a whole. The authority which Dorval might conventionally enjoy as narrator, hero and eye-witness is subverted, and the play is revealed to be a wishful construction which is one of a number of possible versions of the original events. Beneath the official representation of the virtuous, victorious, and self-

23. 'Les drames de Diderot', p.86.
24. 'Les drames de Diderot', p.79-95.

determining Dorval lurk other Dorvals. The Dorval who is described in the *canevas tragique* as only loving Rosalie and as killing himself must be placed next to the Dorval of the play who has put that Dorval aside; and these figures or projections are to be placed beside the various other possible versions sketched out by André, Moi and Clairville. Moreover, the dutiful son is a thin disguise indeed for the son whose hostility towards his father is manifested, though indirectly, throughout the text.

3. *La Religieuse*

A NUMBER of critics have read *La Religieuse* as a kind of *roman à thèse* directed against the monastic system.[1] This is natural, since the case against convents is stated explicitly, emphatically and repeatedly. The most emphatic passage of all is probably Suzanne's summary of Manouri's *plaidoyer*, where it is argued that the environment of the convent, and the vow of celibacy in particular, is unnatural and can lead to forbidden sexual practices:

> Où est-ce qu'on voit des têtes obsédées par des spectres impurs qui les suivent et qui les agitent? Où est-ce qu'on voit cet ennui profond, cette pâleur, cette maigreur, tous ces symptômes de la nature qui languit et se consume? Où est-ce que la nature révoltée d'une contrainte pour laquelle elle n'est pas faite, brise les obstacles qu'on lui oppose, devient furieuse, jette l'économie animale dans un désordre auquel il n'y a plus de remède?[2]

This general argument corresponds in important respects to the details of Suzanne's particular case and that of other nuns described in her account. The memorable passage in which Suzanne comes face to face with a deranged sister who has escaped from her cell is presented as a decisive moment in the tale (p.92-93):

> Je n'ai jamais rien vu de si hideux. Elle était échevelée et presque sans vêtement; elle traînait des chaînes de fer; ses yeux étaient égarés; elle s'arrachait les cheveux; elle se frappait la poitrine avec les poings; elle courait, elle hurlait; elle se chargeait elle-même et les autres des plus terribles imprécations; elle cherchait une fenêtre pour se précipiter. La frayeur me saisit, je tremblai de tous mes membres, je vis mon sort dans celui de cette infortunée, et sur-le-champ, il fut décidé dans mon cœur que je mourrais mille fois plutôt que de m'y exposer.

In the closing stages of the narrative, Mme *** proves to be actively lesbian, and subsequently loses her reason and dies a premature death. In the light of such indications, then, it would seem perverse to deny that *La Religieuse* is at least in some respects an anti-monastic *roman à thèse*.

However, such an approach does not exhaust the possibilities of interpretation offered by the work, and more recent readings investigate

1. See for instance: Georges May, *Diderot et 'La Religieuse'* (Paris, PUF 1954); Robert Ellrich, 'The rhetoric of *La Religieuse* and eighteenth-century forensic rhetoric', *Diderot studies* 3 (1961), p.129-54; and Vivienne Mylne, *Diderot: 'La Religieuse'* (London, Grant and Cutler 1981).
2. *ŒC*, xi.183-84.

its narrative and psychological complexities.[3] Of those interested primarily in the novel's psychological aspects, several adopt a specifically psycho-analytic approach.[4] Here we will reflect on the tension between the novel's potential for conveying an anti-monastic message on the one hand and its exploration of psychology on the other; our conclusion will be that the work's psychological complexities tend to subvert its function as a *roman à thèse*.

The psychological complexities which are particularly relevant here are connected with the family. *La Religieuse* is a work in which family relationships are shown to operate as causal factors. According to Suzanne, beneath her parents' decision to send her to the convent lurks the imperfectly maintained secret of her illicit birth. In the opening pages of her memoirs, it gradually emerges that her mother conceived her in the course of an adulterous love-affair which ended acrimoniously. This fact causes her legal father M. Simonin to hate her, and arouses a mixture of displaced loathing and religious guilt on the part of her mother. In addition, the pretty Suzanne is the butt of her ugly sisters' envy. In the light of this, it seems natural to inquire whether Suzanne's relationships within the convent might not be read as an extension, in whatever respect, of the problematic relationships which bedevil her family. The question is particularly appropriate given that the convent, with its Fathers, Mothers, and Sisters, finds its structure, precisely, as a metaphorical family. The imitation of family by convent facilitates Suzanne's displacement of a range of conflicts from one to the other.

Even if Suzanne repeatedly argues that her suffering within the convent is explicable by the particularities of the monastic environment, many details of her narrative nevertheless suggest that family relationships offer a more convincing explanation. The clearest proof of this, perhaps, resides in two peculiarities of Suzanne's narrative. First, she fails to represent herself as unhappier inside the convent than outside. Indeed, the only moments of

3. See: Walter E. Rex, 'Secrets from Suzanne: the tangled motives of *La Religieuse*', *The Eighteenth century: theory and interpretation* 24, no. 3 (1983), p.185-98; William F. Edmiston, 'Narrative voice and cognitive privilege in Diderot's *La Religieuse*', *French forum* 10 (1985), p.133-44; Julie C. Hayes, 'Retrospection and contradiction in Diderot's *La Religieuse*', *Romanic review* 77 (1986), p.233-42; and P. W. Byrne, 'The form of paradox: a critical study of Diderot's *La Religieuse*', *SVEC* 319 (1994), p.169-93.

4. See in particular the succinct interpretation by Pierre Saint-Amand, 'D'une mère à l'autre: *La Religieuse* de Diderot', in *Dilemmes du roman: essays in honor of Georges May*, ed. Catherine Lafarge (Saratoga, Anma Libri 1989), p.121-32. Although I had completed a version of this analysis before I came across Saint-Amand's piece, there are points of coincidence between his reading and my own, and I have indicated the most important of these.

happiness she relates are within the convent. Second, she repeatedly implies that she is happy when she enjoys the favour of a parent or parent-substitute, and unhappy when this is not the case, irrespective of her environment. In both respects, Suzanne's story fails to exemplify her own anti-monastic argument. Once again, if Suzanne's unhappiness can be said to have an ultimate or at least a principal cause, we must look not to the convent but to the family.

A detailed reading of the novel confirms this position. Of course such a reading raises problems of theory. If we assert that the narrator's discourse combines two accounts of events which are fundamentally contradictory, and only one of which is explicitly and publicly avowed, then we need to characterise the narrator in such a way as to take account of this. This involves reference, be it implicit, to a model of psychology; and whilst in many cases a commonsense or folk psychology model is adequate to a reading of a novel, a Freudian account is more appropriate in the case of *La Religieuse*. The notion of competing causalities embedded in a single discourse can easily be accommodated in a Freudian reading, providing of course that one type of causality is of a nature to be disavowed and the other resembles a systematic but false explanation of the events related. Moreover, it scarcely needs stating that the Oedipus complex and the concept of transference might be used to illuminate *La Religieuse*, given that Suzanne treats her relationships within the convent as extensions of her family relationships. Taken together, Mme Simonin and the Mother Superiors in charge of Suzanne can be read as forming a succession governed by transference; various father figures form a similar chain. Suzanne's unavowed but manifest change of allegiance, from mother to father, will be explained by reference to the pivotal scene in which Suzanne confesses to père Lemoine. Finally, the connected concepts of negation and disavowal can serve as a frame for analysing Suzanne's style of narrative. For the sake of clarity, we will examine passages as far as possible in the order of their disposition in Suzanne's account.

From family to convent

After beginning *La Religieuse*, the reader must wait some two hundred pages for the most complete statement of the case against convents which is Manouri's *plaidoyer*. However, the details of Suzanne's life which are to exemplify it are already being put in place in the earlier part of the novel, which culminates in Suzanne's definitive entry into convent life (p.81-124). The original situation seems designed to show that Suzanne took her vows as the result of the injustice of her family and of the convent which conspires with it. Through the gradual revelation of her parents' guilty secret, it is made clear to Suzanne that she has no place in the original family, no dowry can be made available to her, and that she is expected to atone for her mother's sin by living as a nun.

The ground has been thoroughly prepared, then, for Suzanne to argue that if she took her vows, it was under pressure; that vows taken under duress are not morally binding and should not be legally binding. The issues seem to be clearly delineated, and equally clear is the reader's choice of loyalty, to the sinister establishment or to the innocent victim Suzanne, together with all the young men and women for whom she can be taken to stand. However, present in the opening part of the novel are two important elements which do not fit. First, there is the apparently ideal relationship with Mme de Moni. Thanks to her influence, Suzanne seems perfectly fulfilled at Longchamp; when her superior states that she wishes Suzanne to be happy, the latter replies: 'Si vous m'aimez toujours, je le serai' (p.121). When we further consider that Suzanne's life at home has been effectively one of solitary confinement since her first profession, and a marriage is out of the question, we might well ask ourselves why Suzanne's future in the convent might not consist in a continuation of happiness, with Mme de Moni or a successor.[5]

Second, there is the mysterious trance-like state which overtakes Suzanne as she is about to take her vows. We have just seen that the ground has been prepared for the argument that vows taken under duress should have no force. However, no advantage is drawn from this argument, for it is never finally articulated by Suzanne. Instead, at the pivotal moment of the profession ceremony, she decentres the issue to base her justification on different grounds, adducing the fact that she was *unconscious* when she took her vows. 'On m'a sans doute interrogée, j'ai sans doute répondu, j'ai prononcé des vœux, mais je n'en ai nulle mémoire, et je me suis trouvée religieuse aussi innocemment que je fus faite chrétienne [...] Eh bien, Monsieur, quoique je n'aie pas réclamé à Longchamp comme j'avais fait à Sainte-Marie, me croyez-vous plus engagée? J'en appelle à votre jugement, j'en appelle au jugement de Dieu' (p.123-24).

Why does Suzanne fail to use the argument that she was the victim of duress? The unprepared argument which she substitutes for it implies a weakness in the case which she abandons. The idea that Suzanne might be taken to stand for nuns and monks in general is also weakened, given the exceptional and possibly unique circumstance of her unconsciousness during the profession ceremony; and so the structure of the *roman à thèse*,

5. See Vivienne Mylne, *The Eighteenth-century French novel: techniques of illusion* (Manchester, Manchester University Press 1965), p.203, where an attempt is made to smooth this inconsistency out by lending Mme de Moni a darker side.

which requires that individual characters' experience can as far as possible be matched to a general argument which can be abstracted from the work, tends to break down.[6]

In the opening section of the novel, then, the ideal relationship with Mme de Moni and the argument of unconsciousness do not by any means contribute to the work's anti-monastic rhetoric. However, if we refer to what the same section tells us of Suzanne's attitudes towards her own family and the convent as a substitute family, we discover plausible explanations of the role of Mme de Moni and the 'aliénation physique' of the profession scene. First of all, the exact words which Suzanne uses to characterise Mme de Moni are significant. These are: 'elle avait de l'indulgence, quoique personne n'en eût moins besoin; *nous étions tous ses enfants*' (p.117; emphasis added). The metaphor is telling. Surely Suzanne does not mean to inform the reader of the well known convention by which one woman becomes the spiritual 'mother' of another in a community of nuns. Instead her sentence characterises Mme de Moni in particular; she is a mother in some sense in which the Mère des Novices and other Superiors are not. In fact, Suzanne's remark can only reasonably be understood in one way: in Mme de Moni's case the conventional Church relationship coincides with her affectionate maternal feelings towards younger women. She is a mother-substitute in a human rather than a spiritual sense. The causality of family determinants inhabits the metaphor parasitically, so to speak: for Suzanne, the mothers, fathers and sisters of the convent have a psychological rather than a spiritual significance. Monastic life under the authority of Mme de Moni represents the perfect compensation of Suzanne's situation in her true family; the least favoured daughter at home, Suzanne is the favourite daughter of the Superior.[7] 'Le nom de favorites est celui que les autres donnent par envie aux bien-aimées de la supérieure' (p.117), she states, and her emphasis suggests that her own satisfaction derives largely from the envy of the less favoured sisters. Nevertheless, Suzanne does not willingly enter the convent. This, together with Suzanne's comparison of Mme de Moni with a natural mother, suggests that though Suzanne presents her as an ideal alternative, she is not truly drawn to her as fully as to her true mother. Only the bond with the natural mother seems fundamental to Suzanne's motivation; at once it motivates her aversion to the convent and her ostensible happiness within it, the happiness having the meaning of a

6. There also results an ethical vagueness which is perplexing in a *roman à thèse*. Suzanne does not tell us what she feels she ought to have done had she remained conscious. Would refusing her vows have been a case of having the courage of her convictions, or would taking them have been a case of laudable self-sacrifice?

7. Cf. Saint-Amand, 'D'une mère à l'autre', p.126: 'En d'autres termes, Suzanne exige au couvent le traitement qu'elle n'a jamais reçu à la maison.'

reproach to the true mother who loves her less than the substitute. Thus the original bond of love persists rather than being renounced.[8]

This affords us an explanation of the trance-like state of the profession scene. Being a novice, suspended between world and convent, is a compromise-situation which comports compensations offered neither by secular life, nor by life as a nun. However, Suzanne's advantage cannot easily be prolonged after the day set for her profession. If she takes her vows, everything which Mme Simonin has said indicates that she will hand her over, heartily relieved to be rid of her, and the relationship with the real mother will be dissolved. On the other hand, if she refuses to take her vows, she can only look forward to solitary confinement at home (this was her fate after she publicly refused to take her vows at Sainte-Marie). The 'aliénation physique' which overtakes Suzanne on the day of the profession, preventing her from consciously saying either 'yes' or 'no', should have prevented the due completion of the ceremony. This would provide a solution to Suzanne's dilemma. She could with some justification have hoped that her physical inability to take or refuse her vows would invalidate the profession ceremony, yet without her seeming responsible as at Sainte-Marie. Either one of two outcomes might conceivably have resulted. The novitiate could have been extended, and with it the compromise-situation along with its compensations; or (better still, no doubt) the family might have been obliged to resign itself to the impossibility of its plan, and a re-acceptance of the rejected daughter.

Close examination of the opening section, then, suggests that where the official rhetoric of the anti-monastic narrative with its social causality seems to break down, the causality of family can serve instead as an adequate explanation of events. That this can be said of the novel as a whole will emerge in subsequent sections, where it will be demonstrated that Suzanne is consistently represented as though she has strong unconscious motives connected with her family. These motives can be summarised in the form used above: it is not being inside or outside a convent which decides the question of happiness for Suzanne, but being inside or outside the favour of the parent (-substitute) – father, mother, Mother Superior, confessor or marquis.[9]

8. Freud discusses a comparable process in 'Family romances' (1909), where he speaks of the motive of revenge and retaliation underlying the child's substitution in day dreams of imagined parents for his own; such day dreams are made possible by the fiction that the child is a foundling or a bastard. See *The Standard edition*, ix.235-41.

9. I anticipate here on what follows by extrapolating from mother figures to parent figures in general. For, as I intend to show, it emerges that Suzanne takes as objects of love mother-figures until the confession with père Lemoine, after which she elects instead father-figures. Motivations for this (oedipal) development will be

The onset of persecution: Suzanne and Sœur Sainte-Christine

By a coincidence which reinforces the implicit invitation to compare the two women's roles as mother, Mme Simonin and Mme de Moni both die shortly after Suzanne's profession. From this point on, the work enters its most powerful phase as a satire of convents, for it is here that the story of Suzanne's persecution begins. The depiction of cruelty in the convent seems designed to allow Suzanne to argue that 'l'acharnement à tourmenter et à perdre se lasse dans le monde; il ne se lasse point dans les cloîtres' (p.134) (and later, she recalls a similar statement of Mme de Moni's, p.160). Yet, as in the opening section of the novel, there is here a disturbance of the anti-conventual rhetoric; for here too Suzanne's suffering is not adequately explained by the monastic environment, but is caused by her attitude towards figures of maternal authority. Suzanne herself points out that she provokes her own persecution by adopting a hostile attitude, whilst the new Superior initially views her with indifference: 'Je fus indifférente, pour ne rien dire de pis, à la supérieure actuelle, par la raison que sa précédente m'avait chérie; mais je ne tardai pas à empirer mon sort' (p.129).

The first of Suzanne's provocative actions is to praise Mme de Moni and to contrast her with Sainte-Christine (just as Mme de Moni has been implicitly contrasted with the real mother). This behaviour seems consistent with the familial determinants already outlined: if at first Suzanne is happy in the convent because it offers her the position of favourite daughter in a substitute family, then the failure of Mme de Moni's successor to perpetuate her privileges is enough to antagonise her. It should perhaps be added that Sœur Sainte-Christine's cruelty results in the appearance of a stern father figure (Hébert, whose role will be examined below) who reproves the mother figure for her injustice. This outcome must obviously afford satisfaction to the spurned daughter, and the prospect of it could provide an additional motive for Suzanne's rebellion.

Given that Suzanne seems to be engaged in seeking out figures who will enable her to extend or renew old conflicts which originally concerned her parents, Diderot's novel represents the type of phenomenon which Freud

suggested in subsequent sections. For a late pronouncement of Freud's on the Oedipus complex in the female, see 'Female sexuality' (1931), *The Standard edition*, xxi.221-43, where it is argued that little girls, unlike little boys, must change both their sexual aim and sexual object (which are claimed to be initially active and female respectively) if they are to become healthy adult heterosexuals. It scarcely needs stating that Freud's account, which in any case was tentative, has been radically challenged by subsequent theorists.

terms 'transference'.[10] With Mme de Moni and Sœur Sainte-Christine in mind, we can resume Suzanne's relations with her Mother Superiors as follows: either she requires to have the mother-substitute correct the injustice of the real mother by granting especial affection; or, failing this, she requires a relation of hostility to the mother-figure. This pattern will be confirmed by Suzanne's relations with Mme ***, who clearly favours Suzanne over her peers, as we shall see. However, whilst Suzanne declares affection for one Superior and hostility for another, a fundamental ambivalence always underpins her relations with each. In other words, the two tendencies are in fact manifested not successively but simultaneously. We have already seen that Suzanne conspires in Sœur Sainte-Christine's persecution of her, and in that respect she submits to it with a kind of approval, however obscurely. On the other hand, when a Mother Superior elects Suzanne her favourite, Suzanne herself is instrumental in the decline or downfall of her protectress, which follows closely on their intimacy. Mme de Moni never recovers after the great trial of faith imposed by Suzanne's approaching profession, exclaiming: 'quel effet cruel vous avez opéré sur moi!' (p.120). As if irremediably weakened by this, she dies in the year Suzanne takes her vows. Suzanne's role in the destruction of Mme *** is clearer still; she dies as a direct result of Suzanne's withdrawal of affection.[11]

An explanation of such ambivalence can be found in the relationship with the true mother. Mme Simonin's rejection of Suzanne provides grounds for hostility, and yet Suzanne displays submission, in particular by accepting to enter the convent to expiate her mother's sin. Suzanne's behaviour towards each of the Superiors seems to manifest anew the trauma of rejection by the mother. This trauma can drive her to seek compensation in the form of affection, or to repeat the trauma by provoking a new rejection. In either case, the trauma is expressed as a response to the raw material, so to speak, which is provided by the mother-substitute; the mother's affection elicits affection, though Suzanne's affection veils hostility; and the mother's indifference elicits hostility which in turn veils spurned affection.

10. Freud mainly speaks of transference in relation to psychoanalytic therapy, and discusses it from a technical point of view. Of relevance here, however, is the more general concept which Freud sometimes uses in order to introduce the term's technical sense, or the phenomenon which according to Freud precedes and explains the role of transference in psychoanalysis. I refer to the broad notion that conflicts related to parental figures are taken forward into fresh situations, being 'transferred' onto men or women of a certain age who enjoy a certain authority.

11. See Alice Parker, 'Did/Erotica: Diderot's contribution to the history of sexuality', *Diderot studies* 22 (1986), p.89-106, p.98. See also Rex, 'Secrets of Suzanne', p.54, and Saint-Amand, 'D'une mère à l'autre', p.127.

Sexuality and the narrative voice

The text after Suzanne's departure from Longchamp manifests a deeper exploration of the family causality than hitherto. Suzanne's involvement with Mme *** invites us to connect relationships on the family model with sexuality. The lesbian relation suggests that Suzanne's desire to win the position of favourite daughter might always have had a sexual aspect which first becomes clearly manifest in her relations with the homosexual Mother Superior.[12]

At the same time, the text obliges us to treat Suzanne as an increasingly unreliable narrator; for she claims not to understand sexuality, even whilst making the sexual level of the action clear to the reader. This, together with Mme ***'s confession which is overheard by Suzanne, has caused critics to object to Diderot's technique, as though he had imperfectly mastered some unwritten code concerning point of view.[13] However, the fact that Suzanne manages to convey the story of Mme ***'s homosexual passion clearly and economically, even whilst denying she is doing so, can be seen in a more positive light. Her narrative voice can be read as a discourse of disavowal which amounts to a fascinating experiment in point of view.

The unreliability of Suzanne's narrative voice has often been erroneously connected with another problem of interpretation. A recurrent concern for critics has been the question of *bévues* or alleged slips in narrative technique. For instance, it is by now well known that Suzanne quotes a letter of her mother's which describes events occurring the day after it has been sent (p.126-27), and that Manouri's *plaidoyer* begins in his own voice yet is completed in Suzanne's (p.181-86).[14] But where do *bévues* end and where does narrative complexity begin? Various commentators have seen as particularly problematic the passage in which Suzanne overhears Mme ***'s confession. How, they ask, can Suzanne claim throughout her memoirs that she is innocent of sexual knowledge, only to reveal towards the end that she knows Mme *** to be an 'abominable femme'?[15]

12. Cf. Saint-Amand, p.129: 'Le dernier couvent de Suzanne, Arpajon, rejoue aussi dans toute son ambiguïté la relation avec la mère et actualise sa teneur homosexuelle.'

13. Mylne initially criticises Diderot on this point; see *The Eighteenth-century French novel*, p.199. However, she revises her view in a subsequent article: 'What Suzanne knew: lesbianism and *La Religieuse*', *SVEC* 208 (1982), p.17.

14. For a thorough discussion of Diderot's alleged slips, see P. W. Byrne, 'The form of paradox'; in addition, most of the pieces already mentioned deal with the subject more or less directly.

15. This is the view, for instance, of Georges May: 'Contre toute logique [Diderot] annule du passé de son héroïne le moment où elle acquiert la connaissance

However, we may instead decide that this aspect only enriches the work. Suzanne's account is indeed problematically inconsistent, not only towards the end of the novel but from an early stage, wherever questions of innocence, guilt and sexuality are concerned. Let us first attend to the general problem of Suzanne's voice, in order to discuss it in the light of psychoanalytic theory. Then we can turn to the passages concerning Sainte-Eutrope – the section where Suzanne's narratorial claims to innocence are placed under the greatest strain and raise the most interesting interpretive problems of all.

Negation and narration

Suzanne's statements concerning ignorance, knowledge, guilt and innocence are never straightforward. Let us take as an example a claim which she makes in the course of her account of Longchamp. The hostile community exploits a young nun's hysteria in order to impute 'des désirs bizarres' to Suzanne; and we can only suppose that homosexual desires are meant by this. Suzanne uses this event to contrast her own sexual innocence with the depravity of her accusers (p.164):

> En vérité, je ne suis pas un homme et je ne sais ce qu'on peut imaginer d'une femme et d'une autre femme, et moins encore d'une femme seule; cependant comme mon lit était sans rideaux et qu'on entrait dans ma chambre à toute heure, que vous dirai-je, Monsieur, il faut qu'avec toute leur retenue extérieure, la modestie de leurs regards, la chasteté de leur expression, ces femmes aient le cœur bien corrompu, elles savent du moins qu'on commet seule des actions déshonnêtes, et moi je ne le sais pas; aussi n'ai-je jamais bien compris ce dont elles m'accusaient, et elles s'exprimaient en des termes si obscurs, que je n'ai jamais su ce qu'il y avait à leur répondre.

This passage is problematic in several respects. First of all, the statement 'elles savent du moins [...] et moi je ne le sais pas' may seem contradictory; if Suzanne knows that others know 'qu'on commet seule des actions déshonnêtes', then she knows too, in the usual sense of the word. Her claim is presumably that she does know in an abstract sense that cloistered women can indulge in sexual practices, either singly or together, but she cannot visualise them or imagine in what they consist. Thus Suzanne sets up a fine distinction between different kinds of knowledge, which must have consequences for any attempt to understand her narratorial point of view. Second, Suzanne defends herself by asserting that it is her accusers who are guilty of the corruption with which they charge her. This may seem a mere

terrible qui détruit irrémédiablement la virginité de son cœur'. See *Diderot et 'La Religieuse'*, p.204.

rhetorical flourish at first. Yet as we read the story of Suzanne's relations with Mme *** at Sainte-Eutrope, we find good reason to suspect Suzanne of homosexual knowledge herself. Suddenly then her assertion that other nuns, not she, know what homosexuality is resembles a defence by projection of guilty knowledge, rather than indicating a pure absence of such knowledge. Third, this passage suggests that Suzanne has a deeply rooted motive for remaining ignorant, and this cannot fail radically to alter our perception of her ignorance. For she manifestly equates having 'le cœur bien corrompu' with simply being able to conceive of or visualise sinful actions; she does not accuse the other nuns of actually having performed them.[16] Such an equation of knowledge with guilt is implied in Suzanne's statement, and so the belief that nuns who know of sex are letting themselves in for damnation provides a motive for wanting to resist such knowledge.

In brief, then, knowledge, guilt, ignorance and innocence are closely interwoven for Suzanne, and her own innocence is in some respect willed. Now the passage we have just examined precedes Suzanne's account of Sainte-Eutrope; so far from arising with the overhearing of Mme ***'s confession, the problem of what Suzanne knew, and the nature of that knowledge, is explicitly raised at a relatively early stage. In addition, the problem is consistently emphasised by Suzanne's position and function as narrator during the whole of the account of Sainte-Eutrope, which, after all, commands a third of the whole work. For ignorance of homosexuality seems inconsistent with the fact that Suzanne is capable of telling a coherent story about homosexuality (even or especially when the story is told indirectly). The story of Mme ***'s passion for her is dramatised with economy and a great deal of psychological nuance; the reader is not obliged to grasp at occasional clues. Worked into Suzanne's account there are even anticipations of and defences against the marquis's interpretation of events as somehow not innocent, which suggest some kind of awareness on Suzanne's part of the sexual meaning she is conveying to her addressee. In its economy, clarity, and tone, then, the section on Sainte-Eutrope suggests a narratorial awareness of homosexuality.

It is here that psychoanalysis might help us out. As suggested in the Introduction, in *La Religieuse* Diderot offers a representation of humanity, and in particular of femininity, according to which there is an official surface which conforms to social conventions and an unofficial level of

16. This calls to mind a fundamental Christian doctrine: to think of committing fornication is to commit fornication (see Matthew v.28). It also calls to mind the logic of the Eden parable, where nakedness only becomes shameful when Man knows it to be so, having eaten of the Tree of Knowledge (see Genesis ii.16 to Genesis iii.22).

motivation connected with sexuality. This is expressed both in the choice of story-events and in the characteristics of the discourse which mediates them. In both these respects a Freudian model of psychology seems more relevant than a model which supposes the subject to be unified, coherent and rational.

Of primary interest here is the concept of negation. In his paper entitled 'Die Verneigung' (1925) Freud writes: 'With the help of negation only one consequence of the process of repression is undone – the fact, namely, of the ideational content of what is repressed not reaching consciousness. The outcome of this is a kind of intellectual acceptance of the repressed, while at the same time what is essential to the repression persists.'[17] As far as the speaker's consciousness is concerned, then, the denial is effective; but for the informed listener, as for the unconscious system (in which 'no' does not exist), the denial is an affirmation. According to such a conception, of the speaker and the informed listener the latter alone can reconstruct the truth distorted in the neurotic discourse. Freud proceeds to suggest that the negative expression of the repressed actually facilitates the process of conscious thinking where true non-expression would obstruct it: 'With the help of the symbol of negation, thinking frees itself from the restrictions of repression and enriches itself with material that is indispensable for its proper functioning' (p.236).

Negation, then, has a dual function: to maintain repression and yet to permit the efficient representation or narration of a given state of affairs by covert integration of the material repressed. This simple but radical view helps to throw light on the problematic aspects of the account of Sainte-Eutrope, mentioned above.[18] The clarity and detail of the account of Mme ***'s love can be seen as deriving from Suzanne's repressed knowledge of the story she is telling indirectly, whilst her repeated negation of the true meaning of the story can be understood as the surfacing in consciousness of the idea of homosexuality. This surfacing permits the highly organised articulation (corresponding to Freud's 'proper functioning' of thinking) of the story by providing the requisite associative links under 'the symbol of negation'. Such ideas can be used to understand Suzanne, not as failing to understand her own story in spite of overhearing part of Mme ***'s confession, but rather as positively resisting a sexual interpretation of her

17. 'Negation', in *The Standard edition*, xix.233-39 (p.236).

18. Of course, negation cannot be plucked from Freud's writing without bringing with it certain closely connected concepts which it presupposes, for instance those of repression and resistance, and a general conception of discourse as a compromise-formation marked by significant gaps, contradictions, juxtaposition of elements associated via unconscious links, and so on. Such concepts will also inform our discussion, without implying consent to the whole of Freud's writing.

story (thanks to the motive implicit in the statement of innocence which we have already examined). Repression and resistance seem to have worked their way into the very texture of her discourse; though this is especially clear where negation has the dual function suggested by Freud, there are also significant gaps and contradictions, curious emphases and juxtapositions which can also be read as indicating repression. The close reading which follows will demonstrate the appropriateness of this characterisation of Suzanne's account.

Now let us return to the part of the novel which deals with Sainte-Eutrope. As stated above, this is the section of the novel in which the narrative voice is at its most obviously problematic. Since the strain on Suzanne's claim to sexual innocence is intensified by her account of her relations with Mme ***, it is also the section in which negation is called upon to play an especially important role, as Suzanne disavows the sexual causality even whilst making it increasingly clear to the reader.

Suzanne at Sainte-Eutrope

Suzanne's entry to the convent at Arpajon marks the point from which the sexual causality is indispensable to every reader's processing of the narrative, whether or not the reader is aware of the precise manner in which he or she recuperates the signals concerning sex. From here on, Suzanne's discourse can be understood as having two levels: the official level of disavowal, and the unofficial level of sexual and aggressive drives.

This is how Suzanne relates her installation in her cell: '[Mme ***] me tint cent propos doux et me fit mille caresses qui m'embarrassèrent un peu, je ne sais pas pourquoi, car je n'y entendais rien, ni elle non plus, et à présent même que j'y réfléchis, qu'aurions-nous pu y entendre?' (p.214). Here Suzanne affords all the information which will permit us to read homosexuality into the incident and simultaneously resists sharing this interpretation. It is as if she is erecting screens opaque to her own consciousness but transparent to the addressee. First we register the fact that at the time of the action related, Suzanne was troubled by Mme ***'s caresses. This trouble signals to us that they are sexual rather than merely affectionate, and that Suzanne was in a position to know as much at the time, having, presumably, a sexual response herself. Next, Suzanne the narrator stresses that there was no intention on either woman's part apart from that of exchanging an innocent caress; 'car je n'y entendais rien'; but inscribed in the need to negate the guilty nature of the caress is the knowledge that such a caress between women may indeed be of a guilty nature; and as if aware that she is accusing herself of such knowledge, Suzanne the narrator reiterates that even now she cannot see in what way the caress might not have been innocent. Such a defence of course only serves to indicate her sensitivity to the unspoken accusation. The innocence of these caresses would have been signified by *not* being stated. The surface-statement of their innocence is in fact a statement of the opposite, under 'the symbol of negation'.

In the continuation of the passage just quoted, the contradiction in what Suzanne tells the marquis is also represented on the level of the plot (i.e. the guilt, though negated, gives rise to a significant action). For Suzanne tells us that she mentioned these caresses to her confessor; 'Cependant j'en parlai à mon directeur qui traita cette familiarité, qui me paraissait innocente et qui me le paraît encore, d'un ton fort sérieux et me défendit gravement de m'y prêter davantage' (p.214). Once again, there is a surface contradiction here, marked by a 'cependant', which is the means by which the unofficial truth is conveyed to us; if Suzanne believed the caresses to be innocent, why mention them, precisely, to her confessor, whose role is to listen to reports of sins? It is as if by the fact of telling him about the sinful actions Suzanne can assign him the role of knowing that they are sinful, an attitude which can serve as a disavowal of her unconscious knowledge by projection. However, the contradiction inherent in confessing actions she claims are innocent betrays her knowledge that they are not, even whilst her projection constitutes a denial.

There are many other instances of the way in which Suzanne's discourse seems to indicate repressed knowledge. For instance, she manages to convey to us that Sœur Thérèse is jealous of her as a sexual rival. Negation of knowledge of this rivalry is characteristically the very means by which the rivalry is introduced into the disavowed love-story, and permits it to be articulated in greater detail, thus helping the 'proper functioning of thought'. During the course of the first day at Sainte-Eutrope, Mme *** has Suzanne play the spinet in her cell before a number of assembled nuns, most of whom proceed to disappear. The account continues as follows (p.217):

> Elle était assise, j'étais debout; elle me prenait les mains et elle me disait en les serrant: Mais outre qu'elle joue bien, elle a les plus jolis doigts du monde. Voyez donc, sœur Thérèse ... Sœur Thérèse baissait les yeux, rougissait et bégayait; cependant que j'eusse les doigts jolis ou non, que la supérieure eût tort ou raison de l'observer, qu'est-ce que cela faisait à cette sœur?

Here, Suzanne's use of the interrogative form conveys a message to the marquis which once again takes the form of a disavowal, given that the question 'what did it matter to her?' is apparently a rhetorical recasting of the negation 'it could not and did not matter to her' and begs the answer 'nothing'. Of course, whilst the answer would be 'nothing' for Suzanne the ideally innocent narrator, it is 'a great deal' for the informed reader or the marquis. The one answer confirms a sexual causality, the other denies it, but both are implied by the text.

Furthermore, the very content of the passage contradicts its surface meaning, in that there is a contradiction between the idea that material is unimportant and the fact of choosing to relate it. Just as Suzanne asks what it mattered to Thérèse that Mme *** praised Suzanne's fingers, we can ask what it now matters to Suzanne herself, why she mentions it in the context of the memoirs, what she would suppose it matters to the marquis. Suzanne's surface statement of the unimportance of the incident is a token of its importance in that she mentions it at all. So just like the sexual nature of Mme ***'s caresses, the idea 'this is important' is introduced under the symbol of negation, and this enables the detailed articulation of the love-story to proceed. After all, the role of Thérèse and her jealousy is an integral part of that story.

Thus Suzanne establishes a double level in the narrative of this scene, a narrative which effects a compromise between the meaning the affair with Mme *** secretly holds for her and the desire to hold that meaning under repression. Suzanne can leave all the responsibility for reading homosexuality into the episode with the reader/marquis. Her discourse effects a distribution of knowledge and ignorance; knowledge to others (the sign either of their masculinity or their corruption), and innocence to herself.

The few initial signals already mentioned induce us to supplement Suzanne's ignorance by our own knowledge. She proceeds to relate the dialogue which ensues between Thérèse and Mme ***: 'Mais, Madame, vous m'aviez promis un moment de consolation avant vêpres. J'ai des pensées qui m'inquiètent' complains Thérèse, to which Mme *** replies: 'Je gage que je sais ce que c'est' (p.218). We, too, bet that we know what it is: a jealous lover's complaint. Yet there is nothing intrinsically suggestive about this exchange; it is suggestive purely because we have by now accepted the reading role Suzanne has created for us; she has accustomed us to reading her discourse as having two contradictory levels. Similarly, when Suzanne proceeds to relate that she subsequently interpreted the incident purely in terms of jealousy, we automatically understand sexual jealousy, but just as automatically suppose that Suzanne officially means non-sexual jealousy; and so we can read this as a rationalisation of what Suzanne unconsciously knows to be the case; 'Il me vint en idée que cette jeune fille était jalouse de moi et qu'elle craignait que je ne lui ravisse la place qu'elle occupait dans les bonnes grâces et l'intimité de la supérieure' (p.219).

Such passages can be used, as here, to suggest that Suzanne the narrator manifests repression in her manner of writing about Mme ***. This repression is a constant force in her organisation of reality. The same is not true of Suzanne the heroine. She is less repressed when she arrives at Sainte-Eutrope; she is shown to have become repressed during her stay there. It may seem problematic to claim that such a development might be perceptible, given that the heroine is always mediated by the narrator, and we claim that the narrator's knowledge is constantly repressed. Yet the development is perceptible on the level of story rather than that of discourse. This can be demonstrated in several ways. Most important, perhaps, is the fact that from a certain point in the novel the heroine begins to act in ways which, in spite of the narrator's retrospective disclaimers, imply that at one stage the sexual impulse towards Mme *** was quite unrepressed, and indicates the stages by which the repression was instituted. For Suzanne clearly begins to treat Mme *** and her former favourite Thérèse as lover and rival respectively. Not only the details of the sexual contact with Mme *** – the 'familiarité [...] innocente' (p.214), the 'scène du clavecin' (p.223-24), and so on – but the behavioural extensions of such contact enter her account. The most obvious of these consists in a mixture of aggression and guilt directed towards Thérèse once she has become the rejected rival.

Let us examine several incidents which show Suzanne behaving in this manner. On one occasion when Thérèse has angered Mme ***, Suzanne obtains her forgiveness by letting the Superior kiss her forehead. This intercession provides the model for a whole series: 'Depuis ce temps, sitôt qu'une religieuse avait fait quelque faute, j'intercédais pour elle, et j'étais sûre d'obtenir sa grâce par quelque faveur innocente' (p.222). Suzanne rationalises her motive as simple compassion. Yet that an underlying wish avails itself of this rationalisation is later betrayed by the fact that her 'compassion' is replaced by flagrant aggression. This occurs on the occasion when Suzanne returns to her cell after an encounter with Mme *** which arouses a particularly strong sexual response in her (she is unable to play the harpsichord because of the trembling of her hands), and Thérèse confronts her, asking: 'Oseriez-vous bien me dire ce que vous y avez fait?' (p.229). Suzanne's account of her reaction contains one of her significant contradictions (marked once again by a 'cependant'): 'Quoique ma conscience ne me reprochât rien, je vous avouerai cependant, Monsieur le marquis, que sa question me troubla' (p.229). This statement tells us that Suzanne's conscience – or consciousness – knows nothing of the underlying cause of her trouble, and her statement is characteristically suspended between negation, in the opening clause, and a related confessional urge, indicated in 'je vous avouerai'.

Troubled, then, Suzanne repays Thérèse in her own currency: 'Chère sœur; peut-être ne m'en croiriez-vous pas, mais vous en croirez peut-être notre chère Mère, et je la prierai de vous en instruire' (p.229). The threat is thinly veiled, and the shift in attitude towards Thérèse, from protection to menace, is telling. The physical intimacy which was initiated ostensibly to protect Thérèse is now protected quite aggressively against Thérèse. Moreover, the penalty with which Suzanne threatens her is the Superior's disfavour: precisely what the intimacy was officially intended to avert from her. This clearly shows that sexually influenced behaviour enters the heroine's relations with Thérèse. It is at the point where Suzanne the heroine is more strongly aroused than ever before by Mme ***'s advances that her sexual desire interferes with her compassionate behaviour towards her rival; or indeed Suzanne's compassion for Thérèse may always have been the rationalisation of her own sexual desire.

Having intimidated Thérèse, Suzanne returns to her cell, where she falls asleep in response to an unfamiliar exhaustion. This is how she relates her waking thoughts concerning her relations with Mme ***: 'je m'examinai, je crus entrevoir en m'examinant encore ... mais c'étaient des idées si vagues, si folles, si ridicules, que je les rejetai loin de moi' (p.230).[19] Here what Suzanne is presenting is a turning point in her development. Nowhere else does the reading of Suzanne as neither innocent nor disabused but repressed seem more directly elicited. Until this point, she has merely displayed an affectionate current towards Mme ***, a sexual tendency not repressed so much as pursued only part of the way towards its aim. Now, however, the situation must change; sexual arousal has overtaken her, suddenly and unexpectedly. There is no going back, no possibility of sensing the danger in advance and fending it off; the abstract knowledge of the fact of homosexuality threatens to find a concrete content in her own actions. She is constrained simultaneously to allow an impure thought into her head, in the form of the realisation that her contact with Mme *** has been sexual, and to recognise her own actions as impure. (We have already seen in her original claim to innocence that she considers the thought alone a token of moral depravity.) The conditions in which repression arises are present: a conflict between powerful demands connected with sexuality on the one hand and the moral tendency to censure them on the other. The text here suggests that ideas unacceptable in consciousness can become preconscious, then at the last instant be repressed if they precipitate moral anxiety. Suzanne represses the ideational links which threaten to draw together her own experience and her knowledge that women can perform sinful sex acts together.

Suzanne now produces a rationalisation to serve in consciousness in the place of the repressed material; she explains her symptoms of sexual arousal

19. Diderot had originally written 'obscènes' after 'vagues' and before 'folles', but he suppressed this. It is interesting to notice him hesitating as to the exact degree of consciousness which should be accorded to the idea of homosexuality which threatens to dawn on Suzanne. For the variant, see *ŒC*, xi.230.

to herself by the hypothesis that Mme *** is suffering from some contagious disease, and that she herself is perhaps succumbing to its first effects. In itself this rationalisation seems feeble indeed; but we should not see it in isolation from Suzanne's development. It is only an application to new material of a dual strategy of repression and rationalisation she has already been seen to use. We have just examined how she rationalises her own impulse towards sexual contact with Mme *** as motivated by compassion for Thérèse. If we recall the earlier passage, discussed above, in which Mme *** installs Suzanne in her cell, we can also characterise her conviction on that occasion that the caresses were innocent as a rationalisation covering a repression. We thus discover a chain of rationalisations of the sexual impulse: innocent affection; compassion for Thérèse; illness. Suzanne may well be thought to cross a line dividing the normal from the abnormal by readers who find her rationalisations increasingly implausible. But in order to understand this development properly, it is important to note that it is not the nature of the mental operations which changes, but the weight of the demands made on them by the material to which they are applied. For as her relations with Mme *** evolve, she must find rationalisations to explain away the increasingly manifest nature of her sexuality.[20]

Suzanne's claimed fear of contagion is undermined as clearly as we have seen her other rationalisations to have been. For this 'fear' does not prevent Suzanne from agreeing to tell the Superior her own life story in an episode where they lie affectionately intertwined, and which culminates in both women showing signs of the 'illness' (Mme *** being much more strongly affected than Suzanne). The illness-hypothesis, which looked promising as a deterrent, therefore turns out to aid the wish rather than the prohibition. Suzanne's rationalisation simply becomes a way of keeping her relations with Mme *** away from the scrutiny of her conscience (or the moral tendency in the conscious system). This is to be inferred from the ease with which she puts herself in danger of contagion; functionally, the idea of contagion is really only an acceptable disguise for the prohibited pleasure of sex.

On close examination of the novel it is difficult to understand how critics can have opposed Suzanne the heroine's innocence to what they believe ought to be Suzanne the narrator's insight. For in our reading we have found many indications in the account of her time at Sainte-Eutrope that her resistance to knowledge is to be understood as an event of the story (as

20. From a non-psychoanalytic point of view, Vivienne Mylne argues that 'the conclusion [Suzanne] avowedly opts for, that the Superior must be suffering from some kind of illness, is plausible enough. But Diderot manages to convey, quite subtly, that this explicit diagnosis could mask some deeper doubt' ('What Suzanne knew', p.169).

well as being manifested in her discourse). This resistance is even dramatised in a dialogue between herself and Mme ***, which occurs directly after Suzanne has rejected the 'idées si folles' which suggest themselves (p.230). Without apparently knowing what they are talking about, Suzanne knows she does not want to find out, and so once more she is characterised as resisting knowledge she has already repressed rather than as straightforwardly ignorant: 'Non, chère Mère, non. Je ne sais rien, et j'aime mieux ne rien savoir que d'acquérir des connaissances qui me rendraient peut-être plus à plaindre que je ne le suis' (p.235). The decoded meaning of this statement might run: 'it is bad enough being a nun as it is, given the limited sexual gratification I obtain; but it would be far worse if the new information you offer obliged me to choose between curbing my sexual behaviour in response to my conscience and remaining sexually active only to be tormented by guilt'.

For Suzanne at this stage in her development, not to know of sex is preferable because it enables her to effect a precarious, neurotic but workable compromise through repression. She can satisfy her desire for Mme *** and the demands of her own moral tendencies simultaneously under the cover of the illness-hypothesis. Mme *** consequently comes up against Suzanne's defences when she aims to seduce her from the direction of consciousness by talking her into full initiation into homosexuality. Suzanne resists these ideas vigorously when they threaten to invade her consciousness from without (i.e. through Mme ***'s words). This is not surprising when we recall that we saw her reject them just as vigorously when they came from within in the form of those 'idées si vagues'. We can infer the same simple cause in each case: moral anxiety.

By this stage of the novel it seems that if Suzanne is to be seduced, it is by actions rather than words and the thoughts they convey, for she displays little resistance to physical closeness with Mme ***. She goes on to narrate a scene in which she allows the Superior into her bed, and it is perhaps only the interruption effected by Thérèse knocking loudly at the door which saves Suzanne from being taken by surprise again by her own sexual responses pushed to a new limit (p.241). We can only suppose that if these responses had developed further thanks to further contact with Mme ***, they would have made the illness-hypothesis unserviceable, just as its predecessor, the affection-hypothesis, had had to be abandoned when Suzanne first became markedly aroused.

A delightful evening

Suzanne's relationship with Mme *** is divided into two phases, the tone of the first being one of affection and happiness, that of the second one of pain and despair. The point of transition between the two coincides with Suzanne's confession by père Lemoine, which will be discussed below. First we will pause to analyse the earlier, affectionate phase. Suzanne recounts an evening which she qualifies as a 'soirée délicieuse'. The evening in question represents the highest point of the first phase, and one of its last moments. The passage is intriguing, since like the episode with Mme de Moni it seems to show us the potential for happiness within the convent. We may well wonder once again that Suzanne foregrounds the possibility of such happiness.

Mme *** has invited Suzanne to attend a gathering in her room. Suzanne compares the sight which greets her as she enters to a pleasant tableau; 'Vous qui vous connaissez en peinture, je vous assure, Monsieur le marquis que c'était un assez agréable tableau à voir' (p.244). Ten or twelve nuns between the ages of fifteen and twenty-three are present. The Superior, who had originally been described as having a face which was 'plutôt bien que mal' (p.208) is now represented as a mature, sensual beauty; 'une supérieure qui touchait à la quarantaine, blanche, fraîche, [...] des lèvres vermeilles comme la rose, des dents blanches comme le lait, les plus belles joues, une tête fort agréable' (p.244). Every one of the young nuns present is also beautiful, but amongst all these beauties, Suzanne occupies the position of favourite; she sits on Mme ***'s bed, and special stress is laid on the fact that she alone of all the young nuns is idle; 'toutes travaillaient, excepté moi, comme je vous l'ai dit' (p.245).

The nuns move towards and away from Mme ***'s bed with their work, and they receive 'de petits reproches ou de petites caresses' (p.245). When Mme *** does finally stir from her bed, it is to stroke and caress them. Finally she faces Suzanne, gazing at her tenderly while all the other nuns lower their eyes 'comme si elles eussent craint de la contraindre ou de la distraire' (p.247).

Each of these details, in particular the lowering of the eyes, suggests that all but Suzanne are fully initiated into the significance of Mme ***'s gathering. This is a harem-family in which the dyadic relation between mother/lover and daughter/concubine is only reinforced by the presence of ineffectual rivals or sisters who know their place. Indeed, part of the thrill for Suzanne seems to be the presence of those sister-substitutes at the tribute paid to her by the mother. The scene closes with Suzanne playing the harpsichord while Mme *** listens in rapture, and the other nuns are reduced either to listening 'debout sans rien faire', or to resuming their work.

The fact of being idle whilst other nuns sew, or that of playing music while they listen or work, hardly seems to constitute gounds for recollecting a 'soirée délicieuse'. It is only by recalling that Suzanne is a child expelled from her family and now compensated by a display of maternal/sexual preference that we can see how this uneventful evening can be qualified as delightful. The scene marks a point in the narrative at which Suzanne's position in the convent-family has brought her sufferings to a temporary end. In terms of structure, the 'soirée délicieuse' would have been a fitting happy ending had the situation been perpetuated. It would have manifested the kind of finality which obtains when a conflict or injustice at the origin of a story is resolved or reversed.

We should not allow ourselves to overlook this important point simply because Mme *** is homosexual. Many readers have assumed that Diderot wishes to present lesbianism as an evil and a danger, and this assumption runs counter to the idea that Suzanne might have been happy at Arpajon. However, to adopt such a view is to refuse the evidence of the text. Besides, it is legitimate to read the representation of homosexuality in *La Religieuse* from the point of view of (Diderot's) moral relativism, in which case the lesbian society which flourishes under Mme *** is of course as viable as any other and can notionally form the basis of a happy ending.

Here we see Suzanne perfectly fulfilled, inside the convent but also inside the favour of the mother-substitute, and so once again we are shown that Suzanne's happiness depends on her position in the (substitute-) family rather than the fact of being inside or outside the convent. Why, though, does Suzanne comes to despair at Arpajon and finally effect a hazardous escape? It is not enough to point out that after Mme *** dies, Suzanne is once again refused the position of favourite daughter; for Suzanne herself helps to bring about the death of Mme ***, and the idyll was already over with the destruction of the dyadic relationship. In fact, Suzanne is clearly denied her happy ending by a specific event which disrupts her life with Mme ***: the intervention of père Lemoine. However, the process by which the latter changes Suzanne's situation irreversibly can only be disengaged from her distorting narrative by inference. For she characteristically claims not to understand all that is essential to that process, whilst managing to indicate it all the same.

Suzanne and père Lemoine

La Religieuse is a novel organised episodically, in which the story of Mme *** constitutes the last great episode. The downfall of the lesbian Mother Superior forms a dramatic tale. She defies what counts as divine and natural law in seducing Suzanne, and at one point she might well view her chances of success with confidence. Her personal design has a political dimension; to the patriarchal structure of the Catholic Church, according to which she should defer to the authority of the male Director of the convent, she opposes a matriarchal ambition. For as the episode of the 'soirée délicieuse' shows, she forms the centre of a community of women to whose happiness the presence of men seems superfluous. She goes so far as to reject the authority of the Directeur, causing him to be replaced when it becomes clear that he opposes her lesbian behaviour (p.260-61).[21] She meets with defeat, however, and instrumental in her downfall is her excessive love for Suzanne. For it is quite clear that she is driven insane and killed by this passion once Suzanne begins to refuse her hope of fulfilment. The turning-point in the tragedy of Mme *** is marked by Suzanne's confession by the Directeur, père Lemoine, from which point the Superior's hope gives way to despair.

Suzanne herself, however, tells the story in such a manner that her own role in the Superior's downfall is nowhere directly acknowledged; and it is precisely at the confession which forms the peripeteia of the Superior's tragedy that the account is most opaque. Opacity in this case depends on amnesia, for Suzanne fails to recall most of what was said by her confessor. The reader is obliged to deal with an account which is distorted by the need to disavow guilt. A careful examination of the manner of narration of the pivotal profession scene reveals the full significance of Suzanne's narratorial posture.

On the occasion of a previous confession with the Directeur, there had been a contradiction in Suzanne's behaviour: she confessed her physical intimacy with the Superior whilst maintaining that this intimacy was innocent; but what is innocent should not, of course, be confessed. Suzanne's next confession is a repetition of the earlier one in this respect, except that by now she has more (not) to confess, and so she emphasises still more strongly that the behaviour to which she confesses is innocent (p.254-56). Père Lemoine treats Suzanne 'avec indulgence', but inveighs against her Superior and forbids further contact with her, 'sous peine de péché mortel' (p.254).

The fashion in which Lemoine explains himself requires close examination: 'Sans oser m'expliquer avec vous plus clairement, dans la crainte de devenir moi-même le complice de votre indigne supérieure, et de faner par le souffle empoisonné qui sortirait malgré moi de mes lèvres une fleur délicate qu'on ne garde fraîche et sans tache jusqu'à l'âge où vous êtes que par une protection spéciale de la Providence, je vous ordonne de fuir votre supérieure' (p.254). The Directeur apparently finds himself in a double bind, wishing to avoid corrupting Suzanne and yet wishing to warn her of the danger of homosexuality. Obviously, participation in a complete sexual

21. See Peter V. Conroy Jr, 'Gender issues in Diderot's *La Religieuse*', *Diderot studies* 23 (1988), p.47-66 (p.48).

act with another woman would inevitably corrupt even Suzanne, and this is the risk from which he wishes to protect her. Yet speaking too explicitly might prove as dangerous as keeping silent, since if he does so, he anticipates Mme *** by corrupting Suzanne there and then. This aspect of Lemoine's speech implies a traditional belief that, in God's view, sinning in thought is as grave as sinning in action.[22] For père Lemoine, the question of guilt hinges on knowledge (and Suzanne will follow his lead in this). The sexually experienced Mme *** alone deserves damnation for the moment; but if the Directeur says too much, he will make Suzanne equally responsible, retroactively, simply by imparting knowledge to her.

This is how Suzanne relates her response to Lemoine's warning (p.256):

> Je ne me rappelle, Monsieur, que très imparfaitement tout ce qu'il me dit. A présent que je compare son discours tel que je viens de vous le rapporter avec l'impression terrible qu'il me fit, je n'y trouve pas de comparaison, mais cela vient de ce qu'il est brisé, décousu, qu'il y manque beaucoup de choses que je n'ai pas retenues parce que je n'y attachais aucune idée distincte, et que je ne voyais et ne vois encore aucune importance à des choses sur lesquelles il se récriait avec le plus de violence [...] Certainement, cet homme est trop sévère.

Suzanne suggests here that she recalls being terrifed yet forgets the words which caused her terror. The inference that there is a causal connection between the forgetting and the terror seems justified: the memory is disturbing and *therefore* resisted. However, we should not overlook a significant contradiction in Suzanne's explanation; in the same sentence, Suzanne implies that if she could remember everything Lemoine said to her, her terror would become comprehensible, and yet that there was never anything to be afraid of in the first place.

In fact, this contradiction on the subject of Lemoine's (un)terrifying words corresponds to two strategies of defence which Suzanne adopts in order to fend off the anxiety aroused in her by the confession. One strategy is to rationalise her terror away by characterising the Directeur as fanatically severe in order to reject his picture of the situation out of hand, and this is made explicit. The other strategy, however, is never made explicit. It consists in a pattern of behaviour consistent with the knowledge that Lemoine's representation of the danger is accurate after all, and this involves rejecting Mme *** as though she is satanic.[23] That Suzanne

22. Once again, as we noticed when discussing Suzanne's earlier, general claim to innocence, the intertext is that of the Eden parable, and of the Sermon on the Mount.

23. This recalls Freud's piece 'Splitting of the Ego in the process of defence', in which he explains that if the ego is understood as the agency concerned with defence, it must be 'split' at times, operating both consciously and unconsciously in order to fend off a given danger. See *The Standard edition*, xxiii.271-78.

herself is at a loss to explain this behaviour permits us to infer that the ideas against which it is so clearly a defence are both repressed and unconsciously active.

Those passages in which Suzanne clearly obeys Lemoine's injunction without recognising that she is doing so are marked by characteristic gaps and contradictions. It is always where the narrator emphasises that she is unable to explain her own past behaviour that we find her unconscious motives most clearly revealed. For instance, there is the passage in which Mme *** attempts to draw Suzanne into her cell, claiming that if Suzanne rejects her, she will die. Suzanne flees. This seems clearly to be a case of obeying père Lemoine; in fleeing, Suzanne is hastening the Superior's death in accordance with Lemoine's statement that she deserves to be despatched to hell by a violent death (p.255). However obvious this might seem to the reader, as narrator Suzanne states that she is ignorant of her motive, and registers puzzlement as she reflects on the contrast between her cruel behaviour and her compassionate nature: 'Je fus un moment incertaine si je continuerais de m'éloigner ou si je retournerais; cependant *je ne sais par quel mouvement d'aversion je m'éloignai*, mais ce ne fut pas sans souffrir de l'état où je la laissais: je suis naturellement compatissante' (p.262-63; emphasis added).

Furthermore, there is the incident where the Superior leaves the first of a series of notes on public display. She has written: 'chères sœurs, vous êtes invitées à prier pour une religieuse qui s'est égarée de ses devoirs et qui veut retourner à Dieu' (p.265). Suzanne's reaction to the note is split: 'je fus tentée de l'arracher, cependant je la laissai' (p.265). Though the narrator offers no explanation, it is not difficult to infer the significance of this incident. Leaving the note is a symptomatic act signalling both that evil has occurred, and that it is the responsibility of the Superior. Thus Suzanne is adopting Lemoine's position. She cannot recognise why she is leaving the note, for as we have already seen, recognition of the guilt of Mme *** brings with it guilty knowledge. Suzanne's conscious ignorance of the meaning of these notes is stressed by her reaction to one of the later ones: 'Il m'arriva une fois de demeurer comme un terme vis-à-vis d'un de ces placards. Je m'étais demandé à moi-même qu'est-ce que c'était que ces égarements qu'elle se reprochait [...] je revenais sur les exclamations du directeur, je me rappelais ses expressions, j'y cherchais un sens, je n'y en trouvais point et je demeurais comme absorbée' (p.265).

The outcome of Suzanne's sustained rejection of Mme *** is that the Superior ultimately assumes the role of guilty, satanic party in which Lemoine (consciously) and Suzanne (unconsciously) have cast her. She makes confession to père Lemoine's successor in the chilling words: 'Mon Père, je suis damnée' (p.247). This confession does not restore her peace of mind. Rather, she deteriorates rapidly, and in her final agony she acts out the descent into hell to which Lemoine and Suzanne have condemned her; 'elle se croyait entourée d'esprits infernaux; ils attendaient son âme pour s'en saisir; elle disait d'une voix étouffée: "Les voilà! Les voilà!"' (p.280). Once again, it is worth recalling Lemoine's exact words in order to show that Suzanne has been his instrument, accomplishing the hostile wishes he directs towards Mme ***: 'Si cette malheureuse vous interroge, [...] dites qu'il vaudrait mieux qu'elle ne fût pas née ou qu'elle se précipitât seule aux enfers par une mort violente' (p.255).

Our analysis of Suzanne's motivations and behaviour in her relations with Mme *** shows that Suzanne's experiences there are determined by her developing sexuality on the one hand and by the moral anxiety generated by the idea of her sexuality on the other. This type of causality can be understood as an elaboration of the family causality we discovered to underlie Suzanne's behaviour preceding her entry to Sainte-Eutrope; for through the series of mother-substitutes culminating in Mme ***, the text suggests that family and sexual motivations are inseparable. We are also shown that Suzanne's resistance to sexuality corresponds to what might be called an oedipal submission to figures such as père Lemoine, whose type of morality resembles her own so precisely as to suggest that she has introjected his severity. The fact that Suzanne ceases to obey the mother-figure in the person of Mme *** and begins instead to defer to father-figures indicates a development in her sexuality; this development occurs thanks to the trauma experienced at the key confession, after which her anxiety causes her to surmount her attachment to Mme *** in favour of a male object.

Patterns of repetition: confessions, trials and father-figures

We have seen that the confession with père Lemoine is traumatic. Nevertheless, Suzanne seems keen to re-enact the discussion concerning the disturbing question of Mme ***'s guilt and her own innocence with Lemoine's successor, Dom Morel. This may seem especially bizarre, given that she has no fresh contact with Mme *** to confess. Not surprisingly, Dom Morel is as wary of making explicit statements about Mme *** as his predecessor, and so the outcome of this new confession reproduces that of the first, in that Suzanne emerges as innocent, and Mme *** as guilty.

The basis of Suzanne's relations to her two confessors is that she defers authority to them to pronounce on her innocence, given, of course, that she can expect them to confirm it on the grounds of the equation of knowledge with guilt. In this respect they have a predecessor in 'M. Hébert, homme d'âge et d'expérience' (p.166), who in a much more dramatic way upholds

Suzanne's innocence at Longchamp when her persecutors conspire to make her appear possessed (p.174).

These three male clerics, then, form a series in that each vindicates Suzanne. Moreover, Hébert absolves Suzanne of the same charges as Lemoine and Dom Morel; of being satanic, blasphemous and impious, on the one hand, and of being homosexual on the other (p.166). (These two types of accusation are easily displaced into each other. Mme *** is obviously deemed satanic by Lemoine and later by herself purely because she is homosexual.) A further similarity between these three male clerics, or rather between their functions in the narrative, is that each of them opposes the authority of the Mother Superior; Hébert opposes Sainte-Christine's abuse of power, and Lemoine and Dom Morel oppose Mme ***'s pretension to turn her convent into a harem/gynaecocracy. Finally, a further point of similarity is provided by the fact that, with increasing clarity, a sexual element is indicated in Suzanne's relation to each of these men. In the case of père Lemoine, this is quite clear: 'Le Père le Moine est grand, bien fait, gai, très aimable quand il s'oublie [...]. Il fallait voir le mouvement que son attente produisait dans toute la communauté; comme on était joyeuse, comme on se renfermait, comme on travaillait à son examen, comme on se préparait à l'occuper le plus longtemps possible' (p.251-52).

If it is clear that Suzanne is drawn to père Lemoine, it is equally clear that Dom Morel is drawn to her; for instance, when she ingenuously inquires what can be wrong with expressing mutual love, he betrays his feelings: 'Il est vrai, dit dom Morel en levant ses yeux sur moi, qu'il avait toujours tenus baissés, tandis que je parlais' (p.270). In the case of Hébert, whilst no element of desire is manifested on either side, it is significant that Suzanne stresses the absence of any affective response on his part (in contrast with the reaction of his two 'jeunes acolytes'): 'J'ai la figure intéressante, la profonde douleur l'avait altérée, mais ne lui avait rien ôté de son caractère; j'ai un son de voix qui touche, on sent que mon expression est celle de la vérité. Ces qualités réunies firent une forte impression de pitié sur les jeunes acolytes de l'archidiacre; pour lui, il ignorait ces sentiments, il était juste, mais peu sensible' (p.174). Disappointment, or at least the existence of an expectation on Suzanne's part, displaced onto the young men present, is indicated here. On the basis of these observations, we can maintain that the three male clerics not only repeat a single function in Suzanne's story, but that in each case there is an intimation of a sexual undercurrent.

Finally, all these clerics can be seen as father-substitutes in a human rather than a spiritual sense. A process of transference occurs across Suzanne's relations with successive father-figures, just as such a process obtains in relation to mother-figures. Suzanne describes how the nuns compete to gain the most marked attention from the handsome père Lemoine, as we have seen (p.251-52); if she too competes, she reproduces the aspiration to the position of favourite which we saw to be rewarded in the case of Mme de Moni and Mme *** and frustrated in the case of Sainte-Christine. (Indeed, since each nun is concerned with occupying Lemoine as long as possible, Suzanne's confession of dramatic material might be partly motivated by the desire to engage him more fully than the others can.) The desire to be compensated for the injustice of the original family might be adduced once again here; this time, the hostile (and, significantly, the false) father M. Simonin may seem to stand at the origin of the transference-series.[24]

The relation to the father is of rather a different kind than the relation to the mother, however. The father is always represented as superior in authority to the mother, and no aggression or hostility is detectable in Suzanne's relations with the father figures who follow M. Simonin. Rather, she is consistently submissive, whilst the father figure is either authoritative (Hébert), tender (Dom Morel), or both (Lemoine). The moment from which Suzanne rejects the mother in favour of the father figure can be located in the pivotal profession with père Lemoine, after which continued attachment to the mother generates excessive anxiety. Thus Suzanne is both pushed and pulled into changing object, so to speak; attachment to the father figure coincides with a horror of contact with the mother figure.

Suzanne and the marquis de Croismare

It seems that after the traumatic confession with Lemoine, at the latest, a compulsion to repeat a situation of trial and confession has begun to govern Suzanne's behaviour. It is difficult to trace its beginning, since whilst Suzanne initiates certain trials and confessions, others are imposed on her, so that the question of her own compliance is sometimes undecidable. Now, this compulsion to repeat is clearly carried forward into Suzanne's relations with the marquis. He is a middle-aged aristocrat eminently qualified to take his place in the series of authoritative father-substitutes. In the opening lines of the work, Suzanne stresses his age and experience: 'C'est un homme du monde; il s'est illustré au service; il est âgé; il a été marié; il a une fille et

24. As already indicated, in the present discussion the term 'transference' is used in its broadest sense. For Freud, the tracing of transference is a technical and delicate matter; for instance, 'it would not be correct to conclude [on the grounds of a strong father-transference to the psychoanalyst] that the patient had suffered previously from a similar unconscious attachment of his libido to his father' (*The Standard edition*, xvi.455-56). See also 'The dynamics of transference', *The Standard edition*, xii.97-108, and 'Observations on transference love', *The Standard edition*, xii.165-71.

deux fils qu'il aime et dont il est chéri' (p.81). She also stresses here that he is the father of a family (one which now lacks a mother); yet again, Suzanne destines herself for a substitute family in which she can presumably aim to achieve the position of favourite daughter – or, as at Arpajon, that of daughter/lover.

Having escaped from Longchamp, Suzanne creates a confessional situation around herself and the marquis by sending him the memoirs. The contradiction between the clear, detailed telling of the homosexual story and Suzanne's claim that this story is innocent casts the marquis in the same kind of role as père Lemoine (and indeed his successor, Dom Morel). For he is invited to reduplicate the confessor's judgment, if at a different narrative level, by deciding that Mme *** is responsible for what has passed between herself and Suzanne, and absolving Suzanne of all blame. In showing us that Suzanne is repeating her confession in this way, the text indicates a characteristic of repressed material: it returns, or continues to press towards consciousness, rather than dissipating. Essential to Suzanne's response to this are the dynamics of negation and the relation of interlocutors they can imply: that one negates or avows what the other reconstructs. But since nothing is resolved, this leaves her trapped within a cycle of repetitive 'confessions' (Lemoine/Dom Morel/the marquis) which may extend beyond the close of the memoirs into a narrative 'future'.

At one point the marquis's task comes to resemble exactly that of Suzanne's confessors. The fact of relating the events contained in the account of Sainte-Eutrope, and above all the admission that she has overheard Mme *** confess to Dom Morel, places Suzanne the narrator in a relation to the marquis which reproduces her confessional relation to père Lemoine. Suzanne presumably intends once again to be deemed innocent because she is ignorant, and expects once again that the blame for her own period of homosexuality is to be assumed by Mme *** alone, but the judge this time is to be the marquis.

The position in which Suzanne has here placed herself in relation to the marquis seems unnecessarily uncomfortable. For alluding to Mme ***'s confession obliges her to transmit information concerning Mme *** at the risk of being accused – as critics have indeed accused her – of knowing that their relations have been of a homosexual nature. It is as though the truth which is indirectly expressed in the report of the traumatic confession has drawn the narrative to the report of Mme ***'s confession because it can find, once again, a distorted and partial expression there.[25] Indeed,

25. Is Suzanne repeating the earlier confession as an alternative to remembering it? In this connection, it is interesting to refer to Freud's views on acting out or working through rather than remembering; see, for instance, 'Remembering, repeating and working-through' (1914), in *The Standard edition*, xiii.145-56.

Suzanne's narrative as a whole is symptomatic of her compulsion to repeat traumatic situations whose outcome was repression; and this symptom arises in transference, in a discourse addressed to the marquis as to a figure playing the role of figures appearing in the earlier traumatic situations.

Nor is the sexual element missing from Suzanne's relations with the marquis. The undercurrent which has always fed her descriptions of her own physical attractiveness (and which might be ascribed to an instinct to titillate as well as to a desire to arouse pity) surfaces in the closing lines of the work (p.288):

> Cependant si le marquis, à qui l'on accorde le tact le plus délicat, venait à se persuader que ce n'est pas à sa bienfaisance mais à son vice que je m'adresse, que penserait-il de moi? Cette réflexion m'inquiète. En vérité il aurait bien tort de m'imputer personnellement un instinct propre à tout mon sexe. Je suis une femme, peut-être un peu coquette, que sais-je? mais c'est naturellement et sans artifice.

Here we detect the familiar characteristics of Suzanne's discourse which permit us to glimpse her sexual level of motivation even while she establishes that she bears no responsibility for it. Her argument is that if she does not intend to manifest her sexuality, she is not to be blamed for doing so; being 'naturally' something of a coquette is not a crime; the crime, she implies, would consist in being so intentionally. 'Bienfaisance' or 'vice'; Suzanne leaves the marquis free to read her account as an appeal to either, according to whether he has been horrified or titillated. Whether Suzanne prefers the marquis to rescue her from the danger of lesbian seduction in order to keep her pure or to seduce her himself is not clarified.

We have briefly investigated the major stages of the novel, from Suzanne's original family situation through to the present of narration, in which she pens her memoirs. Throughout we have found that we can account for the events of Suzanne's life more consistently by referring to her family and sexuality than to her own explanation predicated on the convent environment. The emergence of two series of parental figures, the paternal and the maternal, and Suzanne's emotional and erotic investment of first one then the other, is a secret story told by the memoirs in spite of Suzanne's disclaimers. In that this is a story which is intertwined with the official one of the young innocent unjustly forced into the unnatural life of the convent, we are shown once again that desire may inhabit rhetoric parasitically.

4. *Jacques le fataliste et son maître*

THE Oedipus complex, a tale of incestuous desire and rivalry, has provided a framework within which to read the three fictions which we have examined so far, and will remain useful as we move on to consider *Jacques le fataliste* and *Le Neveu de Rameau*. However, a new element is emphasised in the latter two fictions more strongly than before. That is the affective relationship which obtains between two men, and more precisely two men unrelated by family ties but as far as we can tell belonging to the same generation: Jacques and the Master, for instance, and Lui and Moi. This relationship is in each case one of ambivalence forged of hostile rivalry and admiring identification, and in each case such ambivalence can be related to the operation of desire. In *Jacques le fataliste*, the bond between men is revealed as underpinning the attachment which any man might feel for any woman. In other words, emulation between men, in both its affectionate and hostile manifestations, emerges as a precondition of heterosexual desire. In *Le Neveu de Rameau*, rivalry is not particularly centred on the amorous domain, but rather takes the form of a competition whose prize is accession to the Father's place. In each case, however, the operation of desire is connected with a representation of oedipal relationships. The oedipal theme is more obvious in *Le Neveu de Rameau*, which from start to finish turns on the question of what it means to be someone's nephew and someone's son ('someone' being male). In the case of *Jacques le fataliste*, we have to understand 'oedipal' in its reference to affective and amorous relations between men and women unrelated by familial links (or perhaps, in the light of our reading of *Les Bijoux indiscrets* and *La Religieuse*, we should say 'actual rather than metaphorical family links').[1]

1. This question has already been touched on in our analysis of *Le Fils naturel* and *La Religieuse*, in the course of which it emerged that the bond to the parent can scarcely be conceived without its complement, the relation to the sibling-object or the sibling-rival. In *Le Fils naturel*, the sibling (Rosalie/Dorval) is the object of incestuous desire, and the father is in a sense the rival, since his existence brings the incest taboo into operation and forbids the sister's body to the brother. Clairville can be seen as pseudo-father or pseudo-sibling in that he is the rival who lives on after the father's death as the 'tranquille possesseur de Rosalie'. In *La Religieuse*, as we saw, mothers, fathers and siblings are available in both literal and metaphorical form. In the original and the convent family, Suzanne situates herself in relation to the parent on the one hand and sibling-rivals on the other.

In *Jacques le fataliste*, desire is cut loose, so to speak, from the literal family more than is the case for the other fictions. For to decide to see the relationship between Jacques, the Master and the Captain (for instance) as oedipal is to arrogate the right to view relations between any male characters at all on the oedipal model. Yet this is precisely what certain theorists have argued is a perfectly defensible and illuminating perspective on the fictional text. In this case, 'oedipal' is understood as meaning, in terms of relationships between adults, 'constructed on an infantile, triangular model'. Whatever the weaknesses of Freud's account of the Oedipus complex, one of its more compelling strengths is the plasticity and complexity which it introduces into infantile relations with the mother and father or their substitutes. The infant loves each parent; by the same token, the infant is each parent's rival for the other's affections. Built on this is the notion that desire is the desire of the Other.[2] On such a view one defining characteristic of desire is that in adult life it retains the mark of its infantile origins, remaining a question of alterity, of unconscious reference to a 'third party', rather than an unmediated relationship of subject to object, mirrored where love is reciprocal.

René Girard is an important reference point for all those interested in exploring desire as a structuring device within narrative. In *Mensonge romantique et vérité romanesque*,[3] he argues precisely that desire is to be conceived of not as a dyadic relation of subject to object but in triangular terms. The desiring subject is compelled to choose an object which has already been chosen by a 'mediator', who is often an apparently hated but secretly admired rival and/or possessor of the object. The bond connecting subject to mediator is presented as stronger or more determinant of action and affect than the bond connecting either rival to the object. Girard's study has a strong Freudian resonance in that the type of triangle he explores is more often than not evocative of an oedipal pattern of relationships. Moreover there is a specifically Lacanian resonance (and perhaps an influence) in the stress on the role of the Other and the presentation of the subject's desire as fundamentally alienated.[4]

2. For a discussion of Lacan's theorisation of the importance of the Other for psychoanalysis, see Bowie, *Lacan*, p.80-84.

3. (Paris, Grasset 1961).

4. The psychoanalytic resonance of the study has been noted more than once. For instance, Meredith Anne Skura remarks: 'Girard's triangular situation, as he notes briefly in a footnote to his book (which never mentions Freud), has its origins in the complicated play between external and internal realities which characterises the oedipal triangle' (*The Literary use of the psychoanalytic process*, New Haven and London, Yale University Press 1981, p.89).

Girard's model has recently been elaborated on by Eve Kosofsky Sedgwick.[5] Like Skura, Sedgwick remarks on the fact that Girard's triangulation of desire resembles Freud's oedipal scheme. She further remarks that both writers obviate the question of gender within the oedipal triangle: 'in describing the Oedipal drama, Freud notoriously tended to place a male in the generic position of "child" and treat the case of the female as being more or less the same'; similarly, Girard treats 'the erotic triangle as symmetrical – in the sense that its structure would be relatively unaffected by the power difference that would be introduced by a change in the gender of one of the participants' (p.22-23). By contrast, Sedgwick proceeds to argue, recent interpretations of Freud have focused on asymmetries of gender, especially under the influence of Lacan, whose identification of power, language and the Law with the phallus and the 'Name of the Father' reintroduces the role of gender in the Oedipus complex to centre stage (p.24). She goes on to suggest that 'large-scale social structures are congruent with the male-male-female erotic triangles described most forcefully by Girard and articulated most thoughtfully by others. We can go further than that, to say that in any male-dominated society, there is a special relationship between male homosocial (including homosexual) desire and the structures for maintaining and transmitting patriarchal power' (p.25). Finally, she incorporates into her argument that of Gayle Rubin, who stresses that Lévi-Strauss's normative man uses woman as the 'conduit of a relationship' in which the true partner is a man.[6] So Sedgwick aims to show how, once gender asymmetry has been built into Girard's structure of triangular desire, it becomes congruent with the workings of patriarchy; as men designate objects of desire to each other, they perpetuate a structure of power.

Expanding Freudian theory in this direction, opening up the Oedipus complex to the issue of gender differentiation and masculine power, permits us more effectively to delineate the operation of a specifically homosocial form of desire in *Jacques le fataliste*.[7]

5. *Between men: English literature and male homosocial desire* (New York, Columbia University Press 1985).

6. Gayle Rubin, 'The traffic in women: notes towards a political economy of sex', in *Toward an anthropology of women*, ed. Rayna Reiter (New York, Monthly Review Press 1975), p.157-210. In addition to Lévi-Strauss, Rubin's study draws on Freud, Engels and Lacan.

7. The same applies to *Le Neveu de Rameau*, in which, as we will see in Chapter 5, actual family relationships between uncle and nephew, father and son are shown to be the model for other, homosocial relationships, in particular the relationship of rivalry between Moi and Lui.

The object(s) of Jacques's love

The incipit of *Jacques le fataliste et son maître* is well known for its unconventional tone. As we begin to read, we realise that we are attending to a dialogue between an 'author' and his curious 'reader'. Initially the author refuses to answer, except facetiously, a series of questions posed by the reader: 'Comment s'étaient-ils rencontrés? Par hasard, comme tout le monde. Comment s'appelaient-ils? Que vous importe?' – and so on.[8] However, the author finally responds conventionally to the reader's fifth question: 'Que disaient-ils?' The answer consists in the following statement: 'Le maître ne disait rien, et Jacques disait que son capitaine disait que tout ce qui nous arrive de bien et de mal ici-bas était écrit là-haut' (p.23). As that by which the narrative flow is finally set in motion, this answer might be thought to have a special importance for what we are about to read.

But what precisely does this answer tell us? First it repeats the emphasis of the title, in telling us that Jacques professes himself a fatalist. This aspect of Jacques's character invites the reader to reflect, not only on fatalism, but also on fatalism-as-narrative. For a little further on we learn that Jacques's philosophy will dictate the manner of the stories he tells about himself, as he undertakes to prove to the Master that the events of his life 'se tiennent ni plus ni moins que les chaînons d'une gourmette' (p.24). This *pari* on Jacques's part may stimulate readers to inquire whether the author and/or the reader does not carry fatalistic expectations to the narrative act, which tends intrinsically towards an exposition of causality. Therefore it functions as one of the work's many self-referential devices.

There is more, however, to the sentence in question. Not only does it induce us to reflect on the role of fatalism in the narrative act; it also invites reflection on the psychological and situational significance of Jacques's narrative. For the strained syntax ('Jacques disait que son capitaine disait que') emphasises that Jacques does not speak on his own behalf but rather quotes someone he used to know (the Captain). If as we have seen narrative transactions between Jacques and the Master are to be shaped by Jacques's fatalism, then by the same token they are shaped by his imitation of the man from whom he has learnt his philosophy. In his role as narrator Jacques is certainly saying: 'All events are connected by a chain of cause and effect'. However, in narrating as a convert to fatalism he is also inevitably saying: 'This is how I have learnt to see events since meeting the Captain, whom I now emulate'. In the light of this, Jacques's profession of fatalism is not only an origin (of the narrative which it serves to motivate and structure), but also

8. *ŒC*, xxiii.23.

a repetition. First, the Captain teaches Jacques, then Jacques adopts the role of teacher in relation to the Master. This involves a reversal of roles: Jacques 'becomes' the Captain (as the Master 'becomes' Jacques).

Now, such a situation inevitably complicates our interpretation of Jacques's story as a story of love. Jacques's re-enactment of his relation with the Captain can be read as a process of mourning; having lost the object of his love, Jacques identifies himself with him in order that he can be deemed still present. Read thus, the text reveals an interesting tension. As *énoncé*, Jacques's narrative tells us that he loves Denise with a unique and exclusive type of love. As *énonciation*, it tells us that he loves the Captain whose loss he would disavow by identification. As the narrative is set in motion, then, a story which purports to speak of love between man and woman also, or perhaps instead, indicates a love between two men. The notion that where men seem attached to women, they are actually more fundamentally motivated by their relationship to other men is conveniently expressed by the term 'homosociality'. Especially in the light of the text's opening, then, we might profitably re-read *Jacques* as an exploration of the homosocial structures which may lurk beneath stories of love between a man and a woman.

The Platonic text

Jacques's loving imitation of the Captain is emphasised in various ways throughout the text. There is for instance the scene where Jacques sets up an experiment in order to prove to the Master that free will is an illusion. As he dismounts Jacques causes him to slip, then infuriates him by suggesting that the death he has narrowly avoided would have been no great misfortune (p.285-86). Finally he explains that the whole incident was planned in order to show the Master how completely his responses could be predetermined; 'N'est-il pas évidemment démontré que nous agissons la plupart du temps sans vouloir? [...] N'avez-vous pas été ma marionnette, et n'auriez-vous pas continué d'être mon Polichinelle pendant un mois si je me l'étais proposé?' (p.286). The puppet-metaphor seems appropriate; but we should remember that ultimately it is not Jacques but the Captain who has been pulling the strings. For throughout the whole of this scene, Jacques has been subjecting the Master to a trick originally played on himself by the Captain: 'Dites, grâce à mon capitaine *qui se fit un jour un pareil passe-temps à mes dépens*, que je suis un subtil raisonneur' (p.286: emphasis added). So not only Jacques's philosophical dialogue with the Master is revealed (as we have seen) to be a repetition of a past transaction, via a reversal of roles; this is also the case for whole scenes.

However, it is important to note that Jacques does not feel himself to be completely successful in his imitation of the Captain. This emerges early in the narrative, in the well-known incident where he calmly imposes silence on a group of rowdy bandits who are staying at the same inn as the Master and himself. Such *sang-froid* is maintained in the name of fatalism. The Master expresses his admiration: 'Eh bien, Jacques, Jacques? Quel diable d'homme êtes-vous?' Jacques, however, does not accept this response. Instead, he cites the example of the Captain who, the night before a battle, would dine with his friends and sleep soundly in his tent. Jacques concludes: 'C'est bien de lui que vous vous seriez écrié: Quel diable d'homme!' (p.33). We can infer from this that Jacques sees himself as an imperfect reflection of the ideal.

This tendency on Jacques's part may be termed Platonic, in the sense that it installs a tension within the text between real and ideal.[9] Other elements of the text reinforce this suggestion of Platonicism. We might observe, for instance, that just as Jacques peforms an imperfect imitation of the Captain, so the dynamics of the Jacques/Master pair only weakly reduplicates that of the Captain/Jacques pair. (For instance, the servant's attempt to persuade the Master never succeeds as does the Captain's indoctrination of Jacques.) Indeed, the Captain/Jacques pair itself can be seen as a weak reduplication, in affective terms at least, of an earlier pairing: the friendship which unites the Captain to a fellow Captain.

On closer inspection the relation between these two Captains appears to have the status of an origin. We can trace relationships between men 'backwards' as far as them, but no further. In this sense, the two Captains stand at the origin of a series, or rather two series of pairings between men. First, Jacques's Captain is comrade to his fellow-Captain. Subsequently he is master to Jacques, before Jacques exchanges master for master in a long succession closing with his present travelling companion. As for the other Captain, he is 'originally' comrade to Jacques's Captain, with whom he duels. Then, having lost him, he duels with a substitute. The chain of relationships is shorter, but it is a chain nevertheless. Moreover, if we move from structural to behavioural considerations, we discover that the Captain/Captain pair is presented as 'original' for this dual series in another sense. For men in both series (at least, those men we are told about in any detail) tend to mimic or reproduce aspects of the Captains' relationship, as we have seen Jacques attempts to do in relation to the Master. The same could be said of a whole range of male characters locked in relationships of

9. This is not surprising given Diderot's enduring interest in Platonicism, which is especially apparent in his reflection on aesthetics. In particular he makes use of Plato's cavern. See R. Trousson, 'Diderot lecteur de Platon', *Revue internationale de philosophie* 148-149 (1984), p.88-90.

rivalry and/or friendship throughout the text. So by a simple shift of emphasis or perspective, the Captains, who may seem marginal on first reading, can suddenly appear central, both structurally and thematically. To follow this lead and place the Captains at the centre of our concerns as readers of *Jacques* reveals to what extent the text constitutes an exploration of homosocial ambivalence, and so opens yet another thematic route through this seemingly inexhaustible text.

In order to illustrate these points, let us first examine the relationship between the two Captains and the status which the narrator assigns to it. Subsequently we will see how it serves as a model or origin for other relationships between men within the text.

The duelling captains: a paradigm?

Intrigued by the mysterious hearse which may or may not bear the remains of Jacques's Captain, the Master requests his story (p.70). Jacques begins the tale by dwelling on the similarity between the Captain and a fellow Captain; it seems that the Captain's story cannot be told except as a tale of two seemingly identical Captains:[10] 'C'est que mon capitaine, bon homme, galant homme, homme de mérite, un des meilleurs officiers du corps, mais homme un peu hétéroclite, avait rencontré et fait amitié avec un autre officier du même corps, bon homme aussi, galant homme aussi, homme de mérite aussi, aussi bon officier que lui, mais homme aussi hétéroclite que lui' (p.71). Jacques proceeds to state, axiomatically: 'Cette conformité devait produire la sympathie ou l'antipathie la plus forte; elle produisit l'une et l'autre' (p.77). Ambivalence, then, is the stuff of this relationship; and it is ambivalence pushed to the extremes. When the two men hate each other, they do so with a murderous hatred, since they risk killing each other in combat. When they are friends, however, their affection is described in terms which are conventionally reserved for lovers. This becomes particularly clear when the military authorities separate them. To live apart proves unbearable and the Captains plot a secret rendezvous (p.79):

> A peine furent-ils séparés, qu'ils sentirent le besoin qu'ils avaient l'un de l'autre; ils tombèrent dans une mélancolie profonde. Mon capitaine demanda un congé de semestre pour aller prendre l'air natal; mais à deux lieues de la garnison il vend son cheval, se déguise en paysan et s'achemine vers la place que son ami commandait. Il paraît que c'était une démarche concertée entre eux.

10. The only asymmetry in what follows is a circumstantial one introduced by the fact that Jacques's Captain is rich, his comrade poor. This allows the positive aspect of the bond to be exemplified when the Captain twice attempts to ensure the other's well-being, offering him his posting and his money.

Finally, they plan one last, mortal duel as a kind of suicide pact since death is preferable to separation; and when they are definitively parted, Jacques's Captain dies as if from a broken heart (p.80).[11]

If the Captains' affectionate behaviour creates any comic effect, this depends on the absence of a woman as the pretext of their quarrels. The two men's responses seem at once familiar and grotesque, and a certain absurdity results. However, the joke is not based on any suggestion that they might in fact be lovers, or wish to be. The Captain's heterosexuality has already been attested to by Jacques: 'Mon capitaine, Monsieur', he informs the Master, 'était un brave homme, et moi, j'ai toujours été un honnête garçon' (p.69). We might say that homosexuality has been emphatically marked off from homosociality. Neither man, then, is the object of the other's desire; yet their emotional life, full and intense, is entirely comprehended in their relationship to one another.

This observation raises several questions. If the Captains' case had any general import, it would suggest that without being manifestly homosexual other men, too, might live the essential part of their affective existence in relation to men. This in turn might imply that where such men apparently love women, such love functions as the surface expression of a more fundamental transaction between men. But does the text suggest the Captains' case has any general import? In fact, such a suggestion is foregrounded in two distinct ways (which critics used to be fond of calling 'telling' and 'showing'). First, the narrator emphatically argues such a case. Second, various relationships throughout the text can be seen to represent modified versions of the Captains' ambivalent friendship, and where such relationships involve rivalry over a woman, she tends to be presented as the catalyst or pretext of rivalry rather than its true cause.

Let us proceed by examining the narrator's comments on the two Captains. After Jacques has related their tale, a response is attributed to the reader: 'Voilà, me direz-vous, deux hommes bien extraordinaires!' (p.81). However, the narrator asserts that far from being extraordinary the duelling Captains represent the quintessence of relations between men. A series of arguments builds towards the following climax (p.86):

> Et qu'est-ce qui empêcherait de croire que nos deux militaires avaient été engagés dans ces combats journaliers et périlleux par le seul désir de trouver le côté faible de son rival et d'obtenir la supériorité sur lui? Les duels se répètent

11. More precisely, he dies according to Jacques, who is extrapolating this dénouement; the Master questions his certainty, given that they have seen what appears to be the Captain's cortège beating a hasty retreat before officers of the law. As the Master argues, this opens up the possibility that the Captain is still alive (p.80).

> dans la société sous toutes sortes de formes, entre des prêtres, entre des magistrats, entre des littérateurs, entre des philosophes; chaque état a sa lance et ses chevaliers, et nos assemblées les plus respectables, les plus amusantes ne sont que de petits tournois où quelquefois l'on porte les livrées de l'amour dans le fond de son cœur sinon sur l'épaule. Plus il y a d'assistants, plus la joute est vive; la présence des femmes y pousse la chaleur et l'opiniâtreté à toute outrance, et la honte d'avoir succombé devant elles ne s'oublie guère.

The Captains, then, represent a norm by which we can explain the behaviour of such varied categories of men as priests and philosophers. The primary and universal phenomenon is presented here as rivalry between men, and the role of the woman is reduced to that of catalyst of such rivalry. For the Captains themselves fight and love each other without reference to a woman; and whilst other men, in duelling or jousting, may compete for the affections of women, this is only the case 'quelquefois'. Moreover, the narrator nowhere indicates that women can be loved outside the context of such rivalry. Such a scheme suggests the possibility that heterosexual desire must always find its place in a triangular structure, its precondition being the existence of a male/male rivalry. Read thus, the passage is reminiscent of René Girard's argument concerning desire in the novel. The paradigmatic status of the Captains' relationship may be seen as laying bare the 'lie' that a male character's desire for a woman can be a phenomenon arising irrespective of the (male) Other.[12]

As we commented above, the narrator's assertion seems to be borne out by many passages in the novel. For not only Jacques and the Master, but many other male figures in the text can be read as modified reflections of the two Captains. First, there is an extraordinary proliferation of pairs of men who resemble the Captains not only in that they are duellists but even in that they are *serial* duellists. Second, other pairs of men resemble the Captains more weakly but nevertheless significantly by engaging in *metaphorical* duels (which as we have just seen the narrator presents as one way of resembling the Captains). This is exemplified in particular by Jacques and the Master (in relation both to each other and to other men). Finally, the desirability of women is generally shown to depend on the

12. We have already touched on the fact that Girard describes such a mechanism. He argues that certain major novelists represent the triangular structure of desire by introducing the figure of the mediator, thus exposing the Romantic 'lie' according to which desire involves only the subject and its object. The text of *Jacques* affords a different perspective on Girard's theme. It not only dramatises the triangulation of desire, but also boldly represents the possibility of the object (as opposed to Girard's mediator) being removed from the triangle. When this occurs, the underlying mechanism of ambivalence is exposed, as in the case of the two Captains.

desire of the Other, as though the role of women were indeed to serve as a pretext for the enactment of homosocial rivalry. In all these ways, then, the Captain and his comrade prove to be central to the work's exploration of ambivalence and desire in human relations. Let us now proceed to examine these points in detail.

Duellists and lovers

Literal duels: serial duels

We have already seen that whether the Captain is dead is a moot point (p.80). Nevertheless, Jacques proceeds to tell the Master the story of what happens as a result of the Captain's death. The comrade, enriched by the Captain's legacy, takes up gambling. One day he finds himself playing a game of dice against a fellow officer who wins all his money. Falsely believing the dice to be loaded, the comrade pins his opponent's hand to the table with a knife. When the dice turn out to be true, he is delighted to have found a pretext to fight: 'J'ai perdu mon argent, j'ai percé la main à un galant homme, mais en revanche j'ai recouvré le plaisir de me battre tant qu'il me plaira.' The wounded officer ('le cloué') challenges the Captain's comrade ('le cloueur') to a duel. This duel inaugurates a series of duels, after each of which 'le cloueur' is wounded but welcomes the opportunity to duel again. Next, as in the original story, the military authorities intervene to enforce the separation of the duellists. The Captain's comrade 'en fut désolé' (p.134). Finally, the two men meet purely by chance as the 'cloué' leaves a masked ball. The Captain's comrade is 'enchanté d'une si heureuse rencontre', and the two men duel afresh. Yet again the Captain's comrade is wounded. His adversary sends for a doctor before sitting down to eat. Here the story is left in suspension as the Hostess of the *Grand cerf* interrupts.

This narrative is doubly repetitive. On the one hand, repetition is built into the story; after the initial pretext is found, the two men duel some ten times, always with the same outcome. Nor does it conclude; a potentially infinite series of repetitions is arbitrarily interrupted by the Hostess. On the other hand, the story as a whole clearly repeats the story of the Captain and his comrade. The conclusion that the comrade finds a new duelling partner in order to prolong the original relationship with the Captain seems obvious. It seems that, like Jacques, he wishes to retain the lost object by re-enacting the friendship they shared. (It is debatable whether in doing so he 'becomes' the lost object or simply attributes the object's role to a substitute, since in this case self and object are virtually identical in the first place.)

In similar manner even figures who have known neither the Captain nor his comrade also seem to re-enact aspects of their relationship. The story of the Captain's comrade is interwoven in the telling with that of a M. de Guerchy. He too pins his opponent's hand to the table in the course of a gambling game, and he too becomes involved in a series of duels with the new-found opponent. So Jacques decides to tell the two stories as one, as long as they overlap. When he says 'le cloueur', he means both the Captain's comrade and M. de Guerchy; and when he says 'le cloué', he means their respective opponents. According to Jacques, the characters of M. de Guerchy and the Captain's comrade are only separated by a 'grain de folie': 'telle est la différence de deux hommes braves par caractère, mais dont l'un est sage, et l'autre a un grain de folie'. But another perspective is available; for as we have already seen, according to the narrator the Captain and his comrade are not mad but rather represent a paradigm which is reduplicated by men such as M. de Guerchy. This reduplication is foregrounded by the striking manner in which Jacques can tell both stories as one, at least for a time.

So far we have noted the existence of three pairs of serial duellists in the novel: the Captain and his comrade; the latter and his new opponent; and M. de Guerchy and his opponent. This number would have been striking enough corroboration of the Captains' paradigmatic status; but a fourth pair is included in the novel, and that story too should be briefly examined. The Master relates that his friend Desglands was in love with a beautiful widow who began to detach herself from him as she became interested in a new suitor (p.266). Desglands's jealousy of his rival results in a challenge to a duel. The widow eloquently pleads with the two men not to fight: 'Et vous voulez me perdre, et vous voulez me rendre la fable, l'objet de la haine et du mépris de la province! Quel que soit celui des deux qui ôte la vie à son ennemi, je ne le reverrai jamais, il ne peut être ni mon ami ni mon amant, je lui voue une haine qui ne finira qu'avec ma vie' (p.266-67).

Here the widow removes herself as pretext of the duel by declaring that she will belong to neither man if he kills the other, apparently subverting the male game by making fighting the means *not* to possess her. Yet the men do fight, indulging like the three pairs of duellists already mentioned in a whole series of duels. The widow's wishes count for absolutely nothing; nor, indeed, does her possession. Her health gives way and she dies, removing herself definitively from the situation; and finally, with great satisfaction Desglands kills his former rival (p.268). The elements of this tale, then, imply not only that Desglands and his rival duel as compulsively as the Captains, but also that the widow is reduced to false pretext or mere catalyst of a rivalry which exists independently of her. There could scarcely be a clearer dramatisation of the dynamics of male homosocial desire.

This brief glance at the novel's serial duellists shows how they are used to underscore the narrator's argument concerning the paradigmatic status of the duelling Captains. Now let us turn to examine the way in which even men who do not literally duel can be seen to reflect the paradigm by engaging in metaphorical duels of which women are (once again) less the cause than the catalyst. We will examine the love stories of Jacques and the Master, in order to show that both men seem to be caught in a chain of homosocial relations with men (including each other), and that their behaviour towards women is contingent on such relations.

Metaphorical duels: the loves of Jacques and the Master

As suggested by those of his comments we have already discussed, Jacques's imitation of the Captain can be read as a form of competition in which the inferior rival acknowledges his place whilst never ceasing to measure himself against the victor. With men other than the Captain, however, Jacques aspires to the role of successful rival. This seems to condition his behaviour in the erotic sphere especially, as shown for instance in his account of his earliest sexual experiences, which involve three women of his village. For in each case, the presence of the unsuccessful male rival is emphatically foregrounded.

In the first case, Jacques tells how he and his childhood friend Bigre pursued the same young woman of the village, Justine. The main part of this tale effects an elaborate preparation for a climax in which the discomfiture of Bigre as rival is savoured, as he realises that Jacques has seduced or violated Justine in his own bed. His suffering is increased by the fact that he is helpless to protest in front of his father, who is unaware of Justine's presence in Bigre's bed, and the three men sit down to eat together whilst Jacques makes ambiguous remarks alluding to his recent conquest (p.215). Jacques's enjoyment of his friend's agony is patent, and we may well infer that the seduction of Justine is less gratifying in itself than the victory over Bigre which it permits.[13]

This story, which is introduced as that of Jacques's *dépucelage*, is followed by that of two fake *dépucelages* following closely on each other. During a wedding banquet Jacques deliberately plays the role of 'nigaud' or naive virgin, and the husbands of *dames* Marguerite and Suzon mock him (p.219-20). This mockery consitutes a challenge from male to male, and in making love to Suzon and Marguerite, Jacques exacts a sweet revenge on the husband-rivals. Once again this may be the primary source of his

13. In fact, the victory over Bigre is all the more gratifying in that it is also a victory by extension over a crowd of anonymous rivals; Jacques tells us that Justine 'ne passait pas pour autrement cruelle, mais elle jugea à propos de se signaler par un premier dédain et son choix tomba sur moi' (p.210).

gratification during these sexual encounters (and his subsequent narration of them to the Master).[14]

There is in addition a curious scene in which the village priest surprises Jacques with Suzon in a barn, and attempts to part them. This priest is explicitly presented as a rival for the peasant woman's attentions, as we are told he is 'amoureux et peut-être aimé de Suzon'. In this tale the priest is temporarily substituted for the husband as injured third party. Jacques lifts him on a pitchfork and deposits him in the hayloft, from where he watches in powerless rage as Jacques and Suzon make love.

It should be added that Jacques does not always enjoy the position of triumphant rival. Early in the text, he relates at some length an episode in which he is taken in by a poor peasant couple while he recovers from the knee wound he acquired at Fontenoy. This involves relating a dialogue in which the husband persuades the wife to make love to him, in spite of the risk of conceiving a further child (p.40-42). Jacques has heard this dialogue from his sleeping area, adjacent to the parental chamber. On this occasion Jacques must lie helpless and excluded from the sexual union. However, as narrator of his own 'loves' he chooses to include the tale, which the Master enjoys hearing as the servant enjoys telling it. It is, on both counts, an erotic tale, even if the listener (first Jacques in the peasants' home, then the Master riding along with Jacques) is reduced to the role of excluded third party. The third party is never, after all, completely excluded.

Jacques completes the catalogue of his loves by returning to the case of Denise. This tale proves to be something of an anti-climax. The stories concerning Justine, Suzon and Marguerite are mere tales of seduction, told with no intimation of affective involvement on Jacques's part, and we might expect no more than this, given that Jacques professes to have been in love only once in his life. So when the story of Denise is finally told, we might expect something more, or something different. However, in this respect it is a disappointing tale; for it is also merely in terms of manoeuvres leading towards seduction. Pressing Jacques to finish his story the Master states: 'selon toute apparence tu touches à la conclusion de tes amours' because 'quand on est arrivé au genou il y a peu de chemin à faire' (p.285). Clearly the Master cannot conceive of the story of Jacques's love being told except as a progress along Denise's thigh, so that once the genital target is reached the love story is over. Jacques echoes this logic in his reply: 'Mon maître, Denise avait la cuisse plus longue qu'une autre' (p.285).

14. Meanwhile Marguerite and Suzon incidentally show how triangulation of desire may also take place as a doubling of women; Jacques cries out Marguerite's name as he makes love to Suzon, and both women discover that he is not the virgin he had claimed (p.220-25).

The uniformity of tone shared by the stories of Jacques's conquests suggests that the special place Denise holds in his affections does not depend on any innate qualities she may possess, or any intense feelings she may directly inspire. Instead it depends, once again, on the desire of the Other. In the case of Jacques's desire for Denise, the Other is incarnated by the Master, and by a number of his peers who had all sought in vain to seduce her. For as he explains to Jacques: '[Denise] est une des plus belles et des plus honnêtes créatures qu'il y ait à vingt lieues à la ronde. Moi, et la plupart de ceux qui fréquentaient le château de Desglands avaient tout mis en œuvre inutilement pour la séduire, et il n'y en avait pas un de nous qui n'eût fait de grandes sottises pour elle, à condition d'en faire une petite pour lui' (p.177). Jacques's one beloved, then, is one who has rejected the Master, and in the absence of any other indications, Denise's usefulness as a marker of (erotic) superiority is capable of explaining her appeal to Jacques.[15] The Master seems especially sensitive to Jacques's use of Denise as a proof of superiority. For at the point when Jacques reveals his seduction of her, the Master and he quarrel violently. To the Master's incredulous 'La coquine! Préférer un Jacques!' the servant ripostes 'Un Jacques, monsieur, est un homme comme un autre. [...] C'est quelquefois mieux qu'un autre'. The Master wishes to suggest that Denise's love for Jacques reduces her to a mere 'coquine'. Jacques's reply insists that, on the contrary, the love of a woman such as Denise elevates him above the Master. If this dart hits its target, it is perhaps only because the two men have both tried to obtain Denise; and similarly, Denise's value is precisely that she permits Jacques to shoot such a dart at such a man.

We have seen that the tales of Jacques's loves all exemplify the principle that relations between men and women are contingent on rivalry between men. For in each case the figure of the rival is foregrounded in his role as excluded third party, as though desire did not simply bind subject and object but depended in the most fundamental way on the desire of the Other.

Let us now turn from Jacques's loves to concentrate on those of the Master. Apart from his brief mention of Denise, the Master mentions only his pursuit of Agathe, a *roturière*; but this story is told at length. It involves the Master's friend, the chevalier de St-Ouin, and provides a detailed exemplification of the role of the rival in the choice and pursuit of the object. It is the chevalier who designates Agathe as an object of desire and acts the role of go-between. By the same token, he initially plays the role of excluded

15. Admittedly, the Master points out that Denise is exceptionally 'belle', but in the same breath he alludes to her being 'honnête', which is a tribute paid to what is from his point of view her sexual unavailability.

rival. The Master asks him at one point: 'Vous n'avez point eu de prétentions?' to which he replies: 'Pardonnez-moi, s'il vous plaît, elles ont même duré assez longtemps, mais tu es venu, tu as vu, et tu as vaincu [...] faute de mieux, j'ai accepté le rôle de subalterne auquel tu m'as réduit' (p.250).

The Master begins to display impatience at Agathe's resistance of his advances, and the chevalier 'confesses' that he has been her lover all along. This occurs during the course of a tearful supper in which, the Master tells us, the two men share an outpouring of mutual affection such as never before: 'Jamais le chevalier ne m'avait marqué tant de confiance, tant d'amitié... Il buvait, il m'embrassait, il pleurait de tendresse; je buvais, je l'embrassais, je pleurais à mon tour' (p.253-54).[16] The Master's reactions are telling. Friend and mistress, who betrayed him together, are not blamed together. Instead, the friendship between men is recuperated whilst the woman is demonised.

By the same token the Master settles for a reversal of roles. The chevalier needs merely to tell him details of a night with Agathe and the Master will be fully reconciled with him (p.257). If the Master can derive gratification from an act which excludes him, it is presumably because it is more important for him to remain within a triangular structure of desire, be it as spurned rival, than to mark his anger by extricating himself altogether. At this point the Master might appropriately have borrowed the chevalier's own words: 'Faute de mieux, j'ai accepté le rôle de subalterne auquel tu m'as réduit'.

This aspect of the Master's character is manifested elsewhere in the novel. The scene in which he quarrels with Jacques is famously resolved by his acceptance of Jacques's superiority; he will have 'le nom' whilst Jacques will have 'la chose'. He quickly overcomes any jealousy or anger which he feels at the news that Jacques has been successful with Denise and is soon ready to enjoy the consolation of listening to his servant tell him the tale of her seduction. Similarly, he confesses to Jacques that others' tales of the loss of their virginity have an especial appeal for him; and these are of course tales of an act from which he is irrevocably excluded. It does not matter too much who wins the sexual contest; the most important point is that it should occur, as a transaction between men permitted by the woman's body.

The chevalier, however, proposes that his friend should not settle for a narration of a night with Agathe but enjoy it in person, by entering her bed when she expects her lover. Moreover, the chevalier will join the Master and

16. In the use of syntactical and lexical repetition we can detect an echo of the passage in which the two Captains are shown to be psychological doubles, though in this case the mirror effect is to be subverted by the chevalier's duplicity.

Agathe, in order to expose her to public ridicule for her duplicity. In fact, the chevalier secretly intends Agathe's family to discover the Master in her bed so that he will be obliged to marry her and provide for the illegitimate child she is already carrying (p.274-75). In other words, he intends no less than to give the Master to Agathe in marriage. This transaction concerning the Master's body, struck between a man and a woman, is the ultimate betrayal of the homosocial bond. It feminises the Master by situating him in the woman's place. Indeed, we could argue that the Master's subsequent killing of St-Ouin seems to be motivated by the latter's commission of this crime against the code of honour which is patriarchy in its homosocial form. So it is that the metaphorical duel of rivalry in love culminates in an actual duel, and the Master and the chevalier conform in their own way to the model of the two Captains.

Wives, mothers and prostitutes

We have seen how, in *Jacques le fataliste*, the value of a woman is represented as the result of a negotiation between men, and according to the limits of her sexual availability. Through all their varied tales of love Jacques and the Master seem to be repeatedly communicating the same message concerning women as the sultan Mangogul: what is important is not only that she desires me, but that simultaneously she desires no-one else. This is a function of the situation of the Other (male); the woman is valued if she promises to place the rival irredeemably in the place of thirdness, especially since, by doing so, she becomes peerless to the man who tends to debase women in general as available whores. A correlative of such a reading is that the value of a woman is never inherent, but is assigned, and assigned above all by men for the use of men. The basic values attached to the woman are, as in *Les Bijoux indiscrets*, those of *maman* and *putain*. This arbitrary yet communal assignation of value is foregrounded in more than one way within the text. Let us take two incidents as examples.

In the earlier part of the narrative, Jacques returns to Conches to retrieve the Master's purse, which he had at his bedside the night before (p.48-51). Javotte, a servant girl, now holds the purse but claims Jacques exchanged it for sexual favours. The Master's host, who is a magistrate, pronounces that Javotte values herself far too highly by charging a whole purse of money: 'Ah! Javotte! Neuf cent dix-sept livres pour une nuit, c'est beaucoup trop pour vous et pour lui'. He confidently fixes her value at six francs and as he dismisses her he envisages a life of prostitution for her. In fact, she did not sleep with Jacques; her crime is not prostitution but theft. The episode somewhat bluntly invites us to reflect on the arbitrary (authoritarian and absolute) nature of values assigned to women. Javotte has no right of appeal;

Manon-like, she is ultimately treated not as a subject but as an object of male desire and power.[17]

A more elaborate and striking exploration of the process by which women are assigned value is contained in the famous story of the marquise de La Pommeraye. The marquise employs a mother and daughter in order to exact her revenge on the marquis des Arcis. It is the history of these two women which suits them to her purpose. Having been ruined by a court case, the mother is 'réduite à tenir tripot' (p.138), and the pair adopt the name d'Aisnon in the place of their true name, Duquênoi. Mother and daughter alike prostitute themselves: 'On s'assemblait chez elle, on jouait, on soupait, et communément un ou deux des convives restaient, passaient la nuit avec Madame et Mademoiselle, à leur choix' (p.138-39). Here, *maman* curiously converges with *putain*, and the mother becomes a model of vice rather than virtue for the daughter to follow. The marquise, however, has the two women resume a virtuous and austere existence. This creates a dilemma for the marquis: are they to be respected for their virtue or despised for their poverty? Initially he repeatedly treats the daughter as a whore, offering her money and jewellery in exchange for sexual favours. In the face of her resistance, however, he decides she is the type of woman to marry rather than merely bed. Mlle d'Aisnon must be bought at the price of elevating her to the rank of titular equal, by marriage and the sharing of life and reputation. The marquise de La Pommeraye finally reveals her secret, expecting to enjoy revenge. However, somewhat reminiscent of Pygmalion's Galatea, the virtuous young woman who is the object of the marquis's fantasy becomes a living reality as we hear her confess at length to her husband at the close of the tale. It emerges that in fact she has had a virtuous heart all along, and the marquis accepts her as his wife in spite of her past.

From one point of view, the tale indicates a dialectical development on the part of the marquis. Having treated the daughter first as whore then as 'mother' (unique and idealised), the marquis finally realises that she is, like Mirzoza in *Les Bijoux indiscrets*, both these figures, without contradiction. The contradiction was perhaps in his desire and not in her nature.[18] The marquise de La Pommeraye had not envisaged the possibility of such a synthesis; she sees the *maman/putain* dichotomy as inescapable, and that

17. The most forceful case for reading *Manon Lescaut* in this way is made in Naomi Segal, *The Unintended reader: feminism and 'Manon Lescaut'* (Cambridge, CUP 1986).

18. This dialectical process corresponds to the daughter's three names. As a virtuous maiden she is named Mlle Duquênoi; as a prostitute she takes the name d'Aisnon; and of course as a married woman she becomes the marquise des Arcis, the name and position no doubt to which the marquise de La Pommeraye once aspired.

mistake makes of her the unwitting architect of the marquis's happiness. The narrator presents her as a champion of the woman's cause, providing a terrible example of vengeance which might effect a change in the relations between the sexes. However, she botches her revenge precisely because she thinks and acts as a man, i.e. as though women really are to be sorted according to the *maman/putain* dichotomy.[19]

The marquise's mistake is reduplicated at two higher levels of narrative; first by the Master, then by the 'reader' in conversation with the 'author'. Like the marquise, the Master is unable to view women except via the dichotomy of mother and whore; when the tale is over, he complains that Mlle d'Aisnon's character lacks unity and *vraisemblance*, for she exhibits behaviour both sluttish and virtuous, though she must be one thing or the other (p.169-70). The Master's resistance to the story is easily understood, for it threatens the subversion of the very structures of thought and desire through which he views the world. As for the figures of author and reader, the extent of their investment in the *maman/putain* dichotomy is dramatically indicated towards the end of the text, where the author is quoting from a supposedly apocryphal source concerning Jacques's courtship of Denise. As we have seen, an earlier passage suggests that Denise yielded to Jacques's seduction, as implied by the Master's rage when he exclaims 'La coquine! préférer un Jacques!' Nevertheless, the reader seems to have resisted drawing this conclusion, for he is outraged when the author states: 'Il se précipita sur elle, et la baisa'. The reader construes 'la baisa' as meaning that Jacques and Denise had sex. Leaping to the latter's defence, he exclaims 'Insigne calomniateur!' The author quickly reinstates Denise's virtue: 'Il la baisa sa main' (p.290). The misunderstanding turns on the ambiguity of 'la' and of 'baisa', an ambiguity which points to the alternatives of mother and whore, of courtly love and available sex. The parallel with the Master's reception of the story of Mme de La Pommeraye is striking. Just as the Master is disturbed by the 'invraisemblance' of a virtuous-whorish Mlle d'Aisnon, so the reader is rendered anxious by the figure of Denise as she is apparently portrayed by the author. What is disturbing about Denise and Mlle d'Aisnon alike is the suggestion that each can be lent the role of the virtuous woman who serves at first to shape the narrative as an amorous quest culminating in a marriage, yet can suddenly effect an apparent fall from virtue in the closing stages of the narrative.

If the double meaning of 'la baisa' is a mischievous trap set by the author,

19. In other words, on the one hand the marquise is presented as an individual who might transform a widespread moral attitude, and on the other hand it is suggested that such attempts to right the world are necessarily abortive. This is typical of a tension in Diderot's writing between the resigned determinist and the idealistic reformist.

then he is playing with the reader's preconceptions. However, in an alternative reading reader and author can be imagined to be equally shocked; the reader shocked that the author implies that Denise yields to Jacques's advances, and the author shocked in turn that the reader might think that this is what he means. Author and reader would then share in a complicated variation on the Freudian slip, both equally understanding 'la baisa' to mean that Denise yielded, whilst each holds the other responsible for the 'accidental' emergence of that meaning. If this is the case, then at the point where they misunderstand each other both author and reader would understand each other only too well. For their misunderstanding could be read as a lifting of the repression involved in their joint idealisation of the 'respectable' woman (Denise offering a hand to a courtly, respectful kiss, but no more). Each would then (mis)construe 'la' in a sense corresponding to their common repressed fantasy of the available whore whose unconscious link with the respectable woman has never been dissolved. The condensation of both images of woman in the ambiguity of 'la' (a demure hand or an available body) is suggestive of their unconscious identity, an identity which avails itself of a linguistic ambiguity in order to find a route to expression.

All the passages which we have just examined serve to foreground the problematic aspects of assigning value to women, especially within a *maman/putain* dichotomy. The Magistrate, the marquise, the Master, the reader and the author alike struggle to stabilise a dichotomy which threatens at any moment to elude them, since it is based on an unstable repression. By the same token, these passages represent elaborations of the homosocial theme, however much they may problematise the theme in question.

Conclusion

Enough has been said to show in what sense the homosocial theme is present in *Jacques le fataliste*. This is not to suggest that all relationships between all characters can or should somehow be related to the theme. What of characters such as père Hudson, what of Richard, both of whom are the subjects of extended narratives? What of the many subsidiary characters we have not mentioned, some of whom, like Gousse, are the object of especial emphasis? It seems difficult to read them as exemplifying the homosocial theme, except perhaps tangentially.

Does it need to be added that by means of a whole range of devices *Jacques le fataliste* reminds us constantly to avoid falling into the trap of deciding that we have found a key to a text? No such key is proposed here. The patterns which emerge when we place the duelling Captains and homosociality at the centre of our concerns co-exist with many other patterns, some of them contradictory, some of them simply different. It remains the case, however, that when we inquire what the text shows us of desire, what we have called homosociality forms an important part of the answer. This has allowed us to recognise in *Jacques* points of comparison and contrast with the tensions, contradictions and structuring principles of the other texts of the corpus.

5. *Le Neveu de Rameau*

Le Neveu de Rameau offers rich pickings to literary critic and historian of thought alike, and has been approached in a great variety of ways. Here I intend to approach it neither for its social and political implications, nor for its potential contribution to Enlightenment debates on music, aesthetics and ethics, nor for the possibility of relating the beliefs of each speaker to those of the historical Diderot. Instead, the direction of our discussion will be derived from an initial reflection on the structure of the text. This is a framed dialogue, and the dialogue is framed in such a fashion that a single narrating figure controls its various elements. According to the fiction of the work, that narrator has created the text we read by performing the following actions. He selects his subject by recalling, for whatever reason, an encounter with a famous composer's nephew; he records their conversation (exhaustively, selectively, faithfully, or otherwise); he represents his former self as Moi, designating his sometime interlocutor Lui; and finally, not wishing, for whatever reason, to leave the dialogue unframed, he adds a preamble and intercalated comments.

Given this structure, the reader has immediate contact with the narrator's voice, and only mediated contact with that of Lui – and, indeed, with that of the narrator's former self Moi. We might pertinently, then, relate all elements of the text to the controlling narrator's concerns. This permits us to ask the following questions. Why is the narrator moved to recall and record this particular conversation with this particular interlocutor? What is the significance for him of the composer's nephew? And should we not adopt a suspicious attitude towards the care which the narrator takes in order to control the dialogue's significance by adding a preamble and intercalated commentary? This approach soon leads us to perceive the extent to which, beneath its meandering discussion of topics such as music, ethics, aesthetics, and genius the dialogue is inflected throughout by a conflict concerning identity. The narrator is concerned to use Rameau/Lui for a single, overriding purpose: as his other. More precisely, he wishes to set up the composer's nephew as a figure who differs from himself absolutely, in order to be able to disavow aspects of himself by projecting them onto him. The narrator strives to achieve this purpose by two means. First, he is generally concerned to avoid identification with Rameau/Lui. Second, he is concerned to represent the latter as his inferior in the domains of art and ethics. However, Rameau/Lui threatens to escape the narrator's control by crossing his purpose in two distinct ways. First he repeatedly insists that Moi and he are not opposites, as Moi suggests, but are fundamentally similar. Second, he contests Moi's claim to superiority by suggesting that he does not only equal Moi, but surpasses him.

Lui's two moves may seem mutually contradictory; to press towards resemblance or identity may seem to be to preclude claiming superiority. However, the manoeuvring of Lui and Moi alike needs to be understood in relation to an issue which is of the utmost concern to them both. This issue, somewhat neglected by critics, is Lui's relation to his famous uncle. The narrator is concerned to represent his interlocutor as one who is overshadowed by his paternal uncle, indeed by father and uncle alike. In this sense at least, the relation to the paternal uncle is represented as an oedipal one; and accordingly, the otherness which the narrator is anxious to ascribe to Rameau/Lui is itself narrowed at various points to a specifically oedipal one. This leads to a curious conflict. Moi and Lui both wish to see the uncle toppled from his pedestal, and in this they are allies. But each of them wishes to usurp the place of greatness, which can only occur, they seem to assume, by defeating the other, as though their claims are mutually exclusive. In this sense not only is Rameau/Lui an oedipal figure; the dialogue itself can be characterised as an oedipal contest. For its speakers are concerned above all to establish which of them will succeed to the uncle's place.

Taken together, these two conflicts – identity versus difference, and the oedipal contest – explain the contradictory positions which Lui assumes in the course of the dialogue. We will see that when he presses towards identification, it is in order to establish that Moi cannot achieve superiority through philosophical detachment from the general play of need, desire and submission to others which Lui calls the 'pantomime des gueux', but lives on the same terms as Lui and the rest of humanity. When he stakes out his claim to superiority, it is in order to establish that though both interlocutors live in the same (oedipal) world, Lui achieves greatness within it by usurping the uncle's place whilst Moi, not he, is the miserable failure falling short of his forebears.

In order to demonstrate these various points, we will first examine the sense in which Lui represents the threat of identification whilst Moi attempts to use him as his other. Subsequently we will turn to the sense in which Lui is a specifically oedipal other, and engages with Moi in a contest to usurp the uncle's or father's place. This will inevitably involve touching on various topics which they discuss, but only in order to understand how each speaker's discourse, however abstract it may at times appear, is in fact designed to outmanoeuvre the other in order to emerge as victor in the oedipal contest. Nor should we forget that our knowledge of the supposed dialogue depends on the retrospective view of the controlling narrator; and so we will throughout be analysing 'Jean-François Rameau'/'Lui' above all as a figure whom the narrator would have incorporate those aspects of himself which he is anxious to disavow.

Identity versus difference

We will explore the pervasive presence of the issue of identity versus difference by a brief examination of its traces as they can be found in the preamble, the narrative instance, and the main body of the dialogue.

If we turn to the preamble we find that the narrator structures it in order to emphasise the absolute difference between himself and Rameau. He does so initially by characterising himself as unified and Rameau as fundamentally split. The first line of the preamble stresses the constancy of the narrator within a changing world; 'Qu'il fasse beau, qu'il fasse laid; c'est mon habitude d'aller sur les cinq heures du soir me promener au Palais Royal.'[1] The weather may change; he does not. There follows the image of the narrator conversing with himself on various topics: 'Je m'entretiens avec moi-même de politique, d'amour, de goût ou de philosophie' (p.69). This reinforces the opposition between the shifting world and the autonomous self.[2] The narrator is an intellectual perpetual motion machine, needing no Other to fuel his thoughts and observations. When Rameau/Lui accosts him in the Café de la Régence, he is 'écoutant peu, et parlant le moins possible', more interested in pursuing his meditations on chess than any distracting social exchange (p.70).[3]

If the narrator pictures himself as constant and independent, he pictures Rameau as inconstant and dependent. Moreover, he explains his inconstancy by his dependence. The process begins with the epigraph which represents someone (generally assumed to be Rameau) as 'Vertumnis, quotquot sunt, natus iniquis' (p.69), and so constantly subject to change. Further on, the narrator describes Rameau as 'un composé de hauteur et de bassesse, de bon sens et de déraison' (p.70). In doing so, incidentally, the narrator implies that since he can wonder at the contradiction between these qualities in Rameau, he himself possesses 'hauteur' and 'bon sens' without 'bassesse' and 'déraison'. Finally he proposes the striking paradox

1. Denis Diderot, *Le Neveu de Rameau*, *Œ C*, xii.69.

2. The fact remains that the image of the narrator in dialogue with himself inconveniently suggests an inner division, a suggestion which is especially inconvenient given the narrator's desire to contrast his unity with Rameau's internal divisions (a point which we are about to examine).

3. The famous line 'Mes pensées, ce sont mes catins' (p.70) summarises this narcissistic attitude.

that Rameau himself is more unlike Rameau than anyone or anything else is: 'rien ne dissemble plus de lui que lui-même' (p.71). Rameau's mixed nature and his failure to 'resemble himself' are next ascribed in large part to his dependency on the protection of others, including the narrator. For in the following passage, an account of his changing appearance is blended with references to some of those on whom he depends to give him food and shelter of varying degrees of luxury (p.71-72):

> Quelquefois, il est maigre et hâve, comme un malade au dernier degré de la consomption; on compterait ses dents à travers ses joues. On dirait qu'il a passé plusieurs jours sans manger, ou qu'il sort de la Trape. Le mois suivant, il est gras et replet, comme s'il n'avait pas quitté la table d'un financier, ou qu'il eût été renfermé dans un couvent de bernardins. [...] Quand il n'a pas six sols dans sa poche, ce qui lui arrive quelquefois, il a recours soit à un fiacre de ses amis, soit au cocher d'un grand seigneur qui lui donne un lit sur de la paille, à côté de ses chevaux. [...] Il m'empruntait quelques écus que je lui donnais. Il s'était introduit; je ne sais comment, dans quelques maisons honnêtes, où il avait son couvert, mais à la condition qu'il ne parlerait pas, sans en avoir obtenu la permission.

If we now compare the contrasting portraits of Rameau and the narrator, we realise that the narrator uses the composer's nephew in order to confirm his own sense of individuality and wholeness. If Rameau is different from the narrator in respect of being split and dependent on others, then it follows that the narrator is unified and autonomous. Such, at least, is the narrator's implied logic.[4]

Before we move on to consider how the dialogue section returns to the issue of identity versus difference, it would be useful to consider the 'narrative instance', or the choices which supposedly face the textual narrator as he decides how to set out the dialogue. More precisely, we can usefully reflect on narratorial decision to designate the interlocutors 'Lui' and 'Moi' as he presents the dialogue to the reader. The decision, whilst unspectacular in itself, is the result of a significant choice. After all, the narrator could have designated the speakers 'Rameau' and 'Moi', or 'Rameau' and 'Diderot'.[5] This authorises the question: why use the third and/or first person pronouns in the place of proper names? What is at stake in naming or not naming the speakers?

4. The narrator also, of course, takes trouble in the preamble to portray Rameau as the overshadowed nephew of a famous uncle. This point, however, will be more appropriately addressed below, in our discussion of the oedipal question.

5. A glance at other framed dialogues taking place between two interlocutors shows Diderot using such possibilities. For instance, in the *Entretiens sur le Fils naturel*, 'Dorval' and 'Moi' are used, whilst in the *Entretien avec la Maréchale de ****, 'Diderot' and 'La Maréchale' are used. So it is all the more appropriate to inquire why this is not the case in *Le Neveu de Rameau*.

One possible answer, to be derived from linguistics, is connected with the narrator's wish to exclude all possibility of identification with Rameau, which we have just explored. For the result of the narrator's choice is a curious dialogue not between an 'I' and a 'you' but an 'I' and a 'him'. (More precisely, the framing text retrospectively superimposes the form of such a dialogue on a 'natural' dialogue, in which each speaker does indeed say 'I' and address himself to a 'you'.) This can be read as a curious exploitation of the relationship of shifters to each other, as expounded for instance by Emile Benveniste. 'I' and 'you' set up a discursive space which is (potentially at least) alternately occupied by both parties to a dialogue, implying a cross-identification. By extension, 'nous' is an expanded 'je' rather than a true plural: 'D'une manière générale, la personne verbale au pluriel exprime une personne amplifiée et diffuse. Le "nous" annexe au "je" une globalité indistincte d'autres personnes'.[6] The third person, however, is not a person in this respect at all, so that to use 'he' is to exclude and reify (p.230-31):

> 'je' et 'tu' sont inversibles: celui que 'je' définis par 'tu' se pense et peut s'inverser en 'je', et 'je' (moi) devient un 'tu'. Aucune relation pareille n'est possible entre l'une de ces deux personnes et 'il', puisque 'il' en soi ne désigne spécifiquement rien ni personne [...] 'je-tu' possède la marque de personne; 'il' en est privé.

The narrator's choice of 'Lui' and 'Moi', then, can be said to correspond to his wish to mark Rameau out as one with whom identification is excluded, even if this exclusion can only operate on the past dialogue retrospectively and superficially (i.e. at the level of the framing text).[7]

Further attention to the preamble tends to confirm this possibility. There, an absent reader-figure 'vous' is addressed: 'Si vous le rencontrez jamais et que son originalité ne vous arrête pas; ou vous vous mettrez vos doigts dans vos oreilles, ou vous vous enfuirez' (p.71); 'Vous étiez curieux de savoir le nom de l'homme, et vous le savez' (p.73). Now, given Moi's views on greatness and posterity, it seems reasonable to suppose that his later incarnation the narrator is also addressing his text to posterity, so that 'vous' here involves (to use Benveniste's term) a 'globalité indistincte d'autres personnes'. Of course, in the first of these quotations the person addressed is by implication a contemporary, since he may one day meet Rameau.

6. Benveniste, *Problèmes de linguistique générale* (Paris, Gallimard 1966), p.235.

7. For interesting discussions of the use of pronouns in *Le Neveu de Rameau* and their relevance for narrative structure, see Yoichi Sumi, *'Le Neveu de Rameau': caprices et logiques du jeu* (Tokyo, Librairie-Editions/France-Tosho 1975) and Marian Hobson, 'Déictique, dialectique dans *Le Neveu de Rameau*', *Etudes sur 'Le Neveu de Rameau' et le 'Paradoxe sur le comédien' de Denis Diderot*, ed. Georges Benrekassa, Marc Buffat, and Pierre Chartier (Paris, Textuel – Université de Paris VII 1991), p.11-19.

However, it is interesting to note that in *Le Pour et le contre*, the exchange of letters between Diderot and Falconet on the subject of posterity, Diderot frequently draws a parallel between contemporaries geographically distant, absent or merely out of earshot on the one hand and posterity on the other, and so collapses the distinction between these categories. For instance, in Letter VII he states provocatively: 'Londres où vous avez envoyé un chef-d'œuvre dont vous ne recevez point de nouvelle, c'est la postérité'.[8] To frame the past dialogue in terms of a present address to a new interlocutor (an absent 'vous'/posterity) is to set up a situation in which Rameau cannot (can no longer) take up the 'I' position, and any former identification with him can more easily be disavowed.[9] At the same time, the new 'you' cannot pose the same kind of threat as Rameau, because having no textual voice it can never transgress its function of perfect mirror to the speaking subject.[10] In his choice of form and manner of designation of the speakers, then, the narrator reveals what we might term an anxiety of identification just as it is revealed in the elaborate (dis)avowal of the preamble.

Once we are alerted to this aspect of the text, we realise how apt is the analogy with chess implied by the setting – for the dialogue is indeed a contest. Moi is either subject to a fundamental identification with Lui or he is not; Lui claims he is and Moi denies it; each strives to wrest victory from the other. On the other hand, Moi might be thought to possess a tremendous tactical advantage, for it is supposedly he who becomes the arranger and narrator of the text as a whole. Perhaps like Clairville's household in *Le Fils naturel* he might modify the original content after the fact.[11] However, the outcome will be a stalemate in spite of all. For if the text as a whole does indeed constitute an elaborate disavowal of identification with Lui, the very need to disavow can be read as a manifestation of the repressed identification. In a psychoanalytic perspective this would be far from surprising, for all disavowals and repressions, in which the avowable and the unavowable exist in an unresolved tension, are by definition something of a stalemate.

8. *ŒC*, xv.31.

9. The strategy is doomed to incomplete success, since the dialogue section remains. The text as a whole represents a compromise formation in which dialogue and frame manifest the danger and its fending-off without possibility of dialectical synthesis.

10. Indeed, the narrator's choices may be read in terms of a wishful retreat from the symbolic towards the imaginary. For a useful discussion of Lacan's terms, see Bowie, *Lacan*, p.88-121.

11. As we saw in Chapter 2, Dorval explains to 'Diderot' that once he had composed his play, he allowed the various people represented in it to alter the text, which they generally did to their own advantage. See *ŒC*, x.90.

Let us now turn to the dialogue section of the work, where the narrator's control is weaker or at least less obvious, as Rameau, now called Lui, is allowed to oppose his own speech and ideas to those of the narrator's former self, Moi. Suddenly the contrast between a unified narrator/Moi and a disunified Rameau/Lui seems less secure than in the preamble, and ultimately it may well seem that Lui is unified whilst Moi is split.

The importance for both Lui and Moi of the issue of identity versus difference is manifested on the stylistic level by the recurrence of the motif of splitting and fusion. This motif represents identity as precarious, as though the barriers between an 'I' and a 'you' could yield at the slightest pressure. For instance, one person frequently becomes another through performance, which suggests an alienation of 'self' from 'self'.[12] This is mainly the province of Lui, who, declaring 'Je suis excellent pantomime', acts out the gestures of various types of sycophants, in order to illustrate 'les différentes pantomimes de l'espèce humaine' or 'la pantomime des gueux' (p.189-91). Elsewhere, Lui plays himself, as when he improvises the scene between mother, daughter and music master (p.105-108). But Moi becomes involved too. For at one point Moi and Lui perform different functions of a single person. Moi, placing himself in Lui's situation, invents a speech which Lui might deliver to Mlle Hus in order to gain readmittance into Bertin's household. At the same time Lui performs the gestures which he considers to be most suitable to the speech: 'Ce qu'il y a de plaisant, c'est que, tandis que je lui tenais ce discours, il en exécutait la pantomime' (p.90). The two speakers here enact their fusion, which is from another point of view the splitting of one ('Lui' speaking to Bertin) into two (Moi and Lui playing 'Lui').[13] Another striking fusion of persons occurs at the level of word-play; at one point, Lui coins a Latin-sounding name for Bertin and Mlle Hus, presenting them as fused yet separate within the space of a single sentence: 'Si Bertinhus vivait doucement, paisiblement avec sa maîtresse' (p.149).[14]

Splitting and fusion also invade the rhetoric used by Lui and Moi in defence of their respective arguments. In the earlier part of the dialogue

12. At least, it does so according to the logic of the *Paradoxe sur le comédien*, where it is suggested that the great actor effects an emotional separation between the character played and a hidden, detached and controlling self. Lui's performances might fruitfully be measured against the statements contained in the *Paradoxe*.

13. Of this passage, Hobson remarks: 'le *je* de MOI glisse dans le *je* de Rameau qui parle par sa bouche' ('Déictique, dialectique dans *Le Neveu de Rameau*', p.16).

14. See the critical apparatus of *ŒC*, xii for details of previous uses of 'Bertinus' and 'Bertin-Hus' by Diderot and others (p.149).

especially, Moi hypothetically splits various persons into two alternative possibilities. One example is Racine, in the following passage (p.80):

MOI

> Lequel des deux préféreriez-vous? ou qu'il eût été un bon homme, identifié avec son comptoir, comme Briasson, ou avec son aune, comme Barbier; faisant régulièrement tous les ans un enfant légitime à sa femme, bon mari; bon père, bon oncle, bon voisin, honnête commerçant, mais rien de plus: ou qu'il eût été fourbe, traître, ambitieux, envieux, méchant; mais auteur d'*Andromaque*, de *Britannicus*, d'*Iphigenie*, de *Phedre*, d'*Athalie*.

LUI

> Pour lui, ma foi, peut-être que de ces deux hommes, il eût mieux valu qu'il eût été le premier.

Here the 'real' Racine, an evil man but a poetic genius, is set beside an imaginary Racine, an upstanding citizen but not an author. Other figures too are compared with alternative selves, as Moi invents a modest but untalented Greuze and an even-tempered but uninspired Voltaire (p.83):

> Songeons au bien de notre espèce. Si nous ne sommes pas assez généreux, pardonnons au moins à la nature d'avoir été plus sage que nous. Si vous jetez de l'eau froide sur la tête de Greuze, vous éteindrez peut-être son talent avec sa vanité. Si vous rendez de Voltaire moins sensible à la critique, il ne saura plus descendre dans l'âme de Merope. Il ne vous touchera plus.

In one sense Moi is here using the conceit of doubling or splitting to illustrate a deterministic point of view. He is arguing that to change one element in a person is to change the balance of all elements, so that, given his contribution to the general good, we should not wish the genius to be other than himself. Yet since splitting (and fusion) of identities returns in other guises throughout the text, the splitting of Racine and the others acquires a special resonance, permitting us to realise that the device serves a function over and above its rhetorical or expository efficacy.

Another example is afforded when Lui imagines the possibility of remaining himself and yet becoming his uncle. In doing so he borrows Moi's trick of hypothetically splitting one figure into two, whilst charging the device with his own desires and frustrations: 'Tout ce que je sais, c'est que je voudrais bien *être un autre*, au hasard d'être un homme de génie ... J'étais donc jaloux de mon oncle; et s'il y avait eu à sa mort, quelques belles pièces de clavecin, dans son portefeuille, je n'aurais pas balancé *à rester moi, et à être lui*' (p.84-85; emphasis added).

In each of these cases, splitting or fusion is used to illustrate a particular point having its place in the logical unfolding of the discussion: that genius is always good, that kudos and wealth are always to be pursued, that we cannot shake off the heavy hand of heredity, and so on. But once again, the very frequency of the motif, in both rhetorical and non-rhetorical uses, points in another direction. It suggests a joint concern of the speakers, expressed symptomatically. Indeed, in its constant return to images of splitting and fusion the text becomes a context in which Lui's statement 'Je suis moi et je reste ce que je suis' (p.138) is no tautology. For within this text, it would seem, *identity is to be gained and maintained against the pressure towards identification*. This formulation throws light on Moi's characteristic response to Lui; he must resist the threatened (con)fusion of identities by insisting on his difference.

Yet early in the dialogue, Lui and Moi seem to agree that to possess a fixed identity is a desirable state of affairs: 'Lui. Vous avez raison. Le point important est que vous et moi nous soyons, et que nous soyons vous et moi' (p.83). However, the two have differing notions of what constitutes, and what threatens, the state of being oneself. Lui's sense of identity seems undiminished, strengthened even, by his frequent identification with others. When he states 'Je suis moi et je reste ce que je suis', he adds 'mais j'agis et je parle comme il convient' (p.138), as though he can move effortlessly between different social roles or identities without compromising his sense of being identical to himself. Accordingly, in the last lines of the dialogue he intones victoriously: 'n'est-il pas vrai que je suis toujours le même' (p.196). In this closing moment, of which he makes a moment of summary, he seeks above all to emphasise that since his last meeting with Moi, contact with others has not modified his inner self; and perhaps he also implies that the specific contact with Moi which is their dialogue leads to no modification either.

Moi, on the other hand, displays anxiety throughout at the notion of identification with Lui. Or rather, the narrator displays such anxiety, and recalls feeling it during his talk with Lui. In his intercalated commentary he tells us that he was especially disturbed by one of Lui's pantomimes (p.95):

> Je l'écoutais; et à mesure qu'il faisait la scène du proxénète et de la jeune fille qu'il séduisait; l'âme agitée de deux mouvements opposés, je ne savais si je m'abandonnerais à l'envie de rire, ou au transport de l'indignation. Je souffrais. Vingt fois un éclat de rire empêcha ma colère d'éclater; vingt fois la colère qui s'élevait au fond de mon cœur se termina par un éclat de rire... Il s'aperçut du conflit qui se passait en moi.

So the narrator presents his former self as having become, in Lui's presence, a kind of *homo duplex*. There is the disapproving, moralising self which the reader readily recognises; and there is an alien self, willing to laugh with Lui at the notion of debauching a naive young woman. Thus Lui effects a division in Moi, inducing him to identify with Lui in a particular attitude whilst retaining an incompatible attitude. This state of division, or of being at once 'Lui' and 'Moi', is experienced as intensely unpleasant ('je souffrais').

At another point, the subject under discussion is Lui's ability to perform and teach music creditably (p.97-100). Moi wonders that Lui expends a great deal of energy in convincing him of his ability, since Moi did not contest it. It then becomes clear that what really preoccupies Lui is not the subject of teaching *per se*, but the comparison which this permits between Moi and himself. Lui claims that Moi used to teach mathematics as Lui now teaches music, keeping one step ahead of the student, or not even that, and living hand to mouth. So by embarking on an apparent digression Lui is able to move towards the telling comparison. Moi's reaction to this is once again one of manifest anxiety: 'Laissons cela' he protests (p.101). Moi may be disturbed by the memory of poverty, but in the light of those aspects of the text we have so far discussed, it seems more likely that he is rendered anxious by the implied statement which runs: 'you once were as I am now'; or simply: 'you resemble me'. It is as though identification with Lui were equivalent to assimilation by him (and not conceivably vice-versa). This might usefully be connected with Elisabeth de Fontenay's characterisation of Rameau/Lui in terms of stomach and appetite, as when she speaks of 'le Neveu, ponctuel comme le borborygme d'un estomac vide' (p.185).

We are now in a position to compare the rhetoric of the preamble with the tensions introduced to the dialogue by the motif of splitting and fusion. This yields a significant contradiction. Whilst in the preamble the narrator is concerned to present himself as unified and Rameau as disunified, the characterisation of Lui and Moi implied by the dialogue section of the work is the reverse of such a scheme. It is Lui who there claims to possess a core of unalterable identity, whilst it is Moi who feels threatened by his lack of such a core. Therefore it would seem that the narrator is engaged in an attempt to disavow his fractured nature by projecting it onto Rameau/Lui, as he attempts to appropriate Lui's sense of being unproblematically oneself.

The oedipal theme

We have seen that the narrator disavows resemblance with Lui, as though such resemblance constituted a threat.[15] We will now examine the case for arguing that if Moi fears resemblance with Lui, it is largely or entirely

15. The disavowal of Rameau's supposedly split nature and that of his supposedly oedipal nature can be treated as one and the same, or at least as overlapping in large part. The split disavowed by the narrator/Moi is instituted by all the wishes and fantasies which he represses. The contention put forward here is that the latter include, or perhaps are entirely composed of, oedipal wishes and fantasies.

because he perceives the composer's nephew as a specifically oedipal other. As we are about to see, the narrator/Moi represents Lui as being ensnared in an oedipal patterning of relationships. He prefers to perceive Lui so ensnared, in order better to disavow by projection his own oedipal subjection – a gain which would of course be put at risk by identification with Lui. As for Lui, he refutes Moi's claim to stand apart from oedipal subjection. Meanwhile, each speaker, avowedly or not, positions himself to usurp the place of the revered uncle, which makes the contest between them an oedipal one. As in Freud's *Totem and taboo*, as the 'sons' do away with the 'father', they become rivals for his place.

Lui as Oedipus: Moi's perspective

It seems clear that Moi looks on Lui as an oedipal figure. Most strikingly, in the course of a discussion of how Lui should raise his son, Moi produces the formula which Freud was fond of quoting, since it indicates essential aspects of the Oedipus complex: 'Si le petit sauvage était abandonné à lui-même; qu'il conservât toute son imbecillité et qu'il réunît au peu de raison de l'enfant au berceau, la violence des passions de l'homme de trente ans, il tordrait le col à son père, et coucherait avec sa mère' (p.178). In fact, although Moi alludes to incest with the mother on this single occasion, it is the second time he has evoked the possibility that Lui will fall victim to parricide. For a couple of pages earlier, as Lui explains that he will bring his son up to love gold above all, we find the following exchange (p.175):

MOI

> On ne peut rien de mieux. Mais s'il arrivait que profondément pénétré de la valeur du louis, un jour...

LUI

> Je vous entends. Il faut fermer les yeux là-dessus. Il n'y a point de principe de morale qui n'ait son inconvénient. Au pis aller, c'est un mauvais quart d'heure, et tout est fini.

If it seems somewhat marginal in the final version of the dialogue, the theme of parricide may at some stage of composition have struck Diderot as a fitting climax to the whole. For there exists a piece entitled *Lui et Moi*, published by Assézat as part of Diderot's *œuvre*. The authorship of this dialogue has been questioned, but those who attribute it to Diderot are likely to see in it an embryonic version of *Le Neveu de Rameau*.[16] In the earlier

16. The full dialogue can be found in *ŒC*, xii.65-67. The editors of the Hermann edition are amongst those who cast doubt on the authenticity of the piece, largely on

piece, Lui horrifies Moi by indicating that he has perhaps murdered his own father. Moi's reaction is placed in the closing lines (p.67):

MOI

Mais si vous aviez un père âgé qui vécût trop longtemps...

LUI

Je n'ai point de père.

> A ce mot, l'horreur me saisit. Je m'enfuis, lui me criant: 'Philosophe, écoutez donc, écoutez donc. Vous prenez les choses au tragique.' Mais j'allais toujours et j'étais bien loin de cet homme que je m'en croyais encore trop près. M. Le Roy m'a dit qu'il avait beaucoup de pareils. Ma foi, je ne saurais le croire.

It would seem, then, that if *Lui et Moi* is indeed by Diderot, and if it is an early sketch of *Le Neveu,* then it was essential to Diderot's project to connect parricide with the figure of a 'Lui' in dialogue with a 'Moi', in order to show how Moi views Lui in terms of such parricide. There is of course a striking difference: the allusion to the murder of the father by Lui in the earlier piece would seem to have been replaced in the later version by an evocation of the murder of Lui by his own son. But of course the two possibilities are not mutually exclusive. For in *Le Neveu*, precisely, Moi is evoking a process and a set of relations, so that a single subject (Lui or his son) can occupy first one then another position in an oedipal patterning of relationships. As we shall see, as he considers Lui here in the paternal role, elsewhere he represents him in his filial aspect. In neither case does Moi place Lui beyond Oedipus; he simply shifts his position in the oedipal triangle. In doing so, he consistently emphasises Lui's weakness and passivity. As a son Lui cannot compete with his forebears; as a father, he risks being overthrown by the son whom he will have failed to educate or subdue.

Not only does Moi's commentary on Lui's family show that he wishes to represent Lui as caught in such oedipal relationships. If we attend to what it leaves out, we realise that it also shows that Moi is wary of applying the formula, *mutatis mutandis*, to his own family. Once again, in the passage in question, Moi suggests that Lui's son, if unrestrained by education, would have strangled his father and slept with his mother. Now, Moi and Lui are fathers, and each has a single child; so it seems that the statement might have a certain relevance for both men. It is but a small step from stating that the son wishes to kill the father and sleep with the mother to suggesting that

the grounds that it is not previously mentioned or published except in the Assézat edition, although reference is also made to events of Diderot's life and the inferior quality of the piece. However, the discussion is concluded in such a manner as to leave the question of Diderot's authorship open (p.61-64).

the daughter might wish to kill her mother and sleep with her father. And what of the connected proposition that the father might wish to sleep with the daughter? These points are the *non-dit* of Moi's statement on family dynamics. It is revealing that by his silence on this point Moi chooses to see Lui's family and his own as different: one oedipal, the other not. This in turn confirms that Lui is used in order to disavow disturbing aspects of the self; in this case, the possibility of incest with the daughter. It is as though Moi's logic ran: 'I am not the one caught in an oedipal family: you are'.

Incidentally, Lui seems aware of Moi's vulnerability in this respect. For he insists on speaking of Moi's daughter as an object of sexual interest. On the subject of her education, he argues that she should only receive lessons in the feminine graces, or not receive lessons at all, if she can acquire such graces without. He intones catechismally: 'Et laissez-la déraisonner, tant qu'elle voudra; pourvu qu'elle soit jolie, amusante et coquette [...] Laissez-la pleurer, souffrir, minauder, avoir des nerfs agacés, comme les autres; pourvu qu'elle soit jolie, amusante et coquette' (p.103). He thus represents the education of a daughter as a refined form of pimping, a mere prettification in the cause of snaring a rich man.[17] Moreover, he goes to some lengths to represent the business of tutorship, in which Moi and he have both engaged, as a cover for the activity of paid go-between, *procureur*, or pimp. This he does at a moment when Moi's daughter is about to be exposed to various tutors.

Moi betrays his vulnerability on this point in several ways. First, he affects indifference to his daughter's education, passing it off as the responsibility of her mother (p.101). Second, he seeks repeatedly to change the subject. He is especially chary on the topic of the daughter's age, exclaiming 'Cela ne fait rien à l'affaire' and 'Et que diable, laissons là mon enfant et son âge, et revenons aux maîtres qu'elle aura' (p.103). As Lui continues to press he retreats into hypothesis: 'Supposez-lui huit ans' (p.102) – a safely pre-pubescent figure, no doubt. Finally (and somewhat inconsistently, given his affected indifference to the question) he plans an education which stresses the training of the daughter's mind rather than her body. In doing so he projects a development which is more 'masculine' than

17. Whether the man in question is to be husband or lover he does not specify; but when we examine passages in which Lui speaks of his wife, or of the daughter he never had, we find confirmation that he is advising Moi to educate his daughter purely so that he can use her as a sexual bait. In a passage which we will have occasion to discuss below, Lui relates how he once hoped to enrich himself by encouraging his wife to use her charms to attract a wealthy man: 'Elle aurait eu, tôt ou tard, le fermier général, tout au moins' (p.194). When he earlier regrets having a son rather than a daughter, exclaiming 'Ah, si c'était aussi bien une fille' (p.176), he similarly implies that he could have used a daughter's charms for financial gain.

'feminine': '[Je lui apprendrai] à raisonner juste, si je puis, chose si peu commune parmi les hommes, et *plus rare encore parmi les femmes*' (p.103; emphasis added). Such an education, at odds with Lui's suggestions, amounts to a defensive desexualisation of the daughter So it is clearly disquieting to Moi that Lui represents his daughter as an object of sexual interest to men; and he may indeed be particularly anxious on this point because he, precisely, is at risk of desiring her, in accordance with the *non-dit* of his own remark on the incestuous dynamics of the family.[18]

The paternal name

Moi's tendency to view Lui as oedipal is manifested by his later incarnation the narrator in a subtle way: he is reluctant to recognise Rameau's right to be called by his family name, as though he does not deserve to succede his father and uncle. This reluctance is manifested, for instance, when Rameau is first presented in the preamble without being named: 'Un après-dîner, j'étais là, regardant beaucoup, parlant peu, et écoutant le moins que je pouvais; lorsque je fus abordé par un des plus bizarres personnages de ce pays où dieu n'en a pas laissé manquer' (p.70). This initial characterisation extends to some fifty lines before the narrator finally yields the name, and as he does so, he underlines the fact that he has made the reader wait for it: 'Vous étiez curieux de savoir le nom de l'homme, et vous le savez' (p.73). Moreover, he does not yield the name in his own voice. Instead, the chorus of the members of unspecified dining circles (which perhaps include the Bertin clique) is borrowed for the purpose: 'S'il lui prenait envie de manquer au traité, et qu'il ouvrît la bouche; au premier mot, tous les convives s'écriaient, ô Rameau! alors la fureur étincelait dans ses yeux, et il se remettait à manger avec plus de rage' (p.73).

This delegation of the naming of Rameau is significant. As we learn later, the Bertin clique sees in him a miserable failure who falls short of an

18. We might tentatively suggest that Moi's anxiety concerning his daughter's education throws new light on two earlier passages which we have already discussed in order to argue that in both cases Moi reacts with aversion to a threatened identification with Lui. These are: the paragraph of intercalated commentary in which the narrator describes his former self laughing with Lui at the debauching of a pupil (p.95); and the passage in which he objects to being reminded that he was once a tutor like Lui (p.101). These two passages retrospectively acquire an oedipal-incestuous tone when juxtaposed with the passage concerning the education of Moi's daughter. For all three can be linked by an associative path, as follows: Lui (a tutor) = Moi (a [former] tutor); *jeune fille* (a pupil) = Moi's daughter (a *jeune fille* and a pupil). This can be compressed to give: Lui debauching *jeune fille* = Moi debauching daughter. This associative link points to the oedipal underpinning of Moi's horror of identification with Lui.

illustrious relative. So Rameau's inferiority to his uncle is inscribed in the context of the scene in which he is first named. The point is driven home by the narrator's immediate addition: 'C'est le neveu de ce musicien célèbre'. Scarcely has the name been belatedly and indirectly granted than the narrator withdraws it by presenting it as already or 'originally' the uncle's. This may seem natural enough; after all, Jean-Philippe Rameau is the famous and successful member of the family whose name readers acquainted with opera easily recognise, whilst the nephew Jean-François would have remained obscure had Diderot's text not publicised his existence. Yet to find it natural is to underwrite without suspicion the attitude of a narrator who by problematising Rameau's assumption of the paternal name aligns himself with the logic of a patriarchal world; and it is this kind of logic which the text also provides grounds to challenge.[19]

In the preamble, then, we can detect a narratorial reluctance to allow Rameau to accede to the paternal name. A further manifestation of this tendency can be identified in the narrator's decision to use 'Lui' rather than 'Rameau' to precede the relevant speeches within the dialogue section of the work. Above we suggested that the motive underlying the choice of 'Moi' and 'Lui' was the narrator's horror of identification with Rameau. However, nothing prevents us from viewing the narrator's choice as being determined simultaneously by two interrelated motives.[20]

If we now turn from the presentation to the content of the dialogue, we see a parallel tendency reflected on the part of the narrator's previous incarnation Moi, who also tends to avoid addressing Lui by name. A brief glance at the Hermann edition of the text reveals two exceptions (p.117 and 179); but in both these cases variants are indicated, so it is possible to argue that in an alternative version of the text Moi would not address his interlocutor by name at all. However, even if we admit one or two exceptions, it is interesting that Moi uses the name so infrequently (preferring forms such as 'mon cher homme'). This becomes striking when we consider that by contrast, as we shall see, Lui quite often names himself 'Rameau' in self-apostrophe (or cites himself doing so).

In these various ways, the treatment by Moi/the narrator of the paternal

19. It is interesting to connect this with the Symbolic Order as characterised by Lacan, who puns on the 'Nom [non] du Père' in order to connect paternal interdiction/castration with accession to the father's name. For a reliable discussion of such questions, see Bowie, *Lacan*.

20. Of course, ultimately the historical author Diderot has decided to use this form of presentation. However, this fact does not conflict with the idea that within the terms of the fiction we read it is the narrator, a figure distinct from the historical author and constructed by the text, who has supposedly written down the dialogue and made all decisions concerning content and presentation.

name manifests his wish to see Lui as caught in a pattern of oedipal relationships, and above all as occupying a position of weakness and inadequacy as son or nephew. Surprisingly perhaps, Lui himself seems to accept Moi's judgement. At various points, he confesses that he envies the famous composer and wishes to occupy his place. We have already seen that he states: 'J'étais donc jaloux de mon oncle; et s'il y avait eu à sa mort, quelques belles pièces de clavecin, dans son portefeuille, je n'aurais pas balancé à rester moi, et à être lui' (p.85). Elsewhere, he connects this feeling of envious rivalry with the idea of inheriting the paternal name (p.183):

> Et le nom que je porte donc? Rameau! s'appeler Rameau, cela est gênant. Il n'en est pas des talents, comme de la noblesse qui se transmet et dont l'illustration s'accroît en passant du grand-père au père, du père au fils, du fils à son petit-fils, sans que l'aïeul impose quelque mérite à son descendant. La vieille souche se ramifie en une énorme tige de sots; mais qu'importe? Il n'en est pas ainsi du talent. Pour n'obtenir que la renommée de son père, il faut être plus habile que lui.

Lui here argues that whilst the prestige of an aristocratic name increases each time it is inherited, the descendants of a man of talent not only inherit no prestige, but must even surpass the forebear's talent in order to equal him. For Lui, then, the very fact of acceding to the name Rameau is experienced in terms of rivalry and inferiority.[21]

Notwithstanding the fact that Lui claims 's'appeler Rameau, cela est gênant', he does frequently apply the paternal name to himself. However, in many cases he does so in order to admonish himself, precisely, for falling beneath his uncle's stature (or, less frequently, his father's dignity): 'Je n'avais pas quinze ans, lorsque je me dis, pour la première fois; Qu'as-tu, Rameau? tu rêves. Et à quoi rêves-tu? que tu voudrais bien avoir fait ou faire quelque chose qui excitât l'admiration de l'univers' (p.183).

Elsewhere, Lui treats the reproachful voice within himself as autonomous. Naming him 'Rameau' yet again, it speaks to him of what he would have liked to achieve in the uncle's domain. If the formulation 'le grand homme, Rameau le neveu' is used, summing up the oedipal aspiration to inherit the name and with it the greatness, it is only within a conditional structure which once again emphasises that Lui is falling short (p.85-86):

> Le quelque chose qui est là et qui me parle, me dit [:] Rameau, tu voudrais bien avoir fait ces deux morceaux-là; [...] Et c'est ainsi que l'on te dirait le matin que tu es un grand homme; tu serais convaincu le soir que tu es un grand homme; et le grand homme, Rameau le neveu, s'endormirait au doux murmure de l'éloge qui retentirait dans son oreille...

21. Is there a word-play here? Lui laments the fact that within his family the 'vieille souche' (tree-stump or founder) will always split (or 'ramify') itself into less massive branches (*rameaux*).

At other times, by contrast, this voice which names speaks to him in order to reproach him for *not* sinking further beneath the prestige of the uncle and the dignity of his father than he already has (we will discover the sense of this reproach in the concept of sublimity in evil, to be discussed below): 'Rameau, Rameau, vous avait-on pris pour cela! La sottise d'avoir eu un peu de goût, un peu d'esprit, un peu de raison. Rameau, mon ami, cela vous apprendra à rester ce que dieu vous fit et ce que vos protecteurs vous voulaient' (p.89). But either way, self-reproach is inscribed in this curious application of the family name by Lui to himself.

At one point, Lui cites the Bertin clique using his name, and by repetition defamiliarises the act of naming: 'J'étais leur petit Rameau, leur joli Rameau, leur Rameau le fou, l'impertinent, l'ignorant, le paresseux, le gourmand, le bouffon, la grosse bête' (p.88). Lui indicates that the ranks of the Bertin clique are swollen by the failures of the world; failed playwrights, poets, and musicians. As a group, they constitute a grotesque negative of the artistically and intellectually successful, as they devote their energies to the art of ineffectual carping: 'Nous injurions tout le monde, et nous n'affligeons personne' (p.135). The fact that they have a Rameau of their own is naturally an indictment of the Rameau they have. So their use of 'Rameau' cannot fail in this context to function as a reproach.

Lui's sense of falling short helps us to understand the reasons behind his ejection from the Bertin household. As Lui tells it, in one of those passages where he names himself Rameau, it seems that in a moment of filial self-reproach he enacts a wishful identification with the father and uncle by refusing to demean himself before Mlle Hus (p.91):

> Mais cependant aller s'humilier devant une guenon! [...] moi, Rameau! fils de mr Rameau, apothicaire de Dijon, qui est un homme de bien et qui n'a jamais fléchi le genou devant qui que ce soit! moi, Rameau, le neveu de celui qu'on appelle le grand Rameau [...]! Je me sens là quelque chose qui s'élève et qui me dit, Rameau, tu n'en feras rien.

Here the oedipal manner of self-definition is emphasised by the repeated formula 'moi, Rameau! fils/neveu de...'; scarcely has Lui called himself by the paternal name, than he re-assigns it to the father/uncle, showing that he cannot help defining himself by reference to the forebear. (We have already seen that the narrator performs a similar gesture in the preamble.) So uncle and father apparently share the single function of urging him to dignity through identification with them. The 'quelque chose' which names him as it ordains 'Rameau, tu n'en feras rien' has the function of an introjected paternal voice.[22]

22. Incidentally, it is useful to note that whilst closely associating them by repetitive syntax and projecting a similar function on them, Lui here presents father

We have seen that, in a reversal of what might be thought of as a normal situation of dialogue, the narrator/Moi refuses to call Rameau/Lui by name, whilst the latter on the contrary names himself frequently. Indeed, in the passages we have examined, Lui's self-naming becomes almost obsessive. For both figures, however, the significance of this reversal is the same: the refusal/use of the paternal name marks out Rameau/Lui as an oedipal son.

Lui versus father and uncle

We have just seen that Lui openly acknowledges his inferiority towards his father and uncle, to the point of experiencing the paternal name as a burden and a rebuke, and that in defying Bertin he can be said to be acting out an admiring identification with the father and uncle. However, such filial piety is not the whole story. Indeed, it masks an attitude of rebellion. For having set up father and uncle as representatives of goodness and greatness, Lui attempts to topple each of them, and it is important to examine the precise fashion in which he engages in this attempt. Apart from the exceptional moment in which he defies Bertin, Lui does not generally compete with his forebears on their own terms by attempting to be as good as one and as great as the other. Instead, he adopts a dual strategy which enables him to undermine the position of uncle and father in order to establish his own, more solid claim to genius. First he makes out the case that Jean-Philippe Rameau is perhaps not a great composer after all. (This is of course directed at the uncle without touching the father.) Second, he makes out his case for excelling, not in positive but in negative morality, which he calls 'sublimity in evil'. This allows for the possibility that he defeats his father on moral grounds, in that he is more evil than his father is good, and so we might think that the father is primarily aimed at. However, the uncle is in fact equally concerned, for in representing success in negative morality as indicative of a kind of genius, he is able to vie with the uncle on the grounds of genius as he does with the father on the grounds of morality.

Let us examine these points in greater detail, starting with Lui's attack on

and uncle as corresponding to two distinct poles of aspiration. The father is an 'homme de bien', a worthy apothecary, and the uncle is called 'le grand Rameau', a great man. This is reminiscent of the perspective of Moi, who also generally sees goodness and greatness as twin poles of aspiration, as when he speaks of Voltaire and Racine towards the beginning of the dialogue. However, it would be a mistake to see the passage as typifying Lui's attitude, and so as marking out common ground between himself and Moi. The passage as a whole stresses that Lui's behaviour is atypical; the reason his dignity shocks Bertin on this occasion (and amuses Moi) is precisely that as a general rule Lui makes no attempt to live up to his father's or uncle's example.

the uncle's reputation as genius. In one of the speeches from which we have already quoted, Lui echoes Moi's views on genius and posterity as he indulges the day-dream that his musical compositions will survive and be feted whilst his uncle's will be forgotten. For he refers to himself as 'Rameau, le neveu de celui qu'on appelle le grand Rameau, [...] moi qui ai composé des pièces de clavecin que personne ne joue, mais qui seront peut-être les seules qui passeront à la postérité qui les jouera' (p.91).

This is fairly direct and needs no comment. However, in order to bring out the full extent of Lui's defiance towards the uncle, we need to dwell on the psychological significance of his preference for the Italian composers over the French. In doing so, we must place in parentheses the text's exploration of music from an aesthetic point of view. This is not to ignore the fact that the debate on the merits of Italian and French opera, and related theoretical discussions of harmony and melody, are issues of tremendous importance in the eighteenth century. They are also accorded paramount importance in *Le Neveu de Rameau*, both in terms of length of text devoted to their discussion and in terms of their prominent foregrounding, especially in the famous *homme-orchestre* scene.[23] In the present context, however, the importance of the debate is that in championing Italian against French opera, and melody over harmony, Lui is engaging in an attempt to topple his uncle from his pedestal. He aims to prove his uncle's mediocrity by comparing him with greater composers. The quintessentially French, harmony-centred genius of the uncle yields before the Italian composers who emphasise melody. Although it is translated onto the cultural level, this is a classical family romance strategy; out of a motive of revenge towards the parents, superior parents are created in fantasy.

On reflection, it is easy to perceive a certain balance in Lui's attempts to bring down his uncle. Towards the opening of the dialogue, he makes out the case that he is by no means a good man, but rather a hardhearted and pompous monomaniac: 'Il ne pense qu'à lui; le reste de l'univers lui est comme d'un clou à souffler. Sa fille et sa femme n'ont qu'à mourir, quand elles voudront; pourvu que les cloches de la paroisse, qu'on sonnera pour elles, continuent de résonner la douzième et la dix-septième, tout sera bien' (p.76). On the other hand, towards the end of the dialogue Lui expends a great deal of theory and mime in order to prove he is not a truly great man

23. For a discussion of such issues, see for instance Y. Sitbon, 'La musique dans *Le Neveu de Rameau*', *études sur 'Le Neveu de Rameau' et le 'Paradoxe sur le comédien'*, ed. Georges Benrekassa, Marc Buffat, and Pierre Chartier (Paris, Textuel – Université de Paris VII 1991), p.61-74. For further background, see Béatrice Didier, *La Musique des Lumières* (Paris, PUF 1985), Cynthia Verba, *Music and the French Enlightenment: reconstruction of a dialogue, 1750-1764* (Oxford, OUP 1993), and Thomas Christensen, *Rameau and musical thought in the Enlightenment* (Cambridge, CUP 1993).

either. So it is no surprise that when Moi concludes from Lui's arguments that the uncle's music is, along with that of Lulli, Campra, Destouches, and Mouret, 'un peu plate', Lui replies in a whisper 'c'est qu'elle l'est aussi' (p.160).

Now let us turn to the second part of Lui's strategy, which consists in his thesis concerning negative morality. Once again, his hope of superiority over father and uncle is contained in the assertion that it is possible to be sublime in evil, and that such sublimity is the ultimate sublimity: 'S'il importe d'être sublime en quelque genre, c'est surtout en mal' (p.151). Having set out the general principle, he deceptively adopts a humble posture which mirrors his superficial humility in the domain of music. For when Moi goes on the attack, claiming he is far from supreme in evil, he seems to concede that he is outdone by the great sycophants and scoundrels Bouret and Palissot (p.152):

MOI

Mais cette estimable unité de caractère, vous ne l'avez pas encore. Je vous trouve de temps en temps vacillant dans vos principes. Il est incertain, si vous tenez votre méchanceté de la nature ou de l'étude; et si l'étude vous a porté aussi loin qu'il est possible.

LUI

J'en conviens; mais j'y ai fait de mon mieux. N'ai-je pas eu la modestie de reconnaître des êtres plus parfaits que moi? ne vous ai-je pas parlé de Bouret avec l'admiration la plus profonde. Bouret est le premier homme du monde dans mon esprit.

MOI

Mais immédiatement après Bouret; c'est vous.

LUI

Non.

MOI

C'est donc Palissot?

LUI

C'est Palissot, mais ce n'est pas Palissot seul.

However, if Lui seems to concede this point, it turns out to be a case of *reculer pour mieux sauter*. His suggestion that there exists a third figure fit to rank with Bouret and Palissot arouses Moi's curiosity, and Moi duly falls into the trap which has been laid. For this figure turns out to be the renegade of Avignon, whose story Moi requests. Now, as Lui relates how the renegade betrays his Jewish protector, who is cheated of all his possessions, arrested and put to death, he manages to equal or surpass the evil deed by the manner of his telling. As Moi himself states: 'Je ne sais pas lequel des deux me fait le plus d'horreur ou de la scélératesse de votre renégat, ou du ton dont vous en parlez' (p.156). On the basis of this, we might well infer that the effect on Moi of Lui's discourse on evil depends on its performative rather than its constative function. Lui now lays aside his false modesty and crows his victory: 'Et voilà ce que je vous disais. L'atrocité de l'action vous porte au delà du mépris; et c'est la raison de ma sincérité. J'ai voulu que vous connussiez jusqu'où j'excellais dans mon art; vous arracher l'aveu que j'étais au moins original dans mon avilissement, me placer dans votre tête sur la ligne des grands vauriens, et m'écrier ensuite, *Vivat Mascarillus, fourbum imperator*!' (p.156).

Lui's proof of his own supremacy in evil is the crowning moment of his long discussion of negative morality. That discussion, we can retrospectively assume, was from the start intended by Lui to allow him to prove that he can exceed the moderate greatness of his musician uncle and the commonplace goodness of his apothecary father.[24] Hence the importance for Lui and Moi alike of Lui's story of the renegade of Avignon; Lui's success depends on the extent to which he achieves evil performatively in the act of narration.

If by the twofold strategy we have just examined, Lui succeeds both in bringing the uncle/father down and setting himself up, then he has surpassed his forebears and made the paternal name his own. He thus behaves throughout as though the paternal name cannot simply be inherited, but must always be usurped.

Bertin and other 'fathers'

Rebellion agaist the uncle/father can also be seen as a tendency manifested in relation to other key figures of the text. For instance, the ambivalence originally directed towards the uncle/father is transferred onto Bertin. Lui

24. Jean-François's father Claude-François was not in fact an apothecary, but an organist and violinist: see *ŒC*, xii.54. It would be unwise to view Diderot's alteration of Lui's biography as a simple factual error. For the father's occupation is not a negligible detail but permits the thematic opposition of father and uncle as good and great. Lui's attitude towards his family would need to be represented differently if his father resembled him in already falling short of Jean-Philippe Rameau (a more famous musician and his older brother); in particular, such a situation would make it more difficult to represent Lui as overshadowed by father and uncle alike, each in his own domain.

is tolerated in the Bertin household on condition that he consistently shows himself to be 'un ignorant, un sot, un fou, un impertinent, un paresseux, ce que nos Bourguignons appellent un fieffé truand, un escroc, un gourmand' (p.87), and that he must not display 'le sens commun', 'un peu de goût, un peu d'esprit, un peu de raison' (p.89). This implied contract means that he faces a clear choice between submission and rebellion. Bertin and Mlle Hus hold absolute power over him, infantilising him by caressing, punishing and nourishing him according to their whims: 'on fait de moi, avec moi, devant moi, tout ce qu'on veut, sans que je m'en formalise' (p.88). These omnipotent 'parents' are necessary, even cherished providers; once Lui is cast out of the circle of their protection, he cannot adequately meet his own needs, as he concedes. After all, his strategy for life – sycophancy – is infantile dependency rationalised as a kind of philosophy. However, if the parents are needed they are also hated and resented, and rebellion is the irresistible outcome of long submission; for as we have seen, in spite of himself, Lui finally asserts his dignity, self-destructively, and will not abandon it by apologising. 'Faut-il qu'on puisse me dire, Rampe, et que je sois obligé de ramper?' he protests (p.122).

It is interesting to note that the episode of Lui's ejection from the Bertin household, though it is dwelt on at greater length than other such episodes, is one in a series of exits from a nurturing base. At least, this is how Lui tends to tell his own life story, once we reassemble the scattered pieces of his account. The ejection from the Bertin household is prefigured by the rejection by the uncle. If we add to these two scenes the initial departure from the paternal house and the abandonment of the Jewish protector, the story, as told by Lui, is complete. This is a life divided into episodes, and each episode resembles all the others, in relating an exclusion from a nurturing environment. At one point Lui resumes his life in a curious manner. He tells how he once thought of begging on the street beneath a pictorial representation of the main episodes of his life, whilst shouting out an explanatory commentary in the third person (p.186):

> je songeais à me faire peindre un de ces tableaux attachés à une perche qu'on plante dans un carrefour, et où j'aurais crié à tue-tête; Voilà la ville où il est né; le voilà qui prend congé de son père l'apothicaire; le voilà qui arrive dans la capitale, cherchant la demeure de son oncle; le voilà aux genoux de son oncle qui le chasse; le voilà avec un juif, et caetera et caetera.

The serial or repetitive nature of this oedipal existence is emphasised by the tailing off into 'et caetera et caetera'; to pursue the narrative is only to deliver more of the same.

It is tempting to see in a life thus lived, and a life thus narrated, a tendency to repeat on Lui's part, as though unreconciled need and defiance bring him inevitably into conflict with the head of each household he enters. The imagined begging scene is not the only passage in which Lui emphasises the repetitive form of his social experience. Elsewhere he explicitly draws a parallel between the Bertin episode and the story of the Jew of Utrecht, emphasising the strength of his compulsion to break with each protector, however great the discomforts he must undergo as a consequence, together with the repetitive nature of the compulsion: 'Ah, monsieur le philosophe, la misère est une terrible chose. Je la vois accroupie, la bouche béante, pour recevoir quelques gouttes de l'eau glacée qui s'échappe du tonneau des Danaïdes [...] On ne chante pas bien sous ce tonneau. Trop heureux encore, celui qui peut s'y placer. *J'y étais; et je n'ai pas su m'y tenir. J'avais déjà fait cette sottise une fois*' (p.184-85: emphasis added). The fact that the series begins with Lui turning his back on the father's home, and continues with the uncle's rejection of him, strengthens the case for seeing the Bertin household as one on which Lui imposes an oedipal form, just as much as it imposes one on him. For it is a case of repeating the relation to the father/uncle, as in transference. This affords an unexpected point of comparison between Lui and Suzanne Simonin, who, as we have seen, carries forward a familial conflict into new situations which she invests with familial significance.

Finally, there is a sexual dimension to the Bertin episode which is significant. In spending time in the Bertin household, loathing and despising Bertin and his mistress or 'Bertinhus' but always in contact with them, Lui places himself in the sexually inadequate position of injured/excluded third party. He dwells in some detail on a reported scene of love-making between his two patrons, representing it as a grotesque act (p.150-51). The parents, then, are resented not only for their power, but also because they make love. This attitude can be read as prolonging an oedipal mixture of awe, jealousy and rage originally directed towards the true parental couple whose union excludes the son. After Lui leaves the Bertin household, the same attitude is manifested in his aspiration to earn his living as *procureur*. When he evokes his dead wife's charms, it is in the tone of a pimp as he imagines her seducing rich men: 'Outre son talent, c'est qu'elle avait une bouche à recevoir à peine le petit doigt; des dents, une rangée de perles; des yeux, des pieds, une peau, des joues, des tétons, des jambes de cerf, des cuisses et des fesses à modeler. Elle aurait eu, tôt ou tard, le fermier général, tout au moins' (p.194).

All these charms are clearly perceived from the point of view of the Other. Similarly, now Lui has lost his wife, he continues to aspire to the role of *procureur* as his means of subsistence: 'J'ai plus de cent façons d'envisager la séduction d'une jeune fille, à côté de sa mère, sans que celle-ci s'en aperçoive, et même de la rendre complice' (p.129). Lui finds it natural here to lend to the word 'séduction' the meaning 'seduction on behalf of another'; he will set the seduction in motion; another man will consummate it.

Lui versus Moi

We have examined various ways in which Lui's relationship to father and uncle is represented as an oedipal one, and have seen that a certain oedipal ambivalence is manifested in his relation to other providing figures. This leads to the fundamental question: is his relationship to Moi also in some respect oedipal? The point that Moi is likely to be associated with the figure of uncle/father seems an obvious one. Just as Lui's father and uncle achieve a reputation of greatness and goodness respectively, so Moi enjoys a certain reptuation as a renowned *philosophe*. It is clear that Lui, at least, compares the *philosophe* with his famous uncle, as when he says of the composer in the early part of the dialogue 'c'est un *philosophe* dans son espèce' (p.76; emphasis added).

It soon becomes clear that Lui does indeed mean to compete with Moi as he does with the father and uncle; and we shall also see that Moi equally competes with Lui. For Moi aspires to greatness and goodness in the conventional sense of both terms, which makes of Lui's onslaught on the father and uncle an onslaught on himself. If Lui can prove that he exceeds his forebears through the concept of negative morality, then so too may he exceed Moi by being more sublimely evil than Moi is either good or great.[25] However, there is a certain complexity in the situation. Moi and Lui are in fact allies in that they jointly wish to topple the uncle; but they become competitors in that each wishes to usurp the place of greatness.

The issue which opposes Lui and Moi, then, is ultimately this: which one deserves the title of genius denied to the uncle? This issue is manifested from the opening lines of exchange, from which point forward Lui and Moi seem equally fascinated by the figure of the genius (whether he excels in philosophy, music, poetry, or some other area). They begin by discussing chess (after meeting by chance in the Café de la Régence, where the game is played). Lui claims only to enjoy chess, poetry, eloquence, 'et autres fadaises comme cela', if they are practised with genius (p.75). Moi seems disinclined to discuss genius further since he explicitly proposes a change of subject: 'Mais laissons cela'. He broaches instead the topic of Lui's activities since their last meeting. The subject of genius soon returns, however. This time it is Moi who reintroduces it, for Lui's mention of shaving his beard

25. In a sense, then, Moi 'stands for' the father and uncle as in transference, and in so far as he takes on that role he engages in a 'countertransference', as he struggles for supremacy over his interlocutor.

provokes in him the following reflection: 'Vous avez mal fait. C'est la seule chose qui vous manque, pour être un sage' (p.75); and this in turn leads to the image of a bronze sculpture of Lui placed beside ones of Caesar, Marcus Aurelius and Socrates. A second time Moi changes the subject, falling back this time on the most general of gambits: 'Vous portez-vous toujours bien?' (p.75). But this diversion too leads back to the subject of genius. For Lui contrasts his health with that of his famous uncle, whose uncharitable behaviour leads into a general comment on persons of genius: 'Et c'est ce que je prise particulièrement dans les gens de génie. Ils ne sont bons qu'à une chose. Passé cela, rien. Ils ne savent ce que c'est que d'être citoyens, pères, mères, frères, parents, amis' (p.76). In brief, within this opening passage Moi repeatedly changes the subject in order not to speak of genius, while Lui repeatedly returns to the topic; and Moi, as well as Lui, reintroduces the subject. We might regard this as accidental or unimportant. However, we might instead maintain that the repeated return to (or of) the subject of genius, in spite of Moi's resistance, suggests that each speaker is compelled to speak of it in the presence of the other.

Not only the opening but also later sections of the dialogue turn on the issue of genius and greatness. That Moi has the reputation of being a leading *philosophe* is a fact repeatedly alluded to by Lui who addresses him so often as 'monsieur le philosophe' that the phrase becomes a kind of tag. The irony contained in this form of address is clearest when Lui substitutes 'seigneur philosophe' (p.170-71) or states 'Je n'entends pas grand-chose à tout ce que vous me débitez là. C'est apparemment de la philosophie' (p.84). But Moi pretends in all sincerity to this title which Lui ironically accords. He pompously represents himself as hovering between the options of goodness and greatness, as when he uses Voltaire's achievements in each sphere to express a personal preference; 'C'est un sublime ouvrage que *Mahomet*; j'aimerais mieux avoir réhabilité la mémoire des Calas' (p.117). Nor does he hesitate to represent himself as the purveyor of unvarnished truth: 'Je parle mal. Je ne sais que dire la vérité; et cela ne prend pas toujours, comme vous savez' (p.177).

More specifically, Moi identifies with great figures of past and present. Apart from Voltaire, of the models with whom Moi wishes to identify himself Socrates and Diogenes are doubtless the most important; and of all these Diogenes is the figure who is discussed at greatest length (p.192-93). As characterised by Moi, Diogenes is one who stands apart from the general play of desire and frustration which ensnares humanity at large: 'Diogene se moquait des besoins' (p.192). When Lui objects that he experienced sexual needs, Moi replies that he either did without sexual gratification or received what was offered freely (p.193). Now, as a modern-day *philosophe*, Moi is in a position to identify with an Ancient such as Diogenes. To introduce the

Greek philosopher he uses a general formulation: 'Mais il y a pourtant un être dispensé de la pantomime. C'est *le philosophe* qui n'a rien et qui ne demande rien' (p.191-92: emphasis added). Moi repeatedly represents himself in such a fashion as to be included in such a definition. In particular he suggests that he too experiences needs which might be met by others, yet is not enslaved by them. For instance, he claims that sensuous tendencies have less purchase on him than his aspiration to lead a philosophical life of good deeds (p.116-17):

> Je ne méprise pas les plaisirs des sens. J'ai un palais aussi, et il est flatté d'un mets délicat, ou d'un vin délicieux. J'ai un cœur et des yeux; et j'aime à voir une jolie femme. J'aime à sentir sous ma main la fermeté et la rondeur de sa gorge; à presser ses lèvres des miennes; à puiser la volupté dans ses regards, et à en expirer entre ses bras. Quelquefois avec mes amis, une partie de débauche, même un peu tumultueuse, ne me déplaît pas. Mais je ne vous le dissimulerai pas, il m'est infiniment plus doux encore d'avoir secouru le malheureux, d'avoir terminé une affaire épineuse, donné un conseil salutaire [...] Je connais telle action que je voudrais avoir faite pour tout ce que je possède.

Elsewhere he emphasises his philosophical detachment from wordly possessions: 'Mais c'est qu'il y a des gens comme moi qui ne regarde pas la richesse, comme la chose du monde la plus précieuse; gens bizarres' (p.178). It seems clear, then, that when towards the end of the dialogue he says 'Diogenes', he (also) means 'I'. At the same time, Moi uses philosophical genius to mark himself off from Lui, repeatedly insisting in various ways that Lui is a non-philosopher, and a non-genius. If in the opening lines, as we have seen, Moi likens Lui to a philosopher, this is purely in reference to his physical appearance; he only lacks the beard to complete the resemblance: 'C'est la seule chose qui vous manque, pour être un sage'. The unmistakeably ironic tone conveys that, appearance apart, Lui could not be less like a philosopher.[26]

However, Lui however objects to being characterised as a non-philosopher, together with the idea that Moi and other *philosophes* are his superiors. When Moi at one point patronises his theorising, he objects strongly: 'Oh vous voilà, vous autres! Si nous disons quelque chose de bien; c'est comme des fous, ou des inspirés; par hasard. Il n'y a que vous autres qui vous entendiez. Oui, monsieur, le philosophe. Je m'entends; et je m'entends ainsi que vous vous entendez' (p.81). Elsewhere, speaking of his talents as sycophant and *procureur* he states 'Si cela était écrit, je crois qu'on

26. We should no doubt recall that the term 'philosophe' is not generally equivalent to the English 'philosopher', but in this particular text Moi represents ancient philosophers such as Diogenes and Socrates as precursors of the *philosophes*, and so I have used the terms interchangeably.

m'accorderait quelque génie' (p.129). Lui also contests Moi's identification with Diogenes as a great man who stands apart from the rest. When, as we saw above, Moi mockingly ascribes to Lui the greatness to which both men aspire by imagining his bust 'A côté d'un Caesar, d'un Marc Aurele, d'un Socrate', Lui riposts by comparing himself to Diogenes, whom he resembles in being 'effronté': 'Non, je serais mieux entre Diogene et Phrynè . Je suis effronté comme l'un, et je fréquente volontiers chez les autres' (p.75). By appropriating the Greek philosopher in this way, Lui is able to claim an identification with him which challenges in advance Moi's own claim, for that claim will be based, as we have seen, on relative asceticism. Elsewhere, Lui mocks Moi's pretension to be able to view humanity (as Moi claims Diogenes can) from a viewpoint at once philosophical and external: 'Perchez-vous sur l'épicycle de Mercure [...]. Je ne m'en mêle pas. Je suis dans ce monde et j'y reste' (p.188-89). Shortly afterwards, he emphasises that everyone (except perhaps the King) is caught up in the 'pantomime des gueux' (p.190); so by implication no philosopher, even Diogenes, can prove an exception; 'Je vous y prends. Diogene a donc aussi dansé la pantomime' (p.192).[27]

When it is a question of identification with contemporary writers or *philosophes*, Lui similarly refuses to accept Moi's claim to greatness. This is made clear in the passage where Lui explains that the Bertin clique lives to decry men of genius and virtue: 'On n'entend que les noms de Buffon, de Duclos, de Montesquieu, de Rousseau, de Voltaire, de d'Alembert, de Diderot, et Dieu sait de quelles épithètes ils sont accompagnés' (p.134). With a pretence of modesty, Moi uses the fact that his name is included in the list in order to claim his place amongst these great men. After all, to be lampooned by the Bertin clique, with its inverted scale of values, is surely a mark of greatness: 'Tant mieux. Peut-être me fait-on plus d'honneur que je n'en mérite. Je serais humilié, si ceux qui disent du mal de tant d'habiles et d'honnêtes gens, s'avisaient de dire du bien de moi' (p.135). However, Lui's riposte situates Moi precisely in the position of inferiority in which he would situate the musician's nephew. For Lui implies that the reputation of Diderot/Moi is a decidedly second-rank one: 'Nous sommes beaucoup, et il faut que chacun paye son écot. Après le sacrifice des grands animaux, nous immolons les autres' (p.135).

More generally, of course, as we have seen, Lui lays claim to a sublimity in evil which may permit him to surpass uncle, father and worthy *philosophe* alike. Again and again we can notice that Moi seems sensitive to Lui's

27. The corollary is of course that the great man can only be the one who proves himself supreme in the 'pantomime des gueux', which as we have seen Lui threatens to do when he relates the story of the renegade of Avignon.

challenge in this connection. When Lui 'proves' his sublimity by telling the story of the renegade of Avignon, Moi is sickened; to Lui's inquiry 'est-ce que vous vous trouvez mal?' he replies 'un peu; mais cela passera' (p.157). He defensively attempts to force the dialogue back to the field of music; as he asks Lui 'que faites-vous à présent?' it is purely 'pour le ramener à son talent', i.e. music. However, Lui is as keen to stick to morals as Moi is to move him onto music, and the dialogue continues to oscillate between the two. This oscillation does not merely show that one speaker is interested in morality for its own sake, whilst the other is more interested in music. For each speaker, the issue is supremacy. Lui is attempting to establish his genius, Moi to contest it (and vice-versa). This becomes explicit in the following brief exchange (p.177; emphasis added):

MOI

Fort bien. Par cette comparaison, vous me ramenez des mœurs, à la musique dont je m'étais écarté malgré moi, et je vous en remercie; car, *à ne vous rien celer; je vous aime mieux musicien que moraliste.*

LUI

Je suis pourtant bien *subalterne* en musique, et bien *supérieur* en morale.

MOI

J'en doute.

Moi's 'j'en doute' is uttered in bad faith, for it is belied by the strategy according to which he constantly presses for a change of subject. Precisely because Lui is 'subalterne' in music and 'supérieur' in (negative) morality, Moi prefers to keep him to the former subject. Music is the area in which Lui is, by his own avowal and presumably the judgement of society at large, patently inferior. This means at once that he is inferior to his uncle in the domain of music, and inferior to others such as Moi who have achieved distinction in some parallel field (be it artistic, moral, or philosophical). Moi drives the point home in the following speech (in which, several pages on, he is still pushing Lui towards the topic of music): 'Cher Rameau, parlons musique, et dites-moi comment il est arrivé qu'avec la facilité de sentir, de retenir et de rendre les plus beaux endroits des grands maîtres; avec l'enthousiasme qu'ils vous inspirent et que vous transmettez aux autres, *vous n'ayez rien fait qui vaille*' (p.179: emphasis added). These two sentences reveal Moi's strategy as clearly as we might wish; for scarcely does he utter 'parlons musique' than he narrows the field down to a discussion of Lui's inferiority in that realm, pointing out that Lui has produced no worthwhile composition. As long as they talk about music, it seems, Moi can place Lui in the position of the (inferior) nephew/son in order that he himself might accede to the place denied to the uncle/father.[28]

Lui opposes Moi's pretensions in yet another fashion. We have seen that Lui despairs of deserving the paternal name, which he experiences as a rebuke, and we have seen that Lui nevertheless adopts a dual strategy in order to usurp the uncle's place; and so it seems appropriate to speak of an oscillation in his attitude, between ambition and defeatism. However, it is important to understand that he attacks Moi from both positions. When he ambitiously attempts sublimity in evil, he is Moi's rival for greatness, as we have seen. However, when he envisages his own defeat, he threatens Moi no less, since he includes him in that defeat. This becomes clear in the closing lines of the dialogue, when Lui pronounces the following speech on the composer Antoine Dauvergne: 'Il y a d'assez belles choses dans sa musique; c'est dommage qu'il ne les ait pas dites le premier. Parmi ces morts, il y en a toujours quelques-uns qui désolent les vivants. Que voulez-vous? quisque suos patimur manes' (p.195). The Latin quotation included in this speech requires elucidation. The Hermann edition provides the following gloss in a footnote: 'Le texte latin est obscur, mais J.-F. Rameau entend tout bonnement *Mânes* au sens du mot français, qui désigne les âmes des morts, et spécialement des ancêtres: chacun expie les ancêtres à la suite desquels il s'inscrit, Dauvergne est éclipsé par les compositeurs venus avant lui et qu'il imite, un peu comme J.-F. Rameau l'est par la gloire de son oncle' (p.195). So the original's statement that we all determine our own fate in the afterlife has been distorted by Lui into the assertion that we all live in the shadow of our forebears. Dauvergne is not yet dead, but must like Lui undergo in this life a punishment imposed by his dead (musical) forebears, which is to be deemed inferior because he comes later.[29] Now, the interest of Lui's use of the quotation lies as much in the 'quisque' as the rest. Not only does Lui insist on his oedipal vision of life; he also insists that there are no exceptions to the rule; what applies to Dauvergne and himself also applies to Moi. His philosophical interlocutor must not hope to equal his predecessors and models.

28. This is in spite of the fact that, as we have already seen, Moi seeks to distance himself from the Oedipus complex, in which he prefers to see Lui alone confined. We will suggest below that Moi in fact wishes to see himself as a kind of transcendent father-figure.

29. The Hermann edition informs us that the quotation in question is drawn from *The Aeneid*, VI.743, and points out that in the only other place where Diderot names Jean-François Rameau, which is the *Salon* of 1767, he is represented as using the same quotation, similarly misconstrued, in order to talk of the influence of the painter Mignard on the work of Doyen (p.195).

Parenthesis: the 'homme-orchestre' passages

We have suggested that from Moi's point of view, the truly disturbing challenge represented by Lui is in the area of negative morality. Moi only seems to feel threatened by Lui's performance in narrating evil, and not by his mimed performances of musical events. This needs to be emphasised because many critics have argued that Lui achieves his own idiosyncratic form of greatness in the area of mime, which simply happens not to be recognised in the same way as music. This type of reading dwells on the set-piece mimes in which Lui evokes the performance of a piece of music by an individual violinist, harpsichordist, or whole orchestra. In the present context, however, we must distinguish between the extratextual reader's reaction and that of the intratextual narrator/Moi.

The narrator records as follows his former self's reaction to one of Lui's mimes: 'Admirais-je? Oui, j'admirais! étais-je touché de pitié? j'étais touché de pitié; mais une teinte de ridicule était fondue dans ces sentiments, et les dénaturait' (p.166). These comments constitute a fairly clear allusion to neo-classical dramaturgy. Moi seems to dismiss Lui's performance as falling short precisely because he cannot experience catharsis. Terror is left out of account; pity and admiration are experienced, but Lui's very ridiculousness spoils the experience.[30]

On this basis, we can argue that the narrator does not take the trouble to record Lui's frenzies at some length in order that the reader might appreciate their artistry (though this of course may be the result in spite of the narrator). Instead, we could argue, he takes the trouble to record Lui's performances because, however consummate they may be, they ultimately establish that Lui can only *mimic* greatness in music. After all, as we have already seen, Moi inquires pointedly why he has produced nothing worthwhile (p.179). As far as Moi/the narrator is concerned, the composer's nephew is condemned to repetition of the great pieces of others (indeed, he is limited to performing others' performance of others' music). In the musical sphere, then, he falls conspicuously short, being reduced to fantasy performances which hold the crowd only for a moment and provoke not reverence but laughter or (in Moi's case) an imperfect catharsis indicating a blemished artistry.

30. Nor should we forget that in addition to or as an alternative to the usual meaning, 'admirer' can retain the Latin connotation of extreme surprise. Finally, we should note that the narrator records the reaction of the crowd which Lui's mime attracts. The crowd is initially amused and laughs uproariously: 'On faisait des éclats de rire à entrouvrir le plafond' (p.165). However, it would be unwise to conclude that as far as the narrator is concerned Lui's performance is one of great artistry simply because it momentarily amuses the idle crowd.

Conclusion

We began by observing that the theme of alterity versus identity is woven into the texture of *Le Neveu de Rameau*, in preamble, narrative instance and dialogue-section alike. The dialogue-section, however meandering it may appear, consistently implies a contest: Moi insists on his difference from Lui, whilst Lui tends to emphasise the two men's similarities (and potential identity). The various topics discussed (posterity, music, the great and the good, aesthetics, morality and so on) may seem in any case organically interconnected in ways which are obvious even outside the context of eighteenth-century studies. But from the psychological point of view, the interconnections are tighter still; indeed, this is a dialogue strictly without digression, in the sense that the issue of difference and similarity infuses all other topics. In this respect, then, Lui and Moi are engaged throughout in a single contest; and if occasionally the reader loses it from sight, the two speakers do not. Sooner or later any twist or turn of the dialogue is subsumed in the issue of identity versus difference.

We proceeded by connecting the narrator's horror of identification with his representation of Lui as a specifically oedipal other. Lui presents himself as an oedipal son, torn between rebellion and submission. At times he explicitly judges himself as falling short of his uncle/father, whilst at other times he attempts to compensate by vying to achieve greatness in negative morality. Meanwhile, Moi is keen to reinforce Lui's oedipal inferiority on every occasion. In particular he anxiously pushes Lui from discussion of negative morality, where Lui is impressive, back onto the ground of music, where he feels inferior to his uncle, and by extension perhaps to Moi himself (who excels in the parallel area of philosophy).

Examination of these interconnected aspects of the text allows us to naturalise the narrator's speech act in a new way, i.e. in terms of the (dis)avowal of a previously repudiated identification which is still experienced as a threat. He projects onto Rameau/Lui the oedipal tendencies which he would disavow in himself, which is particularly clear when he discusses the dynamics of the family. It is as though Moi's logic runs: 'You are diametrically opposed to me in every respect; you are an oedipal son and father; therefore I am not these things'. Rameau/Lui is perhaps suited to this role of Other precisely because in his presence Moi comes dangerously close to recognising his similarity to him, as if the unconscious identification both facilitated and necessitated the projection.

As constructed by Moi, Lui is on the one hand overshadowed by his uncle/father and on the other hand threatened by his son. If the same law binds his son, he is one of a potentially infinite series of weak and envious sons who can only become precarious Laius-fathers. Moi wishes to avoid such insertion into a series of fathers and sons as just another Oedipus/ Laius. In *Le Fils naturel*, as we have seen, Lysimond dreams of being seen in all perpetuity as the first and only father who really matters, a role which Dorval's play is supposed to allocate him. In *Le Neveu de Rameau* the narrator/Moi manifestly displays a similar aspiration. Myths and images of origin abound in the discourse of both Lui and Moi, but since the text is mediated throughout by the narrator, we can interpret all such imagery in relation to his personal concerns. Racine (whose name of course suggests a root) has become a tree, affording shade in all posterity; Lui suggests that the man who founds an aristocratic name is a trunk, his descendants mere offshoots; and if Rameau's uncle is a genius, which is undecided, he is also a 'souche', or trunk to Rameau's branch. Meanwhile Voltaire, Diogenes and Socrates are breakers with tradition, champions of truth and timeless examples to which posterity might aspire. The narrator/Moi wishes to identify himself with such founding figures, to attain their position of unshakeable precedence. Might he not do so by living in virtuous conformity to his own ideals and perhaps even writing the *belle page* to boot? Or is he just a miserable double for Rameau, failing to live up to his predecessors? Contact with Rameau/Lui creates an uncanny moment where the narrator/Moi comes so close to being (like) him that he must construct a record of their encounter to function as an elaborate disavowal by projection.

It seems that Diderot chose to entitle his dialogue *Satire seconde*.[31] However, the title *Le Neveu de Rameau* was chosen instead by the posterity whose judgement Diderot trusted so implicitly. In this case posterity has indeed chosen aptly. For the preferred title hints already at what the work as a whole seems designed to (dis)avow: the possibility that always being already someone's nephew/son must be experienced as a perpetual falling short, though we have no other choice in respect of our mode of insertion into a pre-existent order which requires us to inherit the Father's name.

31. The critical apparatus of the Hermann edition can be consulted on this point (p.69); see also the general introduction (p.40).

Conclusion

TERMS such as 'literary psychoanalysis' or 'psychoanalytic criticism' allude of course to many different practices. The approach adopted here has been based on notions and formulations drawn from Freud, and also on subsequent thinking such as Lacanian and feminist traditions of psychoanalysis. In addition, narratology has played an important role, for the emphasis throughout has been on the analysis of characters and narrators in their relation to narrative structure.

The question of approach is always a thorny one, and whilst it is inappropriate here to attempt any defence of either narratology or psychoanalysis in general, it is relevant to situate the type of reading proposed against certain trends within both areas. There is a tendency in literary psychoanalysis to claim an evolution through the analysis of author, character, and reader into what might be termed (for want of a more precise term) a purely 'structural' phase. Whilst the present study proposes no psychoanalysis of the author, and does not directly address the question of the reader's psyche, it repeatedly draws on psychoanalytic concepts in order to effect an analysis of the motivations and attitudes of various textual figures, and in this sense effects a psychoanalysis of character. Meanwhile, narratology has tended to minimise analysis of character, especially analysis which involves appeal to any extratextual model of the mind. This follows on the Structuralist attempt to reduce character to the function of 'actant', as a way of insisting on the text's formal aspects. It will be useful, then, to argue that psychoanalysis of character is not incompatible with either a narratological or a psychoanalytic analysis of the text. Indeed, if as critics such as Peter Brooks (to whom we will return) have eloquently suggested, narratology and psychoanalysis are to converge to any significant extent, such convergence must involve analysis of character.

I will focus in what follows on two writers who have proven particularly influential in the rejection of psychoanalysis of character in favour of that of 'structure'. One is Lacan, whose *Séminaire sur la lettre volée* in particular is lent a seminal role; and the other is Brooks, whose *Reading for the plot* is largely responsible for introducing psychoanalysis into Anglo-Saxon narratology. Although these texts are not particularly recent, current theorisation of literary psychoanalysis continues to bear their mark to the extent that to discuss these texts can serve for practical purposes as a kind of 'return to source'.

Discussion of these points will be organised as follows. First, I will suggest that Lacan's famous *Séminaire* does not, as it is often stated, reduce the status of the subject to nothing in order to posit instead the omnipotence of the signifier's role in determining intersubjective relations. From this it follows that to use the *Séminaire* as the basis for showing how literary analysis might focus on 'structure' as the correlative of 'intersubjectivity', rather than on 'character' as the correlative of 'subject', is erroneous. Second, Peter Brooks' practice as critic measured against his theoretical programme will be used to suggest that the most highly sophisticated attempt to exclude the analysis of character from a narratology informed by psychoanalysis necessarily incorporates such analysis, however marginally. Finally, I will suggest that from a narratological point of view, at least one inflected by reader-response theory, the conceptual categories 'character' and 'structure' are mutually implicated, in the sense that character cannot be defined without reference to structure and vice-versa. It follows that there can be no true narratological analysis of form which excessively reduces consideration of character.

Lacan's 'Séminaire sur la lettre volée' and its aftermath

As stated above, there is widespread support for the view that there is an inexorable progression in the field of literary psychoanalysis, usually presented as one from analysis of author to that of character, reader, and beyond, into a new realm which is sometimes defined as a structural one. Since such a view has often been based on the supposed significance of Lacan's writing, and especially the *Séminaire sur la lettre volée*, it will be useful to glance at that piece here.

Poe's *The Purloined letter* analysed by Lacan in his famous seminar includes the following elements. First, a Minister steals an incriminating letter from the Queen, who dare not prevent him since the King is present; indeed, she has left the letter in full view in order to avert the King's suspicion. The Minister realises this letter is important by a process of observation and inference, and steals it while the Queen stands helplessly by. Intending to use the letter for the purposes of blackmail, and knowing his apartments will be searched, the Minister conceals it by placing it in full view on a chimneypiece. Initially his device works, since the police cannot find the letter in spite of a thorough search. However, when consulted by the police, the principal character Dupin guesses the hiding place and secretly recovers the letter.

Lacan's discussion focuses on the striking repetition of a structure of relationships in Poe's story, with characters adopting subject positions previously held by other characters. The Minister moves into the position formerly occupied by the Queen, in that he seeks to draw attention from the letter by exposing it to public view. Similarly, Dupin adopts the position previously held by the Minister, in that he sees what others miss (the location of the secret). Finally, the King, who fails to see the letter or rather to understand that it is concealed by being displayed, yields his place to the police, who also fail to find the letter precisely because it is conspicuous.

In his commentary Lacan not only emphasises the manner in which intersubjective relations seem to allocate predetermined attitudes and responses to the subject, but also makes of Poe's tale an allegory of repetition compulsion which stresses the primacy of the signifier. Drawing together many of his astute observations in a closing section he writes:

> C'est bien ce qui se passe dans l'automatisme de répétition. Ce que Freud nous enseigne dans le texte que nous commentons, c'est que le sujet suit la filière du symbolique, mais ce dont vous avez ici l'illustration est plus saisissant encore: ce n'est pas seulement le sujet, mais les sujets, pris dans leur intersubjectivité, qui prennent la file, autrement dit nos autruches, auxquelles nous voilà revenus, et qui, plus dociles que des moutons, modèlent leur être même sur le moment qui les parcourt de la chaîne signifiante.
>
> Si ce que Freud a découvert et redécouvre dans un abrupt toujours accru, a un sens, c'est que le déplacement du signifiant détermine les sujets dans leurs actes, dans leur destin, dans leurs refus, dans leurs aveuglements, dans leur succès et dans leur sort, nonobstant leurs dons innés et leur acquis social, sans égard pour le caractère ou le sexe, et que bon gré mal gré suivra le train du signifiant comme armes et bagages, tout ce qui est du donné psychologique.[1]

In his authoritative study, Malcolm Bowie refers to this passage in order to illustrate Lacan's mid-1950s emphasis on the role of the signifier:

> [The passage in question] is one of numerous formulations in which the signifier becomes a versatile topological space, a device for plotting and replotting the itineraries of Lacan's empty subject. 'The subject' is no longer a substance endowed with qualities, or a fixed shape possessing dimensions, or a container awaiting the multifarious contents that experience provides: it is a series of events within language, a procession of turns, tropes and inflections.[2]

Bowie's discussion brings out the way in which Lacan calls upon the signifier to perform many tasks and usurp many notions, until 'it can afford to scatter itself across the firmament' (p.78). In his subsequent writing, according to Bowie, recourse to the concept of the Other allows Lacan to remedy the 'severe limitation' which is the incapacity of such a sweeping concept to account for speech 'which takes place between individuals and bears the marks of their conflict' (p.79).

Bowie's study is primarily concerned with effecting an exposition and a

1. Jacques Lacan, *Ecrits I* (Paris, Seuil 1966), p.40.
2. *Lacan*, p.76.

critique of Lacan as a thinker, a theorist of desire and language in general; and in such a perspective, Poe's story is used by Lacan as an illustration of a given theoretical position (which emphasises, as already stated, the intersubjective dimension of the repetition-compulsion, together with the role of the signifier). This is indeed how Lacan explicitly presents his own seminar on Poe, in the quotation above, when he writes 'ce dont vous avez ici l'illustration'. Bowie therefore does not address in detail the question of what Lacan's concept of the signifier, and the *Séminaire sur la lettre volée* in particular, might mean for the practice of psychoanalytic criticism. That question, however, has been addressed by others. Indeed, the *Séminaire* has been held up, not only as an illustration or allegory of a theory but also as a model of literary criticism. This perspective changes everything. Rather than Lacan's argument being that the relations between living human beings are determined by displacements of the signifier, the 'message' is that in the literary text the relations between characters are to be understood in purely structural terms. In other words, just as Lacan's reading considers the actions of the various characters above all in their intersubjective dimension, so it is argued the psychoanalytic critic should eschew the analysis of character in order to concentrate on the literary-critical 'equivalent' of the intersubjective: structure (i.e. the structure which relations between characters yield).

To all appearances pieces such as Shoshana Felman's seminal reading of the *Séminaire* have contributed to this situation.[3] Felman dwells at one point on Lacan's emphasis on structure over character: 'what is repeated [...] is not a psychological act committed as a function of the individual psychology of a character, but three functional *positions in a structure*, which, determining three different *viewpoints*, embody three different relations to the act of seeing' (p.136). We must note the opposition here of the 'individual psychology of a character' to 'structure'. Felman is not exactly arguing that if Lacan is studying the structure which binds three parties, he cannot be studying character; nor is she inviting the inference that the literary critic convinced by Lacan's ideas should no longer study character as such. Indeed, her piece warns of the pitfalls of rushing to draw rules for criticism from the *Purloined letter* seminar.[4] Nevertheless, the piece by

3. 'On reading poetry: reflections on the limits and possibilities of psychoanalytical approaches', *The Literary Freud: mechanisms of defense and the poetic will*, Psychiatry and the Humanities 4, ed. Joseph H. Smith (New Haven and London, Yale University Press 1980), p.119-49.

4. She intends by her piece 'not so much to set this example up as a new model for imitation, but rather to indicate the way in which it suggestively invites us to go beyond itself (as it takes Freud beyond itself), the way in which it opens up a whole new range of as yet untried possibilities for the enterprise of reading' (p.146). In

Felman, together with several others written at around the same period, has helped to launch Lacanian literary theorising on the trajectory which leads to the claim that the analysis of character has been superseded by that of structure.

A good example is provided by a piece written expressly to summarise the history of literary psychoanalysis which declares a debt to Felman, yet goes further than her in projecting a 'Lacanian' future for literary psychoanalysis from which author, character and reader alike are absent. Elizabeth Wright declares: 'The emphasis has shifted from the psychology of the author – or his stand-in, the character – to that of the reader, and further to relations between author, reader, text and language'.[5] In the main body of her discussion she proceeds to argue that, in order to take this progression further, the critic must now embrace a Lacanian method of reading, involving an emphasis on the relationship between language (or the signifier) and desire. More particularly, the *Séminaire sur la lettre volée* is read as showing how the analysis of character should be shunned along with that of author and reader: 'What the seminar will mainly serve to illustrate is the new psychoanalytic structural approach to literature, whereby analogies from psychoanalysis are used to explain the workings of the text as distinct from the workings of a particular author's, character's or even reader's mind' (p.157). Unlike Felman, then, Wright definitively presents the analysis of structure as leaving no room for the analysis of the workings of any textual figure's 'mind' (though Wright does not make it clear how the type of reading she claims Lacan heralds is to be effected).

We might immediately raise two types of objection to this kind of argument. First, as we have seen, Malcolm Bowie suggests that, literary analysis apart, Lacan's *Séminaire* over-inflates the importance of the signifier in relation to the subject (only to modify this position later by according

addition, rather than flattening the characters who successively adopt a given intersubjective position as though they are by that very token identical (e.g. the Queen and the Minister), Felman emphasises that the repetition of the first scene in the second is not a repetition of sameness: 'For Lacan, what is repeated in the text is not the content of a fantasy but the symbolic displacement of a signifier through the insistence of the signifying chain; repetition is not of *sameness* but of *difference*, not of independent terms or of analogous themes but of a structure of differential interrelationships, in which what *returns* is always *other*' (p.139).

5. Elizabeth Wright, 'Modern psychoanalytic criticism', *Modern literary theory: a comparative introduction*, ed. Ann Jefferson and David Robey (London, B. T. Batsford 1986), p.145-65 (p.145). From a narratological point of view, this sentence begs several intriguing questions. In what sense is the character the author's 'stand-in'? And where, in the progress from author and character to reader and beyond, is the figure of the narrator? Is he or she assimilated to the author, subsumed within 'character', or simply left out of account?

greater importance to a Hegelian concept of the Other). If Bowie is correct, it would surely be an error to imitate Lacan's overloading of the signifier by overloading the explanatory force of narrative structure in relation to the category 'character'. Alternatively, we could suggest that, in emphasizing the passivity of the subject/subjects in the passage cited above, Lacan is merely using hyperbole to emphasize the main point which he wishes to convey: that repetition operates intersubjectively as well as at the level of the individual subject. There would then be a danger that Lacan's hyperbole is taken at face value, with the result that his main point is obscured. In other words, whilst he is simply employing a rhetorical flourish to stress how important repetition is at both levels, he would be understood to be presenting the subject as offering, in and of itself, strictly nothing which can be analysed. In any case, Lacan must be seen as analysing the various characters of the tale, however minimally and indirectly, for his reading to make sense. Hence the King is implicitly presented by Lacan no less than by Poe as 'obtuse but potentially jealous', the Minister initially 'perspicacious and ambitious', and so on. Character, it seems, can be de-emphasized in order to stress the role of the signifier, but not dispensed with altogether.

Either way, it would seem a misappropriation of the *Séminaire sur la lettre volée* to use it as setting a programme of 'structural' psychoanalytic criticism from which the character is mysteriously banished. The piece forcefully conveys the insight that there is an intersubjective dimension to the repetition-compulsion as there is to the formation and transformation of character. Its relevance for the practice of psychoanalysis is no doubt to remind the analyst of the importance of the signifier in the situation of transference. By extension, its relevance for literary psychoanalysis is to remind the critic that character is to be treated as neither essential nor fixed. But that was, in a sense, implied by Freud's 'Copernican revolution', which tended to decentre traditional views of selfhood by disintegrating the psyche first into systems, then agencies and their interrelations, and always with a sense that the intersubjective (if under other the guise of various concepts, such as introjection, projection, transference, countertransference and so on) was important. Radical Lacanian reworkings of Freud there undoutedly are, but the claimed eradication of the subject in the *Purloined letter* seminar is not amongst them; nor by extension can the seminar be used to found a psychoanalytic narratology which dispenses with the 'mind' of the character as well as that of author and reader.

Peter Brooks, 'Reading for the plot' and beyond

If psychoanalysis, being a narratology of sorts, was always destined to move into conjunction with formalist narratology, it is in the writing of Peter

Brooks that the conjunction may be said to have occurred in its most influential form. As he brilliantly analyses fairy-tale, detective fiction, nineteenth-century realism or the *nouveau roman* (to name but a part of his range), Brooks borrows a number of phenomena from psychoanalysis in order to throw new light on the workings of narrative. In doing so, he consistently suggests that psychoanalytic concepts are primarily interesting for the light they cast on narrative structure. In this manner the text's textuality is kept in view, whilst psychoanalysis and literary criticism are allowed to illuminate each other in unexpected ways. However, within his writing the critic and the theoretician occasionally part company, and I would suggest that this probably occurs under the sway of the movement we have just explored, against the analysis of author, character and reader alike.

Brooks eschews, amongst other objects of study, the psychoanalysis of character. In a recently published talk he pinpoints three ways in which literary psychoanalysis has 'mistaken' its object. First, there was the analysis of the historical author; next, the character and his or her unconscious; third, the reader. According to Brooks, all these practices are deficient in that they represent a displacement of the object of analysis 'from the text to some person, some other psycho-dynamic structure'.[6] Instead, he asserts, the critic should analyse the rhetoric and structure of the text in so far as they are shaped by the operation of desire. This, it seems, is desire cut loose from any particular subject; at once everyone's desire (the human mind and the text operating on the same principles) and no-one's desire in particular (author, reader and character being eschewed).

This was already Brooks' stated position in *Reading for the plot*: 'We can [...] conceive that there can be a psychoanalytic criticism of the text itself that does not become – as has usually been the case – a study of the psychogenesis of the text (the author's unconscious), the dynamics of literary response (the reader's unconscious), or the occult motivations of the characters (postulating an 'unconscious' for them).'[7] However, it is interesting to inquire whether Brooks' own practice is adequately accounted for by summaries such as these. In his readings, he does indeed demonstrate that the structure of narrative is revealingly analogous with that of the phenomena examined by psychoanalysis. In other respects, however, his practice fails to exemplify his theoretical programme. For whilst it is true that he broadly keeps author and reader out of his concerns, on the other hand he does 'postulate an unconscious' for certain characters

6. *Psychoanalysis and storytelling* (Oxford, Blackwell 1994), p.20.

7. *Reading for the plot: design and intention in narrative* (New York, A. A. Knopf 1984), p.112.

and narrators. In his reading of *Great expectations*, for instance, he writes: 'The fellowship with the convict here stated by Joe will remain with Pip, but in a state of repression as what he will later call "that spell of my childhood" – an unavowable memory' (p.118). Although the word 'unconscious' is duly avoided here, the term 'repression' is by definition accompanied by the concept of the unconscious; and since the repression in question is Pip's, so, by extension, is the unconscious.

Another example is the chapter devoted to Balzac's *Le Colonel Chabert* (p.216-37), in which we find the following passage (p.226):

> Chabert returned from the grave is a curiously infantile figure [...]. He delivers himself to Derville as a dependent, financially as in all other respects, making of Derville the mediator of his affective existence and the representative of all the figures of authority from his past life. Their relationship is propitious to the full development of the transference, where the analyst in dialogue with the analysand becomes the fictive object of all past investments of desire, and where the interlocutionary situation becomes the place of repetition and working through of a past not yet mastered and brought into correct, therapeutic relation with the present.

Here Chabert's 'mind' (as it might be inferred from textual indices) is analysed, and although the word 'unconscious' is once again avoided, the appeal to the concept of transference necessarily implies a gesturing towards the unconscious of Chabert and Derville alike. Indeed, each of the following terms: 'transference'; 'repetition'; 'working through'; 'a past not yet mastered' presupposes the unconscious repressed.

This is not to argue that Brooks surreptitiously indulges in the psychoanalysis of character whilst studiously avoiding the word 'unconscious'. His reading of *Le Colonel Chabert* evinces an interest in the structuring possibilities generated by the psychology and mutual relationship of two characters, as Lacan's *Séminaire sur la lettre volée* insists on the structural relations which obtain between two sets of three characters. But in Brooks's case as in Lacan's, consideration of the structural relations in question must pass through some consideration of characters to whom unconscious attitudes or motivations are attributed; the emphasis brought to the intersubjective, however strong, does not eliminate the subject. And one way of reading Brooks and Lacan on this point is to see them as testing how far the elimination of character can be taken, only to discover that it asserts itself as an irreducible remainder.[8]

8. A related issue is Brooks's insistence that the category of character – regardless of the question of the unconscious – is less important, or has less explanatory force, than that of plot. He does of course repeatedly emphasise plot and plotting over character. In opposition to the Anglo-American tradition of character analysis, he examines a number of theorists, from Aristotle to the Structuralists, who treat plot as

It is interesting to quote a statement from Brooks himself on this point: 'I'm also tempted to do a book on character, a concept neglected in most recent narratological work'.[9] This seems diametrically opposed to the position expressed in *Reading for the plot*, which was as we have seen that narratology should indeed neglect the concept of character. Brooks' intention to investigate character thoroughly, then, perhaps indicates a sense that the relations between character and structure are after all central to a conjunction of narratology and psychoanalysis.

Character and narrative structure

This necessarily brief glance at Lacan and Brooks is intended to suggest that the practice of neither heralds a new version of psychoanalytic criticism in which the (psycho)analysis of character has been superseded. Rather, an attentive reading of both theorists suggest the irreducible necessity of viewing character and narrative structure in terms of each other. Perhaps, however, it would be useful to reinforce the logic of seeing character and structure as mutually implicated in purely narratological terms.

The term 'character' is somewhat unfortunate. It covers meanings which French (for instance) entrusts to separate words, 'personnage' referring to a textual figure, and 'caractère' to whatever motivations, attitudes, values, temperament and so on, may be ascribed to such a figure. One consequence of the English term is that it is not always immediately obvious that the narrator has an analysable 'character' as much as any other textual figure (or 'character') does. In other words, the reader must ascribe to the narrator, as to any character, a number of 'characteristics' (attitudes, motivations, and so on) in order to make him or her comprehensible. This may seem to be a somewhat obvious point, but it does highlight the necessity of breaking down a distinction between characters and narrators which is too often seen as absolute. Instead it is useful to recognise that one

more important than character (and other elements). However, to redress an historical balance by emphasising plot is not the same thing as to demonstrate that the category of character has become redundant, or that plot somehow defines the narrative genre while character is something we read in. Plot, character and other components of narrative, if they are to have any explanatory force in a narratological perspective, are surely to be conceived as interdependent, and the notion of interdependence tends to exclude that of relative degree of importance. Brooks' practice combines attention to the desire of figures represented textually (both characters and narrators) with attention to the textual structures which seem to condition and be conditioned by their desire, integrating analysis of characters and narrators into a new understanding of plots and plotting rather than evacuating them from it.

9. *Psychoanalysis and storytelling*, p.131.

category is a subcategory of the other: not all characters are narrators, but all narrators are characters.

With this in mind we can turn to the question of how narratorial character relates to narrative structure. In an interesting discussion, Jonathan Culler resumes the case for understanding literary texts in terms of the 'naturalisation' which readers perform on them. Readers, the argument goes, necessarily recuperate elements of the literary text as forming part of a motivated speech-act ascribed to a particular figure, the narrator. In other words, readers can scarcely make sense of a narrative, or other literary text, except by reading it in such a way:

> As a linguistic object the text is strange and ambiguous. We reduce its strangeness by reading it as the utterance of a particular narrator [...] the narrator is in a particular situation and reacting to it, so that what he says may be read in a general economy of human actions and judged by the logic of those actions. He is arguing, or praising, or describing, or analysing or ruminating, and the poem will find its coherence at the level of that action. [...] Once a purpose is postulated (praise of a mistress, meditation on death, etc.) one has a focal point which governs the interpretation of metaphor, the organisation of oppositions and the identification of relevant formal features.[10]

Culler's argument is relevant here on two counts. First, his discussion suggests that to naturalise a text involves treating the narrator as an analysable *character*, by the attribution of particular motivations for speaking. This tends to reinforce the point just made, i.e. that narrators are effectively characters. Second, Culler's position implicitly connects narratorial character with the manner in which the reader encounters the *structure* of the narrative. For in Culler's account, to understand why the narrator speaks permits not only the interpretation of metaphor and the 'organisation of oppositions' but also the 'identification of formal features'. Whether these 'formal features' are only certain aspects of the narrative's structure or the whole of it is not stated; but this does not matter greatly. What is of importance here in Culler's passage is the indissoluble connection which it implies between at least one type of character – the narrator – and at least certain aspects of structure. Culler's argument suggests, then, that some, or perhaps all, formal features of a narrative are generated as a function of the reader's ability to construct a particular narratorial character effecting a specific type of speech act for particular reasons.[11] A more concise way of

10. *Structuralist poetics* (London, Routledge and Kegan Paul 1975), p.146-47.

11. A confirmation of this is given by imagining its opposite: without the notion of a single, structuring mind from which the narrative discourse issues and which infuses it with purpose and a type of logic, even of the minimal kind which consists in the desire to 'tell a story', any narrative would be reduced to a succession of disconnected propositions.

putting this would be that the positing of a narratorial character underpins the reader's ability to structure the text, or, more briefly still, *structure is a function of character.*

Culler implies a sequence to events which is problematic. In his account, the reader first postulates a purpose guiding the narrator's speech ('once a purpose is postulated'), and only subsequently engages in 'the organisation of oppositions and the identification of relevant formal features'. However, we might with equal plausibility invert Culler's sequence and argue that until the reader begins to observe the formal aspects of the text, it is impossible to postulate a purpose for the narrator's speech (at least one which will be specific enough, and appropriate enough, to permit a sense of how the text is shaped by the narrator). For in order to construct a sense, however rudimentary, of the narrating figure, the reader must have begun to interpret the text, to 'reduce its strangeness' by becoming acquainted with its structural aspects. In that sense, we might say that *character is a function of structure.*

I would not wish to claim that this inversion of Culler's implied sequence of reading has greater validity than what it inverts; it seems equally impossible that readers posit a specific narratorial motive for speaking before identifying the formal features of the narrative in question, and that they can identify formal features before having some sense of who is speaking, and why. This impasse serves to warn against the dangers of constructing a story of origins for the reading process, which manifestly does not allow itself to be teased out into a simple sequence of moves.[12] Instead, it seems wise to state simply that structure and (narratorial) character are mutually implicated from the outset: we infer what we know of the narrator from how he or she organises the text because the organisation of the text is presumed to be a function of the character of the narrator.

When we reflect on the figure of the narrator and the process of naturalisation as described above, then, we can reasonably conclude that in at least a limited sense it is simultaneously the case that character is a function of structure and structure a function of character.[13] If we turned

12. It should be added that Culler is not proposing such a sequence on his own behalf, but summarising one theory of coherence and *vraisemblance* amongst others, in the course of a sophisticated discussion entitled 'Convention and Naturalisation' (*Structuralist poetics*, p.130-60).

13. This is not to claim that character is *exclusively* a function of structure, or vice-versa. The reader's construction of the character of a narrator depends on many factors – style, for instance, or tone, or degree of sincerity, and so on (though it may be that if we were to investigate such terms from a narratological point of view many might be redefined as aspects of structure). The essential point here is that the reader's sense of the choices made by the narrator as he or she structures the narrative is necessarily connected to the reader's construction of the narratorial character, whatever other processes are involved.

our attention to the relation between structure and character at the level of characters 'proper', any relation of mutual implication between character and structure would have to be argued differently. Obviously, characters in the traditional sense of the word can themselves assume a clear narrative function – a well known example would be Des Grieux narrating his story to the *homme de qualité* in *Manon Lescaut*. In such cases, we would argue as above that the character of the narrating figure serves to structure the narrative (Des Grieux wishes to present himself in a favourable light, and organises his material accordingly), and that by the same token the narrative structure serves to characterise the narrating figure. It is where characters do not become narrators that the mutual implication of character and structure would have to be investigated on different grounds. Such an investigation, whilst of importance in the working out of any narratological taxonomy, is not at issue here. For throughout this study, where psychoanalytic concepts have been used, it has generally been the case that the characters which they have served to illuminate have been narrator-characters. Dorval, Suzanne, Jacques and the Master, the narrator/Moi confronted with Lui and Lui himself are all clearly characters who adopt a narrative role, either supposedly transcribing the entire text or narrating large sections of it. As for *Les Bijoux indiscrets*, the analysis of Mangogul was not proposed as that of a character in the traditional sense, endowed with a pseudo-psychology or an individuality. Rather, the object of the analysis was the narratorial organisation of the text as a whole, which emerged as a structure of disavowal. Whilst Mangogul's quest has an important role in this structure, ultimately the shadowy omniscient narrator was the object of inquiry.

These points are relevant to any conjunction of narratology and psychoanalysis. In brief, consideration of naturalisation and the narrative instance show that far from the text object's structural aspects being a given which can be analysed without reference to character, narratorial character and narrative structure are inextricable and co-determining. This means that narratology should involve reading the text as a motivated discourse whose forms imply an analysable figure's purposes and desires. By the same token, literary psychoanalysis cannot move 'beyond' the analysis of character into the realm of a purely structural analysis, since the analysis of narrative structure is by definition also the analysis of narratorial character.

This closing discussion is appropriate in that my analysis of Diderot's narratives has drawn on psychoanalytic concepts in order to analyse character, and has been informed throughout by the conviction – reinforced by Diderot's practice – that character and narrative structure are mutually implicated. The readings which precede examine structure as a function of a (narratorial) character's desire, and vice-versa. We disengaged from *Les Bijoux indiscrets* a structure in which mother and whore are opposed yet conflated; and this was at the same time an exploration of a desire on the part of the narratorial figure who shapes the text. Similarly, Diderot's two fictions of illegitimacy are structured according to the disavowed motivations of their principal actors and narrators. In *Le Fils naturel*, the wishful narrative structure observable in both the play-section and the dialogues implies Dorval's desire to surpass his father, whilst incorporating ample indications of a contradictory tendency to revere him. Suzanne Simonin's memoirs are structured by her quest for a particular type of relation to parental and sibling figures. The structure of Jacques's superficially fatalistic narrative is generated by his need to identify with the lost Captain, and so to mitigate his loss by 'becoming' him as a thorough-going fatalist. Finally, *Le Neveu de Rameau* is structured as an elaborate disavowal on the part of a narrator who projects his own oedipal subjection onto the famous composer's nephew, so that the disavowal serves to structure and the structure to disavow.

As stated at the outset, the aim of this investigation into Diderot's major narratives is to reveal a tension which persistently recurs throughout texts which are disconnected in other respects.[14] The opposition between sexuality and those forces which would contain it serves not only as a theme but also as a basic structuring device and element of (narratorial) character in all the texts of our corpus. Diderot is well known as an innovator in so many fields that his contribution as a poet of human desire can be overlooked. Yet within his novels we can discover everywhere the trace of a preoccupation with the force of desire and the defences which civilisation constructs against its instigations.

14. This perspective on Diderot's narrative could be pursued in various directions. Obviously, the question arises of how far the various shorter narratives and *dialogues narrés* which we have not examined here might fruitfully be read in a similar perspective. Equally obviously, Diderot's treatment of sexuality in non-fictional texts could be reappraised in the light of a new sense of his novelistic practice.

Bibliography

Diderot

Diderot, Denis, *Contes*, ed. Herbert Dieckmann (London, University of London Press 1963).
– *Correspondance*, ed. Georges Roth and Jean Varloot, 16 vols (Paris, Editions de Minuit 1955-1970).
– *Jacques le fataliste et son maître*, ed. Simone Lecointre and Jean Le Galliot (Geneva, Droz 1976).
– *Le Neveu de Rameau et autres dialogues philosophiques*, ed. Jean Varloot (Paris, Gallimard 1972).
– *Œuvres complètes*, ed. Herbert Dieckmann, Jean Varloot *et al.* (Paris, Hermann 1975-).
– *Œuvres complètes*, ed. Roger Lewinter *et al.* (Paris, Club français du livre 1969-1973).
– *Œuvres philosophiques*, ed. Paul Vernière (Paris, Garnier 1958).
– *Quatre contes*, ed. Jacques Proust (Geneva, Droz 1964).
– *La Religieuse*, ed. Jean Parrish, *SVEC* 22 (1963).
– *Le Supplément au Voyage de Bougainville*, ed. Herbert Dieckmann (Geneva, Droz 1955).

Secondary works

Adams, D. J., 'A Diderot triptych re-examined', *Modern language review* 76 (1981), p.47-58.
– 'An English printing of *Les Bijoux indiscrets*', *Diderot studies* 22 (1986), p.13-15.
– *Diderot: dialogue and debate*, Vinaver Studies in French 2 (Liverpool, Francis Cairns 1986).
– 'Experiment and experience in *Les Bijoux indiscrets*', *SVEC* 182 (1979), p.303-17.
– 'Style and social ideas in *Jacques le fataliste*', *SVEC* 124 (1974), p.231-48.

Bal, Mieke, *Narratology: introduction to the theory of narrative* (University of Toronto Press 1985).
Barchilon, Jacques, 'Uses of the fairy tale in the eighteenth century', *SVEC* 24 (1963), p.111-38.
Barthes, Roland *et al.*, *Analyse structurale du récit* (Paris, Seuil 1981); originally published in *Communications* 8 (1966).
Baudiffier, Serge, 'La parole et l'écriture dans *Jacques le fataliste*', *SVEC* 185 (1980), p.283-95.
Belaval, Yvon, *L'Esthétique sans paradoxe de Diderot* (Paris, Gallimard 1950).

Benot, Yves, *Diderot: de l'athéisme à l'anticolonialisme* (Paris, Maspéro 1970).

Benrekassa, Georges, 'Dit et non-dit idéologique: à propos du *Supplément au voyage de Bougainville*', *Dix-huitième siècle* 5 (1983), p.29-40.

Benveniste, E., *Problèmes de linguistique générale* (Paris, Gallimard 1966).

Blum, Carol, *Diderot: the virtue of a philosopher* (New York, The Viking Press 1974).

Bonnet, Jean-Claude, *Diderot* (Paris, Librairie générale française 1984).

Booth, Wayne C., *The Rhetoric of fiction* (University of Chicago Press 1961).

Bowie, Malcolm, *Lacan* (Cambridge, Harvard University Press 1991).

Bremner, Geoffrey, *Order and chance: the pattern of Diderot's thought* (Cambridge, CUP 1983).

– *Jacques le fataliste* (London, Grant and Cutler 1985).

Brooks, Peter, *Reading for the plot: design and intention in narrative* (New York, A. A. Knopf 1984).

– *Psychoanalysis and storytelling* (Oxford, Blackwell 1994).

Byrne, P. W., 'The form of paradox: a critical study of Diderot's *La Religieuse*', *SVEC* 319 (1994), p.169-293.

Caplan, Jay, *Framed narratives: Diderot's genealogy of the beholder* (Minneapolis, University of Minnesota Press 1985).

Cassirer, Ernst, *The Philosophy of the Enlightenment*; trans. Fritz C. A. Koelln and James P. Pettegrove (Princeton University Press 1951).

Catrysse, Jean, *Diderot et la mystification* (Paris, A. G. Nizet 1970).

Chabut, Marie-Hélène, '*Le Supplément au Voyage de Bougainville*: une poétique du déguisement', *Diderot studies* 24 (1991), p.11-23.

Chartier, Pierre, 'Parole et mystification. Essai d'interprétation des deux amis de Bourbonne', in *Recherches nouvelles sur quelques écrivains des Lumières* (Geneva, Droz 1972), p.203-71.

Chouillet, Anne-Marie (ed.), *Colloque international Diderot* (Paris, Aux amateurs de livres 1985).

Chouillet, Jacques, *La Formation des idées esthétiques de Diderot 1754-1763* (Paris, A. Colin 1973).

– *Diderot* (Paris, Société d'édition d'enseignement supérieur 1977).

– *Diderot: poète de l'énergie* (Paris, PUF 1984).

– *Denis Diderot – Sophie Volland. Un dialogue à une voix* (Paris, Librairie Honoré Champion 1986).

Christensen, Thomas, *Rameau and musical thought in the Enlightenment* (Cambridge, CUP 1993).

Cohen, Huguette, 'La figure dialogique dans *Jacques le fataliste*', *SVEC* 162 (1976).

Connon, Derek F., *Innovation and renewal: a study of the theatrical works of Diderot*, *SVEC* 258 (1989).

Conroy, Peter V. Jr, 'Gender issues in Diderot's *La Religieuse*', *Diderot studies* 23 (1988), p.47-66.

Crocker, Lester, '*Jacques le fataliste*: an "expérience morale"', *Diderot studies* 3 (1961), p.73-99.

– *Diderot's chaotic order: approach to synthesis* (Princeton University Press 1974).

Coulet, Henri, *Le Roman jusqu'à la Révolution* (Paris, Armand Colin 1967).

Cru, R. Loyalty, *Diderot as a disciple of English thought* (New York, Columbia University Press 1913).

Culler, Jonathan, *Structuralist poetics* (London, Routledge and Kegan Paul 1975).

– *The Pursuit of signs: semiotics, literature, deconstruction* (London, Routledge and Kegan Paul 1981).

– *On deconstruction* (London, Routledge and Kegan Paul 1983).

– *Framing the sign* (Oxford, Blackwell 1988).

Daniel, Georges, *Le Style de Diderot. Légende et structure* (Geneva, Droz 1986).

Derrida, Jacques, *De la grammatologie* (Paris, Minuit 1967).

Didier, Béatrice, *La Musique des Lumières* (Paris, PUF 1985).

Dieckmann, Herbert, 'The *Préface-Annexe* of *La Religieuse*', *Diderot studies* 2 (1953), p.21-147.

– *Cinq leçons sur Diderot*, preface by Jean Pommier (Geneva, Droz 1959).

Dirscherl, Klaus, *Der Roman der Philosophen: Diderot, Rousseau, Voltaire* (Tübingen, Gunter Narr Verlag 1985).

Edmiston, William F., 'The role of the listener: narrative technique in Diderot's *Ceci n'est pas un conte*', *Diderot studies* 20 (1981), p.61-75.

– *Diderot and the family: a conflict of nature and law*, Stanford French and Italian studies 39 (Saratoga, Calif., Anma Libri 1985).

– 'Narrative voice and cognitive privilege in Diderot's *La Religieuse*', *French forum* 10 (1985), p.133-44.

Ellrich, R. J., 'The structure of Diderot's *Les Bijoux indiscrets*', *Romanic review* 52 (1961), p.279-89.

– 'The rhetoric of *La Religieuse* and eighteenth-century forensic rhetoric', *Diderot studies* 3 (1961), p.129-54.

Fabre, Jean, '*Jacques le fataliste*: problèmes et recherches', *SVEC* 56 (1967), p.485-99.

Fauchery, Pierre, *La Destinée féminine dans le roman européen du dix-huitième siècle 1713-1807. Essai de gynéchomythie romanesque* (Paris, A. Colin 1972).

Fellows, Otis, 'Metaphysics and the *Bijoux indiscrets*: Diderot's debt to Prior', *SVEC* 56 (1967), p.509-40.

– *Diderot* (Boston, Twayne 1977).

Felman, Shoshana, 'On reading poetry: reflections on the limits and possibilities of psychoanalytic approaches', *The Literary Freud: mechanisms of defense and the poetic will*, Psychiatry and the Humanities 4, ed. Joseph H. Smith (New Haven and London, Yale University Press 1980), p.119-49.

Ferguson, Charles, 'Fiction versus fact in the age of reason: Diderot's *Ceci n'est pas un conte*', *Symposium* 21 (1967), p.231-40.

Fontenay, Elisabeth de, *Diderot ou le matérialisme enchanté* (Paris, Grasset 1981).

France, Peter, *Rhetoric and truth in France: Descartes to Diderot* (Oxford, OUP 1972).

– *Diderot* (Oxford, OUP 1983).

France, Peter and Anthony Strugnell (eds), *Diderot. Les Dernières années 1770-1784* (Edinburgh University Press 1985).

Freud, Sigmund, *The Standard edition of the complete psychological works*, ed. and translated by James Strachey *et al.*, 24 vols (London, Hogarth Press 1957-1974).

Gearhart, Susan, *The Open boundary of history and fiction: a critical approach to the French Enlightenment* (Princeton University Press 1984).

Geary, Edward J., 'The composition and publication of *Les Deux amis de Bourbonne*', *Diderot studies* 1 (1949), p.27-45.

Genette, Gérard, *Figures III* (Paris, Seuil 1972).

– *Nouveau discours du récit* (Paris, Seuil 1983).

Girard, René, *Mensonge romantique et vérité romanesque* (Paris, Grasset 1961).

Goldberg, Rita, *Sex and Enlightenment: women in Richardson and Diderot* (Cambridge, CUP 1984).

Greenberg, Irwin L., 'The *Supplément au Voyage de Bougainville* and Chapter 28 of the *Bijoux indiscrets*', *Kentucky Romance quarterly* 15 (1968), p.231-36.

– 'Narrative technique and literary intent in Diderot's *Les Bijoux indiscrets* and *Jacques le fataliste*', *SVEC* 79 (1971), p.93-101.

Grimsley, Ronald, 'L'ambiguïté dans l'œuvre romanesque de Diderot', *Cahiers de l'Association internationale des études françaises* 13 (1961), p.223-38.

Guedj, Aimé, 'Les drames de Diderot', *Diderot studies* 14 (1971), p.15-95.

Hayes, Julie C., 'Retrospection and contradiction in Diderot's *La Religieuse*', *Romanic review* 77 (1986), p.233-42.

Hobson, Marian, 'Déictique, dialectique dans *Le Neveu de Rameau*', *Etudes sur 'Le Neveu de Rameau' et le 'Paradoxe sur le comédien' de Denis Diderot*, ed. Georges Benrekassa, Marc Buffat, and Pierre Chartier (Paris, Textuel – Université de Paris VII 1991), p.11-19.

– *The Object of art: the theory of illusion in eighteenth-century France* (Cambridge, CUP 1982).

Hunt, Lynn A. *The Family romance of the French Revolution* (Berkeley, University of California Press 1992).

Iser, Wolfgang, *The Implied reader* (Baltimore 1974).

Josephs, Herbert, *Diderot's dialogue of language and gesture* (Columbus, Ohio State University Press 1969).

Kavanagh, Thomas M., 'The vacant mirror: a study of mimesis through Diderot's *Jacques le fataliste*', *SVEC* 104 (1973).

– 'Language as deception: Diderot's *Les Bijoux indiscrets*', *Diderot studies* 23 (1988), p.101-13.

Kempf, Roger, *Diderot et le roman, ou le démon de la présence* (Paris, Seuil 1964).

– 'Des bijoux et de l'opinion', *Colloque international Diderot*, ed. Anne-Marie Chouillet (Paris, Aux amateurs de livres 1985), p.239-44.

Kermode, F., *The Sense of an ending: studies in the theory of fiction* (New York 1967).

– 'Secrets and narrative sequence' in *On narrative*, ed. W. J. T. Mitchell (Chicago and London 1981), p.79-97.

Lacan, Jacques, *Ecrits I* (Paris, Seuil 1996).
– *Ecrits II* (Paris, Seuil 1971).
– *The Four fundamental concepts of psychoanalysis*, trans. Alan Sheridan (New York, Norton 1977).
Langdon, David, 'Diderot and determinism: analysis of a letter', *Diderot studies* 20 (1981), p.175-83.
– 'The message of Diderot's *Entretien d'un père avec ses enfants*', *Diderot studies* 23 (1988), p.115-27.
Larsen, Anne R., 'Ethical mutability in four of Diderot's tales', *SVEC* 116 (1973), p.221-34.
Laufer, R., 'La structure et la signification de *Jacques le fataliste*', *Revue des sciences humaines* 112 (October 1963), p.517-35.
Lecointre, Simone and Jean Le Galliot, 'Pour une lecture de *Jacques le fataliste*', *Littérature* 4 (1971), p.22-30.
Lewinter, Roger, *Diderot, ou les mots de l'absence. Essai sur la forme de l'œuvre* (Paris, Editions champ libre 1976).
Lietz, Jutta, '"Je savais tout cela". Bemerkungen zur Rolle des Zuhörers in zwei Erzählungen von Diderot: *Ceci n'est pas un conte* und *Madame de La Carlière*', *Romanistisches Jahrbuch* 34 (1983), p.118-35.
Loy, J. Robert, *Diderot's determined fatalist: a critical appreciation of 'Jacques le fataliste'* (New York, Columbia University King's Crown Press 1950).

Mason, John Hope, *The Irresistible Diderot* (London, Quartet Books 1982).
Mauzi, Robert, 'La parodie romanesque dans *Jacques le fataliste*', *Diderot studies* 6 (1964), p.89-132.
– *L'Idée du bonheur dans la littérature et la pensée françaises au XVIIIe siècle* (Paris, A. Colin 1960).
May, Georges, *Le Dilemme du roman au XVIIIe siècle* (Paris, PUF 1963).
– *Quatre visages de Denis Diderot* (Paris, Boivin 1951).
– *Diderot et 'La Religieuse'* (Paris, PUF 1954).
– 'Le maître, la chaîne et le chien dans *Jacques le fataliste*', *Cahiers de l'Association internationale des études françaises* 13 (1961), p.269-82.
Mehlman, Jeffrey, *Cataract: a study in Diderot* (Middletown, Conn., Wesleyan University Press 1979).
Mornet, Daniel, *Diderot. L'Homme et l'œuvre* (Paris, Boivin 1941).
Mésavage, Ruth M., 'Dialogue and illusion in *Jacques le fataliste*', *Diderot studies* 22 (1986), p.79-87.
Mylne, Vivienne and Janet Osborne, 'Diderot's early fiction: *Les Bijoux indiscrets* and *L'Oiseau blanc*', *Diderot studies* 14 (1971), p.143-66.
Mylne, Vivienne, *Diderot: 'La Religieuse'* (London, Grant and Cutler 1981).
– *The Eighteenth-century French novel: techniques of illusion* (Manchester University Press 1965).
– 'What Suzanne knew: lesbianism and *La Religieuse*', *SVEC* 208 (1982), p.167-73.

Niklaus, Robert, 'Diderot et le conte philosophique', *Cahiers de l'Association internationale des études françaises* 13 (1961), p.299-315.

– 'Diderot's moral tales', *Diderot studies* 8 (1966), p.309-18.

O'Gorman, Donal, 'Hypotheses for a new reading of *Jacques le fataliste*', *Diderot studies* 19 (1978), p.129-43.

Ozdoba, Joachim, *Heuristik der Fiktion: künstlerische und philosophische Interpretationen der Wirklichkeit in Diderots 'contes' (1748-1772)* (Frankfurt, Peter D. Lang 1980).

Pappas, J. (ed.), *Essays on Diderot and the Enlightenment in honour of Otis Fellows* (Geneva, Droz 1974).

Parker, Alice, 'Did/Erotica: Diderot's contribution to the history of sexuality', *Diderot studies* 22 (1986), p.89-106.

Peeters, Léopold, 'Le style épique dans les contes de Diderot', in *Mélanges de philologie romane offerts à Charles Camproux* (Montpellier, Centre d'études occitanes 1978), p.717-29.

Perol, Lucette, 'Une autre lecture du *Fils naturel* et des *Entretiens*', *Revue d'histoire littéraire de la France* 76 (1976), p.47-58.

– 'Quand un récit s'intitule: *Ceci n'est pas un conte*', in *Frontières du conte*, ed. F. Marotin (Paris, Editions du Centre national de la recherche scientifique 1982), p.95-101.

Pommier, J., *Diderot avant Vincennes* (Paris, Boivin 1939).

Proust, Jacques, 'Nouvelles recherches sur *La Religieuse*', *Diderot studies* 6 (1964), p.197-214.

– 'De l'exemple au conte: la correspondance de Diderot', *Cahiers de l'Association internationale des études françaises* 27 (1975), p.171-87.

– *Lectures de Diderot* (Paris, A. Colin 1977).

Pruner, F., *L'Unité secrète de Jacques le fataliste* (Paris, Lettres modernes 1970).

Rank, Otto, *The Incest theme in literature and legend*, trans. Gregory C. Richter (Baltimore and London, Johns Hopkins University Press 1992).

Renaud, Jean, 'Diderot et le parler d'amour' in *Interpréter Diderot aujourd'hui*, ed. Elisabeth de Fontenay and Jacques Proust (Paris, Le Sycomore 1984), p.217-32.

Rex, Walter E., *Diderot's counterpoints: the dynamics of contrariety in his major works*, *SVEC* 363 (1998).

– 'Secrets from Suzanne: the tangled motives of *La Religieuse*', *The Eighteenth century: theory and interpretation* 24, no. 3 (Fall 1983), p.185-98.

Rimmon-Kenan, Shlomith, *Narrative fiction: contemporary poetics* (London 1983).

Robert, Marthe, *Roman des origines et origines du roman* (Paris, Gallimard 1972).

Roelens, Maurice, 'L'art de la digression dans l'*Entretien d'un père avec ses enfants*', *Europe* 405-406 (1963), p.172-82.

Rosso, Jeannette G., *Jacques le fataliste. L'Amour et son image* (Pisa, Golliardica 1981).

Rubin, Gayle, 'The traffic in women: notes towards a political economy of sex', in *Toward an anthropology of women*, ed. Rayna Reiter (New York, Monthly Review Press 1975), p.157-210.

Saint-Amand, P., 'D'une mère à l'autre: *La Religieuse* de Diderot', in *Dilemmes du roman: essays in honor of Georges May*, ed. Catherine Lafarge (Saratoga, Calif., Anma Libri 1989), p.121-32.

Sarraute, Nathalie, *L'Ere du soupçon* (Paris, Gallimard 1956).

Sedgwick, E. Kosofsky, *Between men: English literature and male homosocial desire* (New York, Columbia University Press 1985).

Segal, Naomi, *The Unintended reader: feminism and 'Manon Lescaut'* (Cambridge, CUP 1986).

Seguin, Jean-Pierre, *Diderot: le discours et les choses* (Paris, Klincksieck 1978).

Sgard, Jean, 'La beauté convulsive de *La Religieuse*', in *L'Encyclopédie, Diderot, l'esthétique. Mélanges en hommage à Jacques Chouillet 1915-1990*, ed. Sylvain Auroux *et al.* (Paris, PUF 1991), p.209-15.

Sherman, Carol, *Diderot and the art of dialogue* (Geneva, Droz 1976).

Showalter, English, Jr., *The Evolution of the French novel 1641-1782* (University of Princeton Press 1972).

Sitbon, Y., 'La musique dans *Le Neveu de Rameau*', in *Etudes sur 'Le Neveu de Rameau' et le 'Paradoxe sur le comédien' de Denis Diderot*, ed. Georges Benrekassa, Marc Buffat, and Pierre Chartier (Paris, Textuel – Université de Paris VII 1991), p.61-74.

Skura, Meredith Anne, *The Literary use of the psychoanalytic process* (New Haven and London, Yale University Press 1981).

Smiétanski, Jacques, *Le Réalisme dans 'Jacques le fataliste et son maître'* (Paris, Nizet 1965).

Spitzer, Leo, 'The style of Diderot', in *Linguistics and literary history: essays in stylistics* (Princeton University Press 1948), p.135-91.

Starobinski, Jean, 'Diderot et la parole des autres', *Critique* 296 (January 1972), p.3-22.

Stowe, William W., 'Diderot's *Supplément*: a model for reading', *Philological quarterly* 62 (1983), p.353-65.

Strugnell, Anthony, 'Les fonctions textuelles du moi dans deux dialogues philosophiques de Diderot', *SVEC* 208 (1982), p.175-81.

Suleiman, Susan R. and Inge Crosman, *The Reader in the text* (Princeton University Press 1980).

Sumi Yoichi, *Le Neveu de Rameau. Caprices et logiques du jeu* (Tokyo, Librairie-Editions France-Tosho 1975).

Thomas, Ruth P., '*Les Bijoux indiscrets* as a laboratory for Diderot's later novels', *SVEC* 135 (1975), p.199-211.

Trousson, R. 'Diderot lecteur de Platon', *Revue internationale de philosophie* 148-149 (1984), p.88-90.

Undank, Jack, 'A new date for *Jacques le fataliste*', *Modern language notes* (1959), p.433-38.

Undank, Jack and Herbert Josephs (eds), *Diderot: digression and dispersion. A bicentennial tribute* (Lexington, Ky., French Forum 1984).

Van den Abbeele, Georges, 'Utopian sexuality and its discontent: exoticism and colonialism in the *Supplément au Voyage de Bougainville*', *Esprit créateur* 24, no. 1 (1984), p.43-52.

Varloot, Jean, '*Jacques le fataliste* et la *Correspondance littéraire*', *Revue d'histoire littéraire de la France* 65 (1965), p.629-36.

Venturi, Franco, *La Jeunesse de Diderot (de 1713 à 1753)*, trans. Juliette Bertrand (Paris, Skira 1939).

Verba, Cynthia, *Music and the French Enlightenment: reconstruction of a dialogue 1750-1764* (Oxford, OUP 1993).

Vernière, Paul, *Diderot. Ses manuscrits et ses copistes* (Paris, Klincksieck 1967).

Vesely, Jindrich, 'Diderot et la mise en question des genres narratifs du XVIIIe siècle', *Philologica pragensia* 27, no. 4 (1984), p.210-17.

Wagner, Horst, 'Diderot: *Madame de La Carlière, ou Sur l'inconséquence du jugement public sur nos actions particulières*', in *Die französische Novelle*, ed. Wolfram Krömer (Düsseldorf, August Bagel Verlag 1976), p.63-71.

Walter, Eric, *'Jacques le fataliste' de Diderot* (Paris, Hachette 1975).

Weisz, Pierre, 'Le réel et son double. La Création romanesque dans *Jacques le fataliste*', *Diderot studies* 19 (1978), p.175-87.

Werner, Stephen, *Diderot's great scroll: narrative art in 'Jacques le fataliste'*, *SVEC* 128 (1975).

Whatley, Janet, '*Un retour secret vers la forêt*: the problem of privacy and order in Diderot's Tahiti', *Kentucky Romance quarterly* 224 (1977), p.199-208.

Wilson, Arthur M., *Diderot*, 2 vols (New York, Oxford, OUP 1972).

Wright, Elizabeth, 'Modern psychoanalytic criticism', *Modern literary theory: a comparative introduction*, ed. Ann Jefferson and David Robey (London, B. T. Batsford 1986), p.145-65.

Index